Tolley's Life and Allied Insurance Handbook

Mike Mead, MSc, FCII
Andy Couchman, FCII
David Smith, FCII
Paul Sutton, FCII, ATII

CII

SUPPORTED BY
THE CHARTERED
INSURANCE INSTITUTE

Tolley
A Member of the LexisNexis Group

Members of the LexisNexis Group worldwide

United Kingdom	Butterworths Tolley, a Division of Reed Elsevier (UK) Ltd,, 2 Addiscombe Road, CROYDON CR9 5AF
Argentina	Abeledo Perrot, Jurisprudencia Argentina and Depalms, BUENOS AIRES
Australia	Butterworths, a Division of Reed International Books Australia Pty Ltd, CHATSWOOD, New South Wales
Austria	ARD Betriebsdienst and Verlag Orac, VIENNA
Canada	Butterworths Canada Ltd, MARKHAM, Ontario
Chile	Publitecsa and Conosur Ltda, SANTIAGO DE CHILE
Czech Republic	Orac sro, PRAGUE
France	Editions du Juris-Classeur SA, PARIS
Hong Kong	Butterworths Asia (Hong Kong) HONG KONG
Hungary	Hvg Orac, BUDAPEST
India	Butterworths India, NEW DELHI
Ireland	Butterworths (Ireland) Ltd, DUBLIN
Italy	Giuffré, MILAN
Malaysia	Malayan Law Journal Sdn Bhd, KUALA LUMPUR
New Zealand	Butterworths of New Zealand, WELLINGTON
Poland	Wydawnictwa Prawnicze PWN, WARSAW
Singapore	Butterworths Asia, SINGAPORE
South Africa	Butterworths Publishers (Pty) Ltd, DURBAN
Switzerland	Stämpfli Verlag AG, BERNE
USA	LexisNexis, DAYTON, Ohio

A CIP Catalogue record for this book is available from the British Library.

ISBN 0 75451 243-6

Typeset by Wyvern 21 Ltd, Bristol BS4 3EH

Printed and bound in Great Britain by Antony Rowe Ltd, Chippenham, Wilts

Preface

Tolley's Life and Allied Insurance Handbook aims to be a wide-ranging and informative guide for those whose main business is not life and related insurances, but who find that some knowledge of the subject is essential for the discharge of their professional duties. The Handbook contains sufficient information to enable the user to cope with enquiries both from consumers and the commercial sector. There are of course detailed textbooks and manuals available of a high technical nature, and readers' attention is drawn to these where appropriate in the text and in the bibliography.

My thanks to the friends and colleagues who collaborated in the writing of the Handbook and without whose expertise the task would not have been possible: Mr Andy Couchman, FCII, who wrote all the material on health and related insurances contained in Chapters 20–25, Mr David Smith, FCII, who undertook the challenging task of writing Chapter 17 on stakeholder pensions, and Mr Paul Sutton, FCII, ATII, who took on responsibility for all the coverage of taxation aspects and whose work can be found in chapters 10, 18 and 26. I also offer my sincere thanks to Jo Moore and her colleagues at Butterworths Tolley – to Jo in particular for her diligent editing – and to Mrs Joan Richards for long hours of typing up my manuscript copy.

Mike Mead, MSc, FCII

Contents

Glossary of Terms

Actuaries: Mathematicians who hold specific actuarial qualifications.

Annual Exemption: The amount that a taxpayer can disburse each year by way of gifts free from inheritance tax liability.

Annuity: An income paid at regular intervals by a life office to an annuitant (in the context of this Handbook).

Bonuses: Percentage additions to the sum assured under with-profits policies.

Certificate of Continued Existence: A certificate called for periodically by life offices whereby annuitants are required to confirm that they remain alive.

Chargeable Gain: The gain arising at a chargeable event relating to a life contract as defined by *section 540* of the *Income and Corporation Taxes Act 1988* and which is taxed as income.

Commorientes Rule: The legal presumption that persons who die in circumstances when it is impossible to establish the order of death die in order of seniority.

Divisible Surplus: The amount of declared surplus which can be distributed as policyholders' bonuses and (where appropriate) as shareholders' dividends.

Fraud: An act or course of deception deliberately practised to gain unlawful or unfair pecuniary advantage.

Lapse Ratio: The proportion of a class or policy which is discontinued (either voluntarily or involuntarily) before becoming due as a claim.

Level Premiums: Premiums which, once set, do not vary with the increase in age of the life assured.

Loading: An addition to a basic premium, for example loading for having a dangerous occupation.

Mortality Tables: Instruments whereby the probabilities of life and the probabilities of death can be measured.

Natural Premiums: Premiums which rise every year as the life assured grows older.

Ombudsman (Insurance): An independent official who, on reference to him, can determine disputes involving personal lines insurances issued by offices subscribing to the scheme. The structure within which this official operates is currently under review (August 2001).

Orphan Funds: Invested premiums held by life offices in respect of policies on which no claim has ever been made or is ever likely to be made.

Premium: The consideration from the assured in return for the life office's obligations in the contract of insurance.

Qualifying Policy: A life policy which qualifies under the rules found in *Schedule 15* of the *Income and Corporation Taxes Act 1988*.

Quantum: The sum involved as potential damages in a legal dispute.

Reassurance: A process by which life offices themselves insure lives upon whom they have granted cover.

Reserves: Sums set aside for future contingencies, for example claims.

Surplus: The amount by which the invested assets of the life fund exceed the statutory solvency margin.

Underwriting: The assessment of risk associated with a proposed life, for example the death risk.

Valuation: The process by which a life office will place a value on its assets and liabilities. The valuation also establishes solvency and surplus(es).

Warranty: A statement whereby the signatory states that a certain thing has been done or will be done, or affirms or negatives a particular set of facts.

Abbreviations

ABI	=	Association of British Insurers
ADL	=	Activity of daily living
ADW	=	Activity of daily working
AEI	=	Average Earnings Index
ASUI	=	Accident, sickness and unemployment insurance
AVC	=	Additional voluntary contributions
CA 1985	=	Companies Act 1985
CA 1989	=	Companies Act 1989
CII	=	Chartered Insurance Institute
CMI	=	Continuous Mortality Investigation
CML	=	Council of Mortgage Lenders
CMO	=	Consultant medical officer
DDA 1995	=	Disability Discrimination Act 1995
DPA 1998	=	Data Protection Act 1998
DTI	=	Department of Trade and Industry
ELT	=	English Life Tables
EM	=	Extra mortality
EPP	=	Executive pension plan
FAT	=	Functional assessment test
FFA	=	Fellow of the Faculty of Actuaries
FIA	=	Fellow of the Institute of Actuaries
FIB	=	Family income benefits
FSA	=	Financial Services Authority
FSAVC	=	Free standing additional voluntary contributions
GISC	=	General Insurance Standards Council
GPP	=	Group personal pension
GRiD	=	Group risk development
IAA 1923	=	Industrial Assurance Act 1923
IAFSA 1948	=	Industrial Assurance and Friendly Societies Act 1948
IB	=	Industrial Branch (insurance)
ICTA 1988	=	Income and Corporation Taxes Act 1988
LAA 1774	=	Life Assurance Act 1774
LAPR	=	Life Assurance Premium Relief
LPA 1925	=	Law of Property Act 1925
LTCI	=	Long-term care insurance
LTDI	=	Long-term disability insurance
MIRAS	=	Mortgage Interest Relief At Source
MPPI	=	Mortgage payment protection insurance
NICs	=	National Insurance contributions
OFT	=	Office of Fair Trading
Opra	=	Occupational Pensions Regulatory Authority
PAYE	=	Pay As You Earn
PHI	=	Permanent health insurance
PPA 1997	=	Policyholders Protection Act 1997
PTDI	=	Permanent and total disability insurance

RPI	=	Retail Prices Index
SERA	=	Self-Employed Retirement Annuity
SERPS	=	State Earnings Related Pension Scheme
SSAS	=	Small self-administered schemes
TPDI	=	Total and permanent disability insurance
WLLP	=	Whole life limited premiums

Section A:
Life Assurance

Chapter 1

Actuarial Principles

- **The nature of long-term business**
- **The evolution of life assurance**
- **The role of the actuary**

The nature of long-term business 1.1

Modern life assurance is long-term business, both in practical terms and by legal definition. Policies may remain on the books of an office for many years (perhaps in excess of half a century), making premium calculations and underwriting a more complicated process than with most types of general branch insurance, where the contracts – with certain exceptions – are usually based on a period of one year. Some policies of life assurance are for short periods only (see 11 TYPES OF LIFE POLICY AND POLICY CONSTRUCTION and 14 USES OF LIFE ASSURANCE), but these tend to be exceptional.

Whereas general branch insurance developed in the large commercial centres of Great Britain from the early 17th century onwards, often based on the conduct of maritime trade, life assurance has its roots in the religious and trade union groupings spread widely throughout the whole country. As the Industrial Revolution brought workers from scattered rural communities into more centralised conurbations, so these 'self-help' organisations often became early pioneers of life assurance on mutual lines. In consequence, what we now think of as the London market had very little involvement in life and related insurance, and the early actuaries found their employment with the emerging life offices, based as much in Scotland, the North of England and in the Midlands as in London.

In simple terms, we can say that people effect long-term life assurance to guard against the risks of 'dying too soon' or of 'living too long'. Premature death can, on occasion, leave family and other dependants not properly provided for; conversely, living beyond the average life expectancy can result in the individual concerned facing old age with an inadequate income. The protection offered by a life policy can guard the assured's dependants financially should the first eventuality take place, and the saving/investment potential of a life policy can help maintain an acceptable standard of living in old age if the second circumstance applies. Today there are variations on these basic reasons for taking out life assurance – some policies are tailored to meet specific situations such as the education of a child or grandchild, or to cover likely commitments notably connected to taxation planning.

The life assurance premium is made up of three basic elements:

(*a*) an allowance for mortality (see 1.5);

(*b*) an allowance for investment; and

(*c*) an allowance for expenses.

To these may be added a loading for the privilege of participating in future profit distributions (see 6 PROFITS, INVESTMENTS AND BONUS DISTRIBUTION) and perhaps a small loading for unexpected contingencies. Investment is an extremely important factor in all calculations relative to life assurance, because the long-term nature of the business means that the insurer has the opportunity to employ to considerable advantage the funds it holds (which are often held for a significant period of time). The interplay of all the above elements of the premium is a key factor in the success of any life office. For instance, the number of early claims can be kept low through prudent underwriting; this can also reduce the amount of money which must be spent on mortality. In addition, office costs should be strictly controlled, leading to a lower allocation to expenses and therefore more money to invest. As projections have to be made many years ahead, past statistics interpreted and extrapolations developed, the role of the actuary becomes extremely important. Only these highly skilled and specialist mathematicians, identified by the title FIA (Fellow of the Institute of Actuaries) or FFA (Fellow of the Faculty of Actuaries, a Scottish qualification) are able to carry out this work, as well as such functions as calculating reserves and undertaking valuations (see 9 RESERVES AND VALUATIONS).

The evolution of life assurance 1.2

The natural premium method 1.3

Given the way that insurance developed, it is perhaps inevitable that the first known life assurance policy was on a ship's captain, at the end of the 16th century. It was short term covering twelve months as the likely duration of a specific sea voyage. For around 150 years such life policies as were issued followed this pattern, payments for the cover being assessed by the natural premium method. Although medical knowledge at the time was relatively primitive, the early insurers did know that a person's risk of dying increased with age. The older you were, the more you were likely to die. Hence a life assured's premium increased each year, and life policies were really a series of annual renewable contracts with an escalating premium. In a sense, we still use something akin to the natural premium method today with group life business (see 3 GROUP LIFE) although the premium does not necessarily increase. The natural premium method is simple to understand and to operate, and the Amicable (the Amicable Society for a Perpetual Life Assurance) used it into the 19th century.

Level premium life assurance 1.4

Despite its simplicity, the natural premium method contained a basic flaw – when an assured grows older and has a greater than ever need for life cover, he/she finds the cost has grown to an extent that it may have become unaffordable (particularly as income may have declined). People spotted this effect and grew disillusioned with natural premium life assurance. What was needed was a system of level premium life assurance, whereby once a person is granted a policy the premium stays constant throughout its duration. However, to operate the level premium method, the forerunners of today's actuaries required mortality tables.

Mortality tables 1.5

Mortality tables are instruments by which the probabilities of life and the probabilities of death can be measured. It seems that Edmond Halley, perhaps better known as an astronomer, was experimenting with mortality tables in the 1680s. However, with no compulsory system of registration of births and deaths, and with the spelling of surnames highly variable and often left to the whim of a parish clerk, data was hard to obtain and inconsistent in nature. Despite this, a very determined mathematician named James Dodson did, by diligent field-work, compile a mortality table in the middle of the 17th century based on baptismal and burial records in Carlisle (the Carlisle Table). This table was by today's standards defective as, *inter alia*, it involved only around 10,000 observed lives and the sample, as well as being inadequate, was not representative of the wider population of Great Britain. The data also contained in-built flaws, as children's birth dates could be considerably different from their baptism dates, and ages at death were often guessed by relatives. The children of poorer families may well not have been baptised and hence were excluded from the sample, giving a skew towards the better-off and hence an 'optimistic' view of mortality. However, the Carlisle Table (to be followed shortly by the Northampton Table, with the same method of compiling data broadly followed but around 3000 more lives considered) was better than no table at all, and we know that as early as 1761 the Equitable Life Assurance Society was using it as the basis for level premium life assurance. (See *Figure 1* overleaf.)

As can be seen from *Figure 1*, the natural premium would follow the risk of dying, making the cost prohibitive in later years. Fixing a level premium gives a new entrant joining at the point where the y and x axes converge a consistent cost throughout his/her policy, although paying more than the death risk truly warrants in the early years. This enables the life office to build up out of the shaded area in the illustration a reserve, which after payment of some early claims and expenses can be invested to provide for the future, when in our example the premium may be less than the death risk would on its own justify. As previously stated, the interplay of these factors of investment, mortality and expenses lies at the heart of the success or otherwise of a life office. In very simple terms, set the level premium too low and the office will probably attract a lot of business but will have problems meeting its solvency requirements (see 9 RESERVES AND VALUATIONS); set the level premium too high and

Figure 1

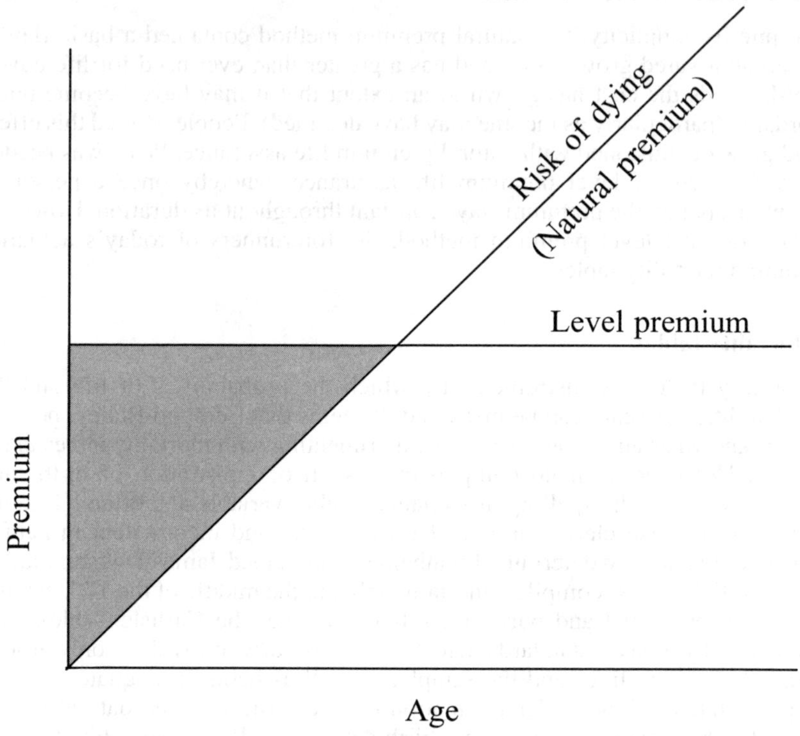

Notes: The above graph is illustrative only. The risk of dying is far from being a straight line, and although it increases with age as a general rule (for young male lives there may be an actual decrease in the death rate in the late 20s due to the relatively heavy incidence of accidental deaths amongst this group between ages 17 and around 25) this increase is not consistent year by year.

the office is likely to be uncompetitive and fail to attract enough premium income to survive.

At one time tables were based on observations over a set period of time (e.g. A 1924–29 and A 1949–52, the 'A' standing for 'Assured', meaning they were based only on lives who had been accepted for assurance). Care was taken to avoid years with an abnormal statistic of deaths – for example, the first of the above tables started in 1924 so as to miss the heavy incidence of deaths post-First World War from the flu epidemic.

Mortality tables in the current market **1.6**

The calculation of mortality tables is now very sophisticated and capable of producing all sorts of refinements. Mortality tables do get out of date quite quickly as the longevity of the nation improves, and using obsolescent tables gives offices a type of concealed profit as premiums are based on an assumption of mortality that has become unduly pessimistic. Nowadays the Institute of Actuaries maintain the Continuous Mortality Investigation (CMI), and every effort is made to ensure that data which by its nature is inevitably historic is updated and used to provide forecasts for the future.

As well as the tables of assured lives, the English Life Tables (ELT) are available based on statistics for the whole population derived from census returns. For many years these tables were used as the basis of industrial branch premiums (see 4 INDUSTRIAL LIFE ASSURANCE).

Mortality tables are a prerequisite of modern life assurance. Problems arise in countries where accurate data is unavailable, as tables based on other nations' experience may not fit local circumstances. However, registration of births and deaths has been compulsory in the United Kingdom for over 150 years, facilitating the build-up of an impressive body of statistics.

The role of the actuary 1.7

Actuaries do not only work in life assurance. An increasing number specialise in general branch insurance, applying their skills to all aspects of this area of the industry. Some operate outside of insurance altogether, working for the Government, in the banking and investments sectors, and in the academic world. There are a number of independent firms of consulting actuaries. However, life assurance has always been heavily reliant on the skills of actuaries, and in the past has attracted leading actuarial figures, some of whom have become famous authorities.

Actuaries employed by insurers, like all employees, owe their prime loyalty to their employer. However, actuaries in all areas of business regard themselves as also owing a high degree of loyalty to the actuarial profession. This is demonstrated by the contribution which qualified actuaries make to the mentoring and tutoring of actuarial students by, for example, assisting with the examining process and preparing and updating technical material.

As well as determining premium tables, life assurance actuaries have responsibilities for the valuation of life funds, the setting of reserves (see 9 RESERVES AND VALUATIONS) and the presentation of statutory annual returns. Bonus distributions will depend heavily on actuarial calculations. Virtually every aspect of the operation of a modern life office, for example such activities as the setting of cash surrender values and loans (see 5 POLICY CONDITIONS AND ENDORSEMENTS), will involve actuarial input.

Chapter 2

Claims

- **Claims procedure**
- **Fraudulent claims**
- **Death claims**
- **Maturity claims**
- **Assignments and trusts**

Claims procedure 2.1

The claimant is usually one of two parties, depending on the type of claim. In the case of a claim by maturity, the claimant is the policyholder. In the case of a claim by death, the claimant(s) will be the policyholder or the legal representatives of the deceased policyholder. It is up to the claimant to establish the facts which support his or her claim. Once this is done, the burden of proof switches to the insurer to prove either that an exception within the policy applies, or that the claim can be resisted for some other reason(for example non-payment of premiums, or non-disclosure or breach of warranty).

Documents held by a third party 2.2

Sometimes relevant documents supporting a claim might be held by a third party, such as a solicitor, who has (or purports to have) a lien over them, typically against payment of a debt. Ideally the documents should be presented to the insurer, but the lien holder is neither the legal nor the equitable owner of the documents and certainly has no entitlement to the proceeds of the policy. If the rightful claimant makes a declaration stating where the policy is and why it cannot be obtained, and then makes a second declaration discharging the insurer from further liability under the policy, and agreeing to indemnify the insurer against the consequences of any future claims under that policy, there is no reason why the insurer should not make a full settlement.

Loss of policy documents 2.3

The loss of policy documents does not affect the validity of the policy; the difficulties created are merely practical and procedural. Obviously there is a danger of the insurer being exposed to a further claim if the policy is subsequently found, and there is the possibility that it may have been in the possession of a third party who could then seek to present a claim on *bona fide* or spurious grounds. The insurer's record-keeping procedures should be able to guard against these risks, but the correct practice is to require the recipient of the policy proceeds to give an undertaking to produce the missing document(s) to the insurer if they are subsequently found, together with a signed indemnity against the risk of a justified claim by a third party. Often the claimant is asked to swear a statutory declaration regarding the loss.

Old policies 2.4

In the case of a very old policy, the problem may surround the very existence of the insurance. There may be no records available, a situation often encountered in relation to Friendly Society policies, and industrial branch policies in general (see 4 INDUSTRIAL LIFE ASSURANCE), which became paid-up many years ago. The discovery of documents apparently relating to such a policy, either by the alleged policyholder or by his/her legal representatives, can lead to a claim, although settlement may have already been made in the past. Insurers are reluctant to consider a claim based only on the production of documents, with no other evidence that a claim is outstanding, and the Insurance Ombudsman has generally supported this reluctance. In law the position depends on the ability of the policyholder to prove that there exists a genuine claim and that it has never been paid.

Policy title 2.5

Disputes frequently arise as to title to a policy. In these situations, the insurer does not dispute that a claim exists, but there is uncertainty as to who is entitled to the proceeds. It is possible for the insurer to interplead between the parties, leaving them to fight it out amongst themselves, although this course is only possible where both parties have started legal proceedings. A better method would seem to be for the insurer to protect its position by paying the proceeds into court under the *Insurance Companies (Payments into Court) Act 1896*, after which it will be up to the rival claimants to conduct the dispute between themselves.

Policy construction 2.6

The construction of life policies follows the normal rules of insurance policy construction. By the *contra proferentem* rule any genuine ambiguities in wording will be construed against the insurer. Words will be taken as having their natural and ordinary meaning unless they have a technical legal meaning by which they should be interpreted. Wordings inserted into a standard form policy, either by writing, typing or specific printing, will take precedence over the standard wording; a good 'common-sense' rule is that 'special provisions take precedence over general provisions'.

Fraudulent claims **2.7**

The effect of a fraudulent claim renders the policy voidable at the option of the insurer. Fraud is by no means as widespread as in general branch insurance as quantum is not an issue: a person is either wholly dead or wholly alive; an endowment policy has either reached maturity or it has not. Cases do arise of feigned death, or of actual deaths where the circumstances of death do not fall within the cover provided by the policy, but the deceased's legal representatives (or the proposer, if it is a life of another contract) attempt to pursue the claim.

If the claimants are not parties to the fraud, then it can be argued that it is not a fraudulent claim. However, if the original policyholder (e.g. the life assured) is or was a party to the fraud, then he/she has committed a breach of the duty of utmost good faith and the claim is voidable on those grounds. If the claimants are themselves parties to the fraud the position is clear.

In certain cases claimants presenting a fraudulent claim may be liable for prosecution for the criminal offence of attempting to obtain money by deception.

Fraud discovery after payment **2.8**

Occasionally the insurer does not discover the fraud until after the policy monies have been paid. In such cases the money is recoverable. If the claimant has been responsible for the fraud, not only is the claim payment recoverable, but any further costs incurred by the insurer ought to be recoverable by way of damages for the tort of deceit. If the claimant is not responsible for the fraud then the existence of a mistake of fact (i.e. the mistaken belief that the life assured is dead) can be relied upon by the insurer. This is supported by the case of *Kelly v Solari (1841) 9 M & W 54*, although the circumstances surrounding this case are less than clear due to the inadequate law reporting of that time.

Forgery **2.9**

Very occasionally with death claims and maturity claims, and more often with surrenders, forgery is encountered. A forged claim is a nullity and an insurer who pays out on a forged claim does not get a good discharge. The true policyholder can still submit a claim which, if *bona fide*, the insurer must pay. The insurer's only remedy is to sue the perpetrator of the fraud for the return of the money, but this is, in practice, a remedy rarely worth taking up.

Death claims **2.10**

Prompt payment of death claims is one of the best possible advertisements for a life office. The Association of British Insurers' (ABI) *Statement of Long-Term Insurance Practice* provides for the payment of interest on death claims which are not paid promptly. Such interest runs from two months after the date of death. The Statement does not specify the rate of interest.

The insurance company is entitled to require proof of death before settling, and it is common practice in the United Kingdom to accept a death certificate in respect of deaths in the home territories and in most developed countries. As far as the United Kingdom is concerned, the *Births and Deaths Registration Act 1953* governs the position and although the Act, rather oddly, does not make a death certificate conclusive proof of death, it is very hard indeed to imagine a modern insurer disputing the document. Mere production of a grant of representation (see 2.14 below) is not of itself proof of death (*High Court, Chancery Division Practice Direction 13-2-70*).

In parts of the world where the registration of death is not an integral part of the legal process, the insurer can only take the view it considers a court would take should a case go that far; namely, it is for the claimant(s) to prove on the balance of probabilities that the life assured is dead. The best evidence would probably be the testimony of a responsible person who has witnessed the death, but this may not be forthcoming and the insurer cannot insist on it.

Presumption of death **2.11**

Presumption of death is allowed at common law at the instigation of interested parties when a person has not been seen alive or heard from for seven years, although very occasionally such presumption is allowed after a shorter period. The interested parties, normally relatives, get leave from the court to 'swear the death' of the life assured. This is not quite the same as proof of death and the insurer can produce evidence to rebut the presumption of death, but unless there is good evidence to support such a rebuttal the court is likely to hold that death has been established. The common law presumption of death does not resolve the question of when the life assured died, and in cases where such timing is an important issue it can only be determined on the balance of probabilities. If two or more persons die in such circumstances that it is impossible to tell which of them died first, then there is a statutory presumption (under *section 184* of the *Law of Property Act 1925* (*LPA 1925*)) that they died in order of seniority with the younger (or youngest) surviving the other (or others). This so-called *Commorientes Rule* was used in deciding the case *Re Grosvenor, Peacey & Grosvenor (1944)* (reported under *Hickman v Peacey [1945] All ER 215*).

Suicide **2.12**

The suicide of the life assured under an own life policy presented problems prior to the enactment of the *Suicide Act 1961*, as suicide was then a criminal act and no person should benefit by his/her criminal action (the *Forfeiture Rule* (see 2.13 below)). Therefore claims in such circumstances were not paid, although some modest *ex gratia* settlements were made. Suicide was not a crime if the life assured's balance of mind was disturbed, and claims in such cases had to be paid as the policyholder had done nothing wrong (assuming he/she had not aided or abetted the suicide, actions which have remained crimes post-1961). The case of *Beresford v Royal Insurance [1938] AC 586*, which involved a deliberate suicide and confirmed that no claim should be paid, related to an unusual set of circumstances.

Today it is possible for an insurer to dispute a suicide claim on the grounds of non-disclosure of a material fact, such as the life assured's history of depressive illness. A number of insurers issue policies containing an exclusion clause, whereby no payment, beyond possibly a refund of premiums, will be made should the life assured die by his/her own hand within a specified period from the inception of the policy; this period is usually, but not always, twelve months. Some authorities contend that an insurer imposing a suicide exclusion clause binds itself to paying all suicide claims arising *after* the exclusion has expired without possibility of recourse to a non-disclosure contention.

Unlawful killing **2.13**

Unlawful killing of the life assured by a person trying to claim title to the policy proceeds would normally be covered by the common law *Forfeiture Rule*, which precludes a person from gaining benefit from his/her wrongdoing. The classic formulation of this principle was given in the case of *Gray v Barr [1970] 2 QB 626*; although this related to the seeking of an indemnity, it would undoubtedly apply to life assurance policies. The *Forfeiture Act 1982* does give the courts some discretion to relieve a person from the full rigour of the Rule where it seems just so to do. Even where a person has been tried and acquitted in connection with the death of the life assured, the insurer could seek to prove such person responsible at civil law, the case being decided on the balance of probabilities. However, an insurer would be well advised to think very carefully before embarking on such a course of action.

Payment of death claims **2.14**

It is obviously important that a death claim should be paid to the correct person. In a life of another policy this is normally the proposer, technically called the assured, as distinct from the life assured. If such person is unable to claim, then the insurer must normally await direction from the court as to how to proceed. An example would be a proposer who is a certified mental patient; here the Court of Protection would be the directing party. Similar rules would govern assigned policies or policies in trust (see 2.13 below).

If it is an own life policy, or the proposer is deceased, the claim will be paid to the deceased's personal representative(s). If the deceased left a will and probate has been obtained, then the claimant will be the executor(s). If the deceased died intestate then the rightful claimant, on production of letters of administration, will be the administrator(s). Occasionally wills are left but no executor is appointed, or the executor cannot or will not act. In such instances, 'letters of administration with will annexed' will be required before settlement can be made.

Age of the life assured **2.15**

If the age of the life assured has not been proved by production of a birth certificate during the currency of the policy, the normal practice is to ask for a birth certificate to verify the age before making payment. If the age has been understated (cases of overstatement are extremely rare), then rather than collect unpaid premiums the insurer normally reduces the sum assured by the ratio premium paid : correct premium. Technically it might be open to the insurer to seek to avoid the claim on the grounds of misrepresentation of a material fact, i.e. age, but this would only seem possible if it could be proved that had the insurer known the true age no policy would have been issued. However, insurers today do not take this step as in all probability a court would say that they have waived their rights by not asking for the birth certificate, as they are entitled to do, at inception. The same principles regarding age discrepancies will apply to maturity claims (see 2.16 below).

Maturity claims 2.16

Claims by maturity arise when endowment policies reach the end of the designated term, the life assured not having died in the meantime. In the past policies matured at a specific age, but the modern practice is to fix a term of years with an expiry date set out in the contractual document.

Most claims by maturity are very straightforward, with payment in own life cases made to the life assured. Life of another policies will be paid to the proposer, or the latter's legal representative(s). Similar procedures will apply to policies assigned or written under trust (see 2.17 below). As stated in 2.14 above, if the policyholder is disabled at law from receiving the proceeds then the insurer will act as directed by the relevant court.

The onus to claim is on the person seeking the policy proceeds, but insurers invariably notify policyholders well in advance of the pending maturity of policies. This enables cheques to be despatched at the maturity date and is excellent marketing practice, as payment of claims by maturity is a good source of further business.

If payment is made to the wrong person, the consequences will fall upon the insurer due to the strict obligation to pay the person entitled. Misappropriation by a stranger, or by an employee, will not be a discharge although the insurer will normally have the right to seek recovery from such a person. If the cheque is misappropriated by a broker or an independent financial adviser the position is less clear. In principle, such broker or adviser will be the agent of the policyholder, and payment to him will be treated as payment to the policyholder himself provided they have actual or apparent authority to receive maturity cheques. However each case will be decided on its merits having regard to the facts.

Assignments and trusts 2.17

Assignment of a life policy 2.18

Assignment was only possible in equity and not at common law until the *Policies of Assurance Act 1867* made provision for statutory assignments. The assignment must be executed in writing, written notice given to the insurer, and the assignee have a good equitable title. Interestingly, insurers still appear not to have permitted anything other than equitable assignments until the passing of the *Judicature Acts 1873* and *1875*. *LPA 1925* subsequently allowed the making of statutory assignments without the requirement of having a good equitable title. Some assignments of life policies are made under *LPA 1925* but assignment under the *Policies of Assurance Act 1867* is probably the more usual option. Assignment of a policy does not of itself discharge the original assured from the duty to pay the premiums. Today many life policies are assigned by way of mortgage.

Assignments made under statute do not have to be supported by consideration. Notice of the assignment must be served upon the insurer (see above) and mere delivery of documents does not constitute an assignment (*Howes v Prudential (1883) 49 LT 133*). An insurer that pays an assignee in good faith obtains a good discharge. If there are successive assignments and they are all of the same type (e.g. all statutory), the insurer's responsibility is discharged if the assignee who gave the first notice of assignment is paid.

It seems as if by assigning a life policy or by placing it in trust (see 2.19 below) the policyholder can evade the strict rules governing the need for insurable interest laid down in the *Life Assurance Act 1774*. Certainly the situation may need clarification before too long, notably with policies assigned very shortly after inception. In *M'Farlane v Royal London Friendly Society (1886) 2 TLR 755* the rule was laid that an assignment will hold good '... provided the assured paid the first premium and the assurance is *bona fide*'. Obviously an assured may 'pay' a premium on reimbursement by the assignee, and the term '*bona fide*' is open to various interpretations. One can only say that life policies have now been freely assigned for over a century and that modern commerce would be made difficult were provisions to be restricted.

Transfer into trust of a life policy 2.19

Just as many life policies are assigned, so are many transferred into trust. A common and simple example is where a parent insures his or her own life and places the policy in trust for the children. The insurer obtains a good discharge by settling a claim or the signature of the trustee(s) – the insurer should not pay the beneficiary or beneficiaries. For many years *section 11* of the *Married Women's Property Act 1882* was used as a vehicle for the creation of trusts in the life assurance sector, but with socio-economic changes in lifestyle this Act is not invoked so much today.

Details of the law and practice governing trusts can be found in *Butterworths Tolley's A Practitioner's Guide to Trusts, John Thurston (3rd Edition)*, available from Butterworths Tolley, price £42.95. Telephone 020 8662 2000.

Chapter 3

Group Life Assurance

- **The principles of group life assurance**
- **Group life assurance in operation**

The principles of group life assurance 3.1

In theory any affinity group can be the subject of a group life assurance scheme, but in the UK modern group life assurance is almost always associated with the work-place environment and with an employer-employee relationship. In some countries, for example in Latin America, if it were not for group business then the life assurance sector would be relatively insignificant. As marketing opportunities are identified, interesting overseas variations of the standard group life contract have developed. For example, in parts of the USA supermarkets admit regular customers to group life plans as a type of 'loyalty bonus' scheme.

History of group life assurance 3.2

Group life assurance in the UK employment context, which is the focus of this chapter, is free of contribution by the employee and is a valuable fringe benefit in the remuneration package. Many families and dependent relatives of deceased employees have found that the group life pay-outs have provided them with a financial life-line at their time of bereavement. During periods of statutory pay restraint in the post-war years, there was a degree of increase in new group life business as employers were barred from anything other than a very modest rise in salaries at best. As a way of improving their workers' conditions, and thus hopefully retaining staff, they opted for a group life scheme. This is analogous to the US experience in the Second World War when many employers, prevented by federal law from offering pay increases, instead offered free group health insurance. However, quite how much workers, especially younger workers, value their group life cover is uncertain, and there is no indication that non-contributory group life 'ties' staff to a particular firm as non-contributory pensions have done in the past.

A collective term assurance 3.3

Effectively group life is a collective term assurance, written on a one-year (or perhaps more often today a two-year) basis. The assured group will obviously vary over time, calling for periodic changes in the sum assured and premiums. This distinguishes it from normal life assurance, where the life assured does not change, and hence a level premium throughout the currency of the policy can be calculated at inception (see 1 ACTUARIAL PRINCIPLES).

Premiums **3.4**

Premiums are based on population statistics and the English Life Tables (see 1 ACTUARIAL PRINCIPLES), with modifications made by insurers to deal with occupational and regional factors. Group life assurance is costed on a unit rate system, based on average age and total sum assured. The initial premium may be based on current salaries, and then adjusted at the end of the policy year if salaries have risen significantly. This follows the pattern of the adjustable premiums common in general branch insurance (e.g. for cover on stock), and is well suited to businesses where the earnings are capable of wide fluctuations, such as City financial institutions.

Types of schemes **3.5**

Group life assurance in the UK can be offered on a stand-alone basis, but it is more commonly linked to an occupational pension scheme. Indeed, the regulations imposed by the Inland Revenue (see 3.7 below and 18 TAXATION IMPLICATIONS OF PENSION/ANNUITY BUSINESS) which cover the business are based on the assumption that a group life scheme is incorporated in an approved occupational pension scheme. These regulations must be adhered to if the employer is to take full advantage of tax concessions and be able to have the premiums allowed as an expense of the business. Special schemes can be arranged for groups of workers in particular circumstances, typically those who travel and/or operate abroad. Here the normal underwriting process will come into play, as clearly there will be specific hazards to be taken into account. It is worth noting that on isolated occasions insurers have been known to act *pro bono* and allow ordinary rates for workers travelling to hazardous areas if their business is essentially humanitarian and aimed at the relief of suffering.

Group credit life assurances **3.6**

Group credit life assurances are an aspect of this business which cannot be ignored. The lender, typically a finance company, is the policyholder and the borrowers are not parties to the contract. Premiums will be calculated on the basis of a type of modified decreasing term assurance (see 11 TYPES OF LIFE POLICY AND POLICY CONSTRUCTION).

The aim of the policy will be to cover any debts remaining outstanding on the debtors' deaths. The policyholder's insurable interest will be that of creditor/debtor (see 7 PROPOSALS AND NEW BUSINESS PROCEDURE).

Some policies are written on a 'profit-sharing' basis. If claims in a year are less than X per cent of premiums, then a proportion of the premiums minus X will be returned to the policyholder. This type of deal is attractive to prospective assureds, as obviously the number of likely claims is very difficult to assess in advance.

Group life assurance in operation **3.7**

Group life benefits are often known, especially in the staff handbooks of insured firms, as 'death in service' benefits. Some misunderstandings have arisen in the past over this terminology – for a legitimate claim to *prima facie* arise, the employee must die while in the firm's employment, but does not have to be physically present in the workplace at the time of death. Benefits are usually expressed in terms of multiples of salary and hence are easy to understand, and change with movements of remuneration levels without the need for constant revisions of wording. A death benefit of four times the salary is the maximum allowed by the Inland Revenue provided the group life plan is incorporated in an approved occupational pension scheme (see 3.5 above).

Underwriting **3.8**

The underwriting criteria for cover to be given within the normal group life scheme limits (or free limits) without evidence of health are:

(*a*) at least a minimum percentage of the workforce must join (this percentage should be set quite high, say at least 80–85 per cent) in order to prevent adverse selection against the insurer (see 12 UNDERWRITING OF LIFE BUSINESS);

(*b*) the scheme members must actually be at work on the day they become eligible for membership (or be physically and mentally capable of working should they be absent on that day for some legitimate reason such as annual holiday) – this hopefully 'screens out' the medically unfit and permits cover without evidence of health on an individual basis;

(*c*) the group must exist for some purpose other than the obtaining of assurance (usually the carrying on of a commercial or business-related enterprise); and

(*d*) there must be a minimum number of people (usually twelve) in the scheme.

As has been stated, if these criteria all apply health evidence will not normally be called for, although the insurer can call for at least a declaration of good health if circumstances so dictate (e.g. if the trade carried on is especially hazardous or a significantly ageing work-force is involved).

Discretionary trust **3.9**

Group life schemes are usually written on a discretionary trust basis. The trustee may be the employer, but many firms favour a group of trustees with staff and employer representatives. One of the principal advantages is that this facilitates the payment of claims. The recommended procedure is as follows:

- the employees each complete a nomination form specifying the beneficiary of their group life cover (these forms can be changed during the currency of scheme membership);
- these nomination forms are not legally binding, but by convention the trustees will always follow the nominations; and
- there will be no inheritance tax liability on the benefit as the deceased employee is held to have neither owned the sum assured nor had the power to dispose of it.

This inheritance tax concession only applies to normal benefits under the scheme.

Employees leaving the firm **3.10**

Insurers do not wish to lose business, so workers who leave the firm are given the option of taking their 'free cover' (i.e. a normal scheme sum assured) with them as an individual policy without evidence of health. A tariff of potential individual policies may be made available. Obviously from the commencement of the cover on an individual basis the ex-employee will have to pay appropriate premiums.

Schemes do often place restrictions on this privilege. For example, the option to take an individual policy will not be granted to employees who are dismissed other than by reason of redundancy. Sometimes the option is also withheld from employees who leave for reasons of ill health, or if not withheld completely is only offered subject to individual underwriting.

Conclusion **3.11**

Group life assurance generates good premium income with, as far as can be assessed, no selection against the insurer. It is a valuable 'fringe benefit' to many workers, albeit one rather lacking the immediate appeal of other arrangements in this category.

Chapter 4

Industrial Life Assurance

- **Development and operations of industrial life assurance**
- **Principles of industrial life assurance**
- **Friendly Societies**
- **Summary**

Development and operations of industrial life assurance 4.1

Foundations and development 4.2

The origins of industrial life assurance probably lie in the village 'box clubs' of the late 18th and early 19th centuries, where rural communities saved on a mutual basis to provide for their coffins (funeral expenses policies would stay a strong element in the business for nearly all its existence). As the rural population moved in large numbers to the cities and towns with the Industrial Revolution, so its members took this tradition of thrift on a mutual basis with them. Early offices were often based around centres of religion, notably nonconformist chapels, and the trade union movement. Some of the pioneering insurers active in the industrial branch grew to become household names, and giant companies of today owe the foundation of their wealth to premiums collected from industrial branch policyholders.

Industrial life assurance has nothing to do with 'industry' in the commercial sense. It began as life assurance aimed at the 'industrial classes' of Victorian Britain, with the objective of offering a service to workers and their families who depended on a weekly wage and who would have had no propensity to save without the discipline of regular collections from their homes. Legally this was classified as 'Industrial Branch (IB)' business. In the 20th century the offices transacting IB insurance moved to calling it 'Home Service Insurance' as this was regarded as a more suitable title.

Definitions **4.3**

The most commonly accepted definition of IB insurance is:

> 'The business of effecting insurances on human life, the premiums in respect of which are received by means of collectors.'

However, a statutory definition appears in the *Industrial Assurance Act 1923* (see 4.10 below):

> 'Insurance business under which premiums are collected at policyholders' homes at intervals of not more than two months.'

It can be seen that a high priority was placed on this characteristic of door-to-door collection, which continued on a weekly basis well into the post-Second World War era.

Criticisms of industrial life assurance 4.4

Transaction expenses 4.5

The expenses of transacting IB business have always been high, mainly due to the labour-intensive nature of an activity based on having a large workforce out on the streets collecting premiums and interacting with the public. At various times the Government has sought to intervene, mainly basing its case on these high expense-ratios. In the mid-19th century a scheme was set up whereby the Post Office offered IB-equivalent policies in competition with the insurers, although it eventually foundered. A more serious threat came in the 1940s, when Clement Attlee's Labour Government proposed the nationalisation of the IB business. The insurers mobilised a campaign, spearheaded by the Industrial Life Offices Association, to counter this threat. Although this threat receded with the virtual collapse of Labour's majority in 1950 and the Conservative victory of 1951, insurers maintained their campaign to keep industrial life assurance in the hands of private enterprise for many years. However, one of the main reasons for the eventual decline of IB business was the cost of running the business, combined with problems recruiting and retaining agents, and the changing pattern of working life (meaning that far fewer homes were occupied during the day to receive callers).

High policy lapse ratio 4.6

Another criticism of the IB offices has been the very high lapse ratio of policies over the years. This has undoubtedly been a source of concealed profit for the insurers, with substantial 'orphan funds' building up, and means hundreds of thousands, possibly millions, of policies and related documents being tucked away in people's possession with little or no indication of what value they might represent (see 2 CLAIMS).

Protection of policyholders 4.7

Governments have, certainly throughout the 20th century, had a particular regard for the welfare of IB policyholders, feeling that they need special protection. This rather paternalistic approach reflects the belief that, as a class, these policyholders lack the ability to stand up for themselves and could be exploited. More than any other class of insurance business, industrial life assurance has been the subject of much legislation (see 4.10 below), most of it designed to safeguard policyholders' interests. In 1923, the Office of the Industrial Assurance Commissioner was created by statute, creating a unique role in Great

Britain, and one which was akin to the State Insurance Commissioners in the USA. The Industrial Assurance Commissioner was a civil servant who doubled as Chief Registrar of Friendly Societies, and had powers to:

(*a*) regulate the IB sector;

(*b*) determine disputes, both between policyholders and insurers and between individual policyholders; and

(*c*) (if necessary) fine insurers and/or members of their staff who broke certain of the strict rules which governed their day-to-day operations.

In 1992 a new regulatory body entitled the Friendly Societies Commission took over from the Chief Registrar of Friendly Societies and the Industrial Assurance Commissioner.

Industrial life assurance in today's market 4.8

Virtually no new industrial life assurance business is being written today, and most of the insurers have ceased door-to-door collections. For many years the high costs and administrative difficulties were looked at askance by insurers, but these were outweighed by the volume of attractive business which flowed in as a result of having agents calling on families and being well-known to them. At one time these agents, although loosely employed by the insurers, owned their collecting books and had an asset value in them, as well as being remunerated by new business and collecting commission. This 'book interest' system was generally phased out over the years in favour of salaried agents, the salary invariably being reinforced by a commission element, but it lingered on in certain areas throughout the 20th century. As previously stated, it will be very many years before IB policies cease to be submitted for attention.

Principles of industrial life assurance 4.9

Although there was never a statutory limit on the size of IB policies, such policies were usually for relatively small sums assured at modest weekly or monthly premiums. Policies were basically whole life or variations of endowment assurances, with little individual underwriting, and there was a strong focus on funeral expenses as the reason for the cover. During the 20th century other motives were also catered for, such as saving for a child's coming of age or just general investment. Policies were issued with profits, although bonus rates were invariably lower than with ordinary branch business. Some interesting ideas were experimented with; for example, during the Second World War policies were allied with 'Victory Bonds' to help the war effort. This was, in some limited respects, a forerunner of today's linking (see 13 UNIT LINKED POLICIES).

Legislation 4.10

Two major statutes dominate industrial life assurance: the *Industrial Assurance Act 1923* (*IAA 1923*) (which took effect from 1 January 1924) and the *Industrial Assurance and Friendly Societies Act 1948* (*IAFSA 1948*) (which was amended in 1958 to raise the permitted sum assured to £30). *Section 5 of Part II of IAFSA 1948*, which must be read in conjunction with *Schedule 2*, lays down that the activities of a Friendly Society can fall into any of the following categories (note that a Society can be in more than one category).

- Life and annuity.
- Marriage and birth.
- Linked long-term.
- Permanent health.
- Tontines.
- Capital redemption.
- Pension fund management.
- Accident.
- Sickness.
- Miscellaneous financial loss.
- Contractual activities for the relief of persons during sickness or when in distressed circumstances, or to meet any funeral expenses.
- Discretionary activities for the education of any persons, relief during sickness or when out of employment, in distressed circumstances or to help meet funeral expenses.

As stated at 4.7 above, the heavy incidence of statute law governing industrial life assurance reflects a governmental desire to protect the interests of IB policyholders. *IAA 1923* paid particular attention to the need for policyholders to receive prompt and correct attention, with penalties for insurers and their employees who kept documents more than 21 days without resolving the problem which had led to their retention or who failed to give a proper receipt for premiums. *IAFSA 1948* is of particular interest in that it took the bold step of creating four new classes of statutory insurable interest:

- child in parent;
- step-child in step-parent;
- adopted child in adoptive parent; and
- grandchild in grand-parent;

to the extent of £20 (uprated in 1958 to £30) with the purpose of assisting with funeral expenses. This financial limit applied to all the policies taken out and ran across insurers, leading to much petty administration and consequent annoyance to many claimants. It was well-meaning legislation that clearly did not keep pace with the escalating cost of funerals; however, it did generate a volume of business and premium income over the years.

Friendly Societies 4.11

Origins and history 4.12

Friendly Societies have their origins in the middle of the 19th century as voluntary organisations based on a principle of mutual self-help. Although at least two grew to be major national participants in the insurance industry, and others converted to become major companies or mutual societies, the vast majority were small in size and regional in nature. Some related to particular trades or professions, perhaps with a purely regional dimension as well. Life assurance was the business of the Collecting Friendly Societies, and there were many other societies which specialised in cattle insurance or operated working men's clubs and old people's homes. The life assurance side started as voluntary funds which evolved into industrial assurance funds over the years.

Mergers, windings-up and transfers of engagements meant a steady decline in the number of Friendly Societies. By the mid-1960s the number had fallen to 57, of which several were moribund. The great advantage of Friendly Societies has long been tax concessions, typically those conferred by *section 460* of the *Income and Corporation Taxes Act 1988.*

Current legislation 4.13

The current legislation governing Friendly Societies is the *Friendly Societies Act 1992*. Significantly, this allows the creation of incorporated Friendly Societies, able to enjoy the advantages of limited liability, either by the conversion of existing Societies or the creation of new ones. In addition to their basic insurance functions these organisations can engage in benevolent activities, reinsurance and group insurance. However, their range of activities is limited to *either* long-term business *or* general business (not both). Full details of what constitutes these classes is in *Part II* of the *Friendly Societies Act 1992*.

Friendly Societies today 4.14

One vestige of the earlier wide-ranging and anomalous activities of Friendly Societies remains. They have the discretion to issue policies to provide for the education of specified persons, even when such policies would otherwise be void under the *Life Assurance Act 1774*. In general Friendly Societies are now found to be a good vehicle for writing attractive contracts, and they can transact linked long-term policies and permanent health insurance as well as life and annuity. Limits on premiums remain but these are purely for the purposes of tax exemption on the profits arising – societies can issue policies with larger premiums but if they do so they will not be exempt from tax on investment gains made under such policies.

Summary 4.15

Even though new IB business is no longer written, industrial life assurance must never be scorned. Although it does relate to an age that has passed – an age of ready cash payments, door-to-door collections, benevolent paternalism and an ultimately cumbersome and bureaucratic system – it did bring insurance into homes where otherwise saving would have been unknown. Many agents became family friends and advisers, and gave some limited financial security, especially at time of bereavement, to the poorer sections of society.

Chapter 5

Policy Conditions and Endorsements

- **Legal principles governing policies, premiums and conditions**
- **Policy conditions**
- **Endorsements**

Legal principles governing policies, premiums and conditions 5.1

The policy 5.2

The policy is the document prepared by the life office to express the terms of the contract which has already been made, and with which it must conform. The office must prepare the policy in accordance with its marketing literature and the proposal form, otherwise the proposer need not accept it. However, preliminary statements and documents form no part of the contract unless they are incorporated into the policy, normally by direct reference, in which case they are read as part of the policy. A mere reference to the proposal in the policy will not constitute incorporation; there must be a positive statement, e.g. that it forms the basis of the contract.

Evidence extrinsic to the policy may be admitted in order:

(*a*) to show that the policy does not truly set out the full terms of the agreement between the parties and should be rectified accordingly (*Sun Life Assurance Company of Canada v Jervis [1944] AC 111*);

or

(*b*) to show that there is a collateral agreement which represents a supplementary part of the bargain.

This must be more than a mere statement as to practice or probable benefits.

A mutual mistake over the agreement which has led to it being mistakenly recorded in the policy can lead to the document being rectified, although the burden of proof on the party seeking rectification is strong. A unilateral error by one party will usually afford no relief (*Royal Liver Friendly Society v Shearer [1930] IAC 9NI0 Rep 73*).

Legislation **5.3**

The common law does not require a contract of life assurance to be in any particular form, or indeed to be in writing at all. *Section 100* of the *Stamp Act 1891* did call for a life policy to be stamped within one month of issue, and it was usually contended that this *de facto* if not *de jure* meant that written policies were required. However, *section 100* was repealed by *section 173(3)* of the *Finance Act 1989*, which abolished stamp duty on life assurance policies. Despite this, whatever the legal position, it is now the general practice to issue policies of life assurance. The advent of unit linked business (see 13 UNIT LINKED POLICIES) has led to the introduction of policies issued in 'clusters', with one document to be treated as the principal contract of assurance alongside a number of separate schedules of benefits which expressly incorporate the contract by reference.

Under the *Unfair Terms in Consumer Contracts Regulations 1994* (*SI 1994/3159*) (as amended by the *Unfair Terms in Consumer Contracts Regulations 1999* (*SI 1999/2083*)), there is the possibility that a policyholder may seek to have the terms of an insurance policy varied if the contract was not individually negotiated and they appear to cause a significant imbalance in the parties' rights and obligations. The 1994 Regulations have caused insurance companies to think carefully about their policy wordings, not least because virtually no policies, certainly no life policies, are individually negotiated. Immunity from the *Unfair Contract Terms Act 1977* gave insurers something of a false sense of security in this area. It has now been established that a policy containing an onerous term against the policyholder's interests can be subject to variation by the courts.

It is not the intention that references under the *Unfair Terms in Consumer Contracts Regulations 1994* (*SI 1994/3159*) come to court; they are dealt with by the Director of Fair Trading via the Office of Fair Trading (OFT). As yet there seem to be no reported references relating to insurance, but the following is a typical example of a reference under the 1994 Regulations. In *Re Penerlie Lodge Residential Home*, reported in the OFT bulletin of August 2000, residents had to have all their possessions cleared from the home within 48 hours of their death, but were still liable for one month's rent with no requirements at all on the management of the home. The rules also stated that no resident could go for a walk without the matron's consent. The latter term was ordered to be completely struck out and the former term varied to all belongings to be removed within three days and the home to claim only three days' rent.

Premiums **5.4**

The premium is the consideration from the assured in return for the life office's obligations in the contract of life assurance. Premiums may be periodic or single, and periodic premiums may be annual or of greater frequency. A policy may be effected at an annual premium payable by a series of *instalment* premiums (or indeed a quarterly premium could be payable by monthly instalments). Any instalments not already paid at the time of claim will be deducted from the policy proceeds. Instalment premiums must be contrasted with *true* premiums (e.g. true quarterly – these are 'stand-alone' premiums in their own right and are not regarded as a part of a greater item).

Renewal notices 5.5

With many policies now paid for via direct debit or through standing order arrangements, renewal notices are not as relevant as in times past. However, offices still send renewal notices where applicable, but non-service of a notice does not excuse the policyholder for not paying the premium. It is extremely important that the renewal process is double-checked to ensure that notices are not despatched in respect of lives assured who are in fact deceased, as apart from revealing inefficiencies in the system this can cause great offence. One office that, as a marketing instrument, despatched renewal notices relative to children's deferred assurances (see 14 USES OF LIFE ASSURANCE) with 'furry animals' around the borders sent several such notices to policyholders whose children had recently died – the consequences, as can be imagined, were horrendous.

Conditions 5.6

Conditions of a life assurance policy can be considered under the headings privilege, restrictive and explanatory. Explanatory conditions are not nowadays generic as the wording of modern life policies tends to be clear, so such conditions are only required on a case-by-case basis. The privilege and restrictive conditions will be looked at in detail at 5.7 *et seq* below.

Policy conditions 5.7

Suicide 5.8

This is the only generic restrictive condition to be found in a life assurance policy, and even then around 50 per cent of life offices do not include it. The typical clause states that the policy shall be void in the event of the life assured dying by suicide within a specific period (usually, but not always, 12 months) of inception of the contract. Generally the insurer will refund the premium(s) paid. It is contended that an insurer who puts a suicide exclusion clause in its policies commits itself to paying claims in all suicide cases outside the exclusion period, with no possibility of contending some form of non-disclosure (typically of previous depressive illness), but this has not been tested.

Days of grace 5.9

If a life policy is issued with an annual or other periodic payment, the assured has the right to renew the policy from time to time on payment of the premium. On the other hand, he/she may allow the policy to lapse unless there is some covenant in existence to maintain it.

As a general rule, a certain number of days of grace (often 28 days) are allowed for payment of the renewal premium. The assured can pay the premiums within this period of time and keep the policy in force without penalty.

The terms of the days of grace and the conditions attaching to them will be construed very strictly. Time is of the essence, and equity will give no relief against lapse for non-payment as the assured and the life office are not on an equal footing. The assured has the right to renew but the life office cannot compel payment (*Rowan v Atlas Assurance Co. Ltd [1928] 72 Sol Jo 285*). Tender of payment without acceptance may suffice to keep the policy in force (*Farquarson v Pearl Assurance Co. Ltd [1937] All ER 124*).

Non-forfeiture regulations **5.10**

Conventional whole life and endowment policies usually contain a non-forfeiture condition, a provision intended to preserve the cover (or some part of it), perhaps for a limited period, if the premium is not paid by the end of the days of grace. There must be a surrender value for this condition to come into action. Variations of the non-forfeiture conditions are:

(*a*) the assurance is held in force as long as the surrender value exceeds the overdue premiums;

(*b*) the assurance is held in force for a set period (typically one year) and then converted to a paid-up policy of such reduced amount as the balance of the surrender value will permit;

(*c*) the surrender value is applied as a single premium for a term assurance for such period as it will cover; and

(*d*) the assurance is automatically converted at the end of the days of grace to the paid-up value of the policy at that date.

At one time there was speculation that non-forfeiture conditions might fall within the scope of the *Consumer Credit Act 1974*, notably *section 9(1)*. However, this is now generally accepted as not being the case, as the main purpose of the overall transaction is not the provision of credit.

Revival (or reinstatement) conditions **5.11**

Insurers do not wish to lose policyholders, and this condition allows application to be made for the reinstatement of the policy on its original terms within a fixed period of lapse and/or the expiry of the period represented by the non-forfeiture regulations (see 5.10 above). Outstanding premiums, as well as a modest rate of interest on top of the premium, will have to be paid, and the insurer will reserve the right to ask for evidence of continued good health and confirmation that there has been no material change in the risk. There is clearly the prospect of selection against the insurer, as the policyholder's desire to revive his/her policy might have been motivated by a deterioration in the health or other circumstances of the life assured. Often a simple declaration will be accepted and no further evidence sought.

Paid-up policy conditions **5.12**

In the past paid-up policies were frequently called 'free policies', although this term never really had a great deal of meaning and is now becoming uncommon. The assurance remains in force on the life assured on its original terms except that no further premiums are payable and the policy is endorsed with a new (and almost always reduced) sum assured. Continued participation in profits for appropriate policies is possible – this can only be determined by examining the wording of both the conditions and the contract. Many paid-up policy values are determined on the 'proportionate' basis, with the new sum assured being calculated by the formula:

$$\frac{\text{Original sum assured}}{} \times \frac{\text{Premiums paid}}{\text{Total premiums paid}}$$

Cash surrender values **5.13**

This condition really relates to conventional policies, as unit linked assurances usually employ some other term to refer to the early termination of the contract and cashing-in of the units accrued by the assured. However, the principles of cash surrender values hold good across the spectrum of life policies, as offices invariably hold back some of the value represented by the policy to cover their initial expenses and other charges.

The surrender value comes out of the policy reserve (see 9 RESERVES AND VALUATIONS), so if a policy does not have a reserve it will not carry a surrender value. Therefore, for example, it is extremely rare for any policy to have a surrender value in its first one or two years of existence. Also, no surrender value will be permitted if it would give rise to selection against the insurer, so term assurances and contingent assurances will not possess this type of privilege condition (see 11 TYPES OF LIFE POLICY AND POLICY CONSTRUCTION).

Surrender values are a source of great misunderstanding, and conflict between policyholders and insurers. In the early years of policies surrender values almost always fall below the policyholder's expectations as something akin to a full return of money paid in is being sought. Some offices print in the policies, or publish in their marketing literature, tables of guaranteed surrender values, or guaranteed minimum surrender values, but the danger inherent in this practice is that policyholders are given the idea that surrender is an 'easy option', and in any event it merely transfers the timing of disputes. It can also be argued that no surrender value can really be 'guaranteed', as the amount available in the policy reserve will depend on future uncertain factors, so such guarantees are not true surrender values but fixed periodic cash options.

Some of the reasons why cash surrender values frequently fall short of policyholders' expectations are as follows.

(*a*) The insurer will have incurred heavy initial expenses (e.g. commission, medical fees, costs of policy preparation) and these must be recovered to preserve equity with other policyholders.

(*b*) Paying the surrender will itself involve expense to the insurer.

(*c*) The policyholder will in a sense be 'breaking' his/her contract and exercising a one-sided option, as the insurer cannot unilaterally cease to provide cover. This argument is not strong, as the relevant condition in the contract does give the policyholder the legal right to surrender.

(*d*) High incidence of surrenders will lead to a deterioration in the insurer's mortality experience, as there is empirical evidence that sound lives tend to surrender in times of financial stress. Impaired lives will retain their cover and seek to raise money by other means.

(*e*) The insurer will lose anticipated investment income.

(*f*) Surrenders are not meant to be attractive.

Policy loans 5.14

As an alternative to surrendering the policy the policyholder can seek to borrow money under it. Loans can be sought to pay premiums. Insurers lend within the surrender value (usually 90 per cent or even 95 per cent), charge a commercial rate of interest, and take a charge on the policy as security. Policy loans represent a good investment for a life office, as they can always deduct the loan from any future claim if it has not by then been repaid.

Endorsements 5.15

Endorsements are not as common in life assurance as in general branch insurance, but when used they apply specific conditions and warranties to the policy. Examples would be premium waiver options (whereby the policyholder is excused payment if they are disabled or undergo redundancy – the element of the premium required for the redundancy cover should not go into the life fund, as it does not relate to life assurance), inheritance tax options, and options to increase the sum assured with guaranteed insurability on the happening of named events such as the birth of a child. Endorsements can be used to restrict cover, typically excluding death arising out of private aviation or motor racing/motor trials.

Special provisions will be held to override general provisions, so endorsements printed on after the main body of the policy text has been set will take priority, yielding to endorsements subsequently affixed to the document.

Endorsements are discussed in more depth in 11 TYPES OF LIFE POLICY AND POLICY CONSTRUCTION.

Chapter 6

Profits, Investments and Bonus Distribution

- **With-profits business**
- **The investment of life funds**
- **Types of bonus**

With-profits business 6.1

It may well be that conventional with-profits life assurance will never again be a force in the financial sector. Most insurers now concentrate on unit linked or unitised contracts (see 13 UNIT LINKED POLICIES), where policyholders can identify the manner in which their premiums are being invested, exercise their own judgement over the best use of money, and see the value of their policies (or plans) expressed on a day-by-day basis. Yet for well over a century offices transacted a high volume of with-profits business and did so very successfully, with generations of assureds gaining excellent returns and benefiting from the growth in life funds. Many people have good reason to be grateful for having effected, in particular, with-profits endowments and receiving claim payments representing a tripling or even quadrupling of the original sum assured.

The philosophy of with-profits business 6.2

With-profits life assurance depends on trust, loyalty and confidence as much as on the technical performance of fund management. In the past policyholders have had a high degree of loyalty to specific insurers, with this loyalty often going back through generations of families, and they trusted the judgement and financial probity of the insurers' officers. At the same time actuaries and senior employees saw the insurer for whom they worked as offering them a career for life, with service of 40 years and upwards the expected norm, and they had complete loyalty to their employer. Their working life would be spent with one insurer, and its success would be their success. These individuals thought long-term and their working practices were long-term. The insurers, although they could be criticised for being paternalistic in attitude, felt a confidence and certainty in their senior work-force, nearly all of whom would not have worked for anybody else and who would have grown up professionally in a common culture.

In this environment with-profits business flourished. Policyholders trusted the insurer, the insurer trusted the judgement of its senior staff, and the senior staff felt completely secure and could plan long-term. The essence of with-profits business is that the investment of the appropriate part of the premium – often over 90 per cent – is at the discretion of the actuaries or investment managers, although subject to the overall concurrence of the Board of Directors. Policyholders do not necessarily know where the funds are being placed, and the results may not be known for many years. Certainly, until quite recently, investment policy and criteria were not regarded as anyone's business outside the tightly-knit group of technical professionals which both the insurers and the policyholders trusted implicitly. It must be said that for many years their performance justified this trust.

The current situation 6.3

We now live in a very different world. This essential trust has disappeared. In today's market policyholders want, and with good reason, to know where their money is going, and financial journalists are always querying company practices and looking for short-term yardsticks by which to measure performance. Investment products and life assurance have become mixed, and this is largely due to selling practices in the latter years of Life Assurance Premium Relief (LAPR) (see 10 TAXATION AND LIFE ASSURANCE). Year-on-year returns are now what many policyholders are seeking, and they are encouraged by the media to 'shop around' rather than stay loyal to one insurer. Senior staff switch from employer to employer, and even when taking jobs make no secret of the fact that they anticipate moving on after two or three years. They will not be there in the long-term, so why should they think in the long-term? Even Chief Executives can and do move around, often with bewildering speed, a process encouraged by the ever-increasing trend towards mergers and take-overs. The stability essential in order for with-profits business to flourish has gone and is unlikely to return.

Recent mis-selling 'scandals', and the failure of bonuses to meet over-optimistic forecasts, have been of serious, possibly mortal, injury to the with-profits concept. The sight of with-profit policyholders – especially those holding pension policies – appearing on television either in person or via 'action groups' to express their worries and even despair does nothing to help the image of the insurance industry. It seems that few future policyholders will be content to trust their funds entirely to the discretion of company insiders.

Investment of life funds 6.4

The importance of investment 6.5

Investment is a vital element in the calculation and utilisation of life office premiums, along with mortality and expenses. Because of the long-term nature of the business life offices can place much more emphasis on investment than can their general branch counterparts, for whom investment returns are very much 'jam' on their bread and butter. In life assurance investments are definitely part of the bread and butter of the sector, and the investment manager is a key player.

Life policies build up reserves, and these reserves are invested by the insurers in assets which exist within the life fund(s). At one time, provided a life office's invested assets exceeded its liabilities, it was deemed to be solvent, and the excess was called the 'surplus'. Of this surplus the Board of Directors, acting on the advice of the actuary, would apportion the 'divisible surplus' and this would be distributed as bonuses to entitled policyholders and, where appropriate, as dividends to shareholders. Nowadays a life office has to achieve the statutory margin of solvency before it can show a surplus and work out the divisible surplus, out of which it can declare bonuses and dividends; however the principle remains the same.

The statutory margin of solvency is a calculation based on actuarial liabilities. A ratio is established which the funds of the life office must meet and maintain in relation to these actuarially calculated long-term liabilities, always subject to the maintenance of a minimum fund which varies between proprietary, mutual and reassurance companies. The requirement for a statutory margin of solvency for life offices was laid down in the *EEC Life Establishment Directive 1979* (*79/167/EEC*) and brought into English law by way of the *Insurance Companies Act 1981*. This Act has now been consolidated into the *Insurance Companies Act 1982*, which in the context of margins of solvency should be read in conjunction with the *Insurance Companies Regulations 1981* (*SI 1981/1654*).

The predictability of claims **6.6**

Another factor helping the role of investment in life assurance is the predictability of claims. Future maturity claims can be accurately forecast and death claims, thanks to the sophistication of modern mortality tables (see 1.6 MORTALITY TABLES IN THE CURRENT MARKET), predicted relatively precisely. Hence large amounts of investments can be kept in non-liquid form, with subsequent potential for high return. 'Matching' is carried out, with attempts made to match a future year's investment return with the future year's likely claims. Long-term and potentially lucrative, but notoriously non-liquid, types of investment such as property and long-dated bonds and stock can be used. In the mid-19th century insurers invested premiums in Post Office accounts – steadily they moved into progressively more 'adventurous' types of investment until we had the 'cult of the equity' post-Second World War.

Potential problems with investment **6.7**

From time to time hints of discontent with life offices' investment practices surfaced. In the 1930s one very large office was the subject of allegations, which were always resisted, that it had undermined the depressed British coal mining industry by investing in Polish coalfields. However in general offices were given a free hand where and where not to invest. The nationalisation proposals of the 1945 Labour Government (see 4.5 TRANSACTION EXPENSES) were followed by ill-defined plans for 'investment control', but in practice until unit linking began (see 13 UNIT LINKED POLICIES) life offices had wide freedom as to where they invested their funds, subject to general legal constraints.

Life offices have massive funds at their disposal, but at the same time it can be said that they 'owe' a great deal of money to policyholders in terms of contractual obligations. To this can be added promises of potential returns they have made over the years. Failure to meet contractual obligations means insolvency, and failure to meet promises means at the very best a serious loss of goodwill. In between these two lies failure to meet guarantees, which constituted a breach of duty with severe consequences for one very well-established insurer, who as a result was forced to cease taking new business (an almost certain recipe for eventual extinction unless a buyer can be found).

Types of bonus 6.8

Uniform simple reversionary bonus 6.9

The reversionary bonus method formed the bedrock of British profit distribution for many years. Offices declared the bonus rate as a percentage of the sum assured at their periodic valuations and the appropriate bonuses were attached to the policies to be paid at time of claim. Policyholders received notification in the form of bonus cards as to their entitlement and knew that all the bonuses would be added together when the eventual claim fell due. For the privilege of participating in profits, policyholders would pay a modest loading on top of the standard non-profit premium, but for most of the 20th century the return on with-profit assurances far outstripped the extra premium. Non-profit policies were only really to be recommended in the relatively brief periods when bonus rates were disappointingly low, such as parts of the 1930s and the late 1940s, or if only a fixed sum assured was all that was needed, for example to meet a known future commitment.

Compound reversionary bonus 6.10

This system was akin to the uniform simple reversionary bonus, with the exception that bonuses, once declared, themselves earned bonuses. This compounding effect could give quite spectacular returns on policies in force for a lengthy period of time. Generally the percentage rate of sum assured quoted for compound bonuses would be slightly lower than that for simple bonuses, but it would not take long for the 'compounding' to take effect and returns thereafter would expand.

Cash bonuses 6.11

From time to time offices would introduce classes of with-profits policies that paid the policyholder periodic cash bonuses. It is fair to say that these were quite legitimate marketing ploys, but they involved extra administration and really represented nothing new as reversionary bonuses could always be surrendered for cash. The so-called cash bonuses were really the immediate surrender value of reversionary bonuses declared at pre-set intervals.

Bonuses in reduction of premiums 6.12

These were another example of offices seeking to gain a competitive edge by varying the method of bonus distribution, and instead of adding bonuses to the value of the sum assured they were employed to reduce future premiums. Experience varied, but the method never seemed to become popular and during the years of LAPR (see 10 TAXATION AND LIFE ASSURANCE) reductions in premiums meant a reduction in income tax relief and consequently in many cases were quite counter-productive.

Contribution method bonuses **6.13**

These were pioneered by a mathematician named Dr. Sprague and mainly offered by Commonwealth life offices, notably the very active Canadian life insurers. There was great emphasis on equity between policyholders, and the idea was that classes of policy would share in the divisible surplus in the proportion that they had contributed to the creation of that surplus (hence the name). The mortality experience of different groups of policyholders would be taken into account, as would their share of the office's expenses and contribution to investment profit. Working out contribution bonuses was rather complicated, and whether the end-result justified the effort was uncertain. The number of policyholders who (a) realised and (b) appreciated the efforts being made on their behalf to ensure fairness of reward was questionable.

Tontine bonuses **6.14**

The tontine method was only followed in very limited operations in the UK, but policies issued overseas, notably in the USA, could carry tontine bonuses. The concept was that all bonuses added to a class of policy (such as 10 year endowments effected in 1988) were held back in a pool and then distributed amongst the survivors at the expiry of the term.

Interim bonuses **6.15**

These were bonuses awarded to policies in between valuations, which at one time needed only to be conducted every five years (triennial valuations became very common). Before computerisation, indeed before the mechanisation of records in the late 1940s/early 1950s, valuations were labour-intensive operations and very time-consuming. The interim bonus was anticipatory of the next valuation and a charge on the forthcoming valuation surplus. For obvious reasons interim bonuses erred on the side of caution and the percentage rate was invariably lower than that which was declared for the reversionary bonus.

Terminal bonuses **6.16**

These have become matters of controversy in recent years, mainly as a result of over-optimistic forecasting. Indeed, it can be argued strongly that terminal bonuses should never be forecast as they depend on future factors which cannot be predicted with any accuracy.

In the mid-1960s offices found themselves with embarrassingly large surpluses and came under pressure to increase bonuses, not least to compete with other financial institutions in investment returns. Actuaries were understandably reluctant to increase reversionary bonuses significantly and thus store up heavy commitments for future years, but the idea of a 'one-off' enhanced payout on policies becoming claims in the calendar year was attractive as it could be costed relatively accurately and involved no ongoing involvement. In the 19th century the first bonuses had been the rather oddly-named 'mortuary bonuses' paid as an addition to claims occurring in a particular year, and this was the concept up-dated to provide terminal bonuses. The initial terminology varied with 'special bonuses', 'final bonuses' and even 'special final bonuses' each having their advocates, but although some practitioners disliked the term 'terminal bonus' on the grounds that the public might somehow associate it with terminal illness, this is the name that has stuck.

Terminal bonuses on with-profits policies are usually expressed as a percentage addition to the reversionary bonuses already accrued. As has been stated, they are declared for a year on all eligible policies becoming claims in that year. They need not be renewed for the next year, and if terminal bonuses *are* again declared they can be at a different percentage rate. It is this possibility of declining a terminal bonus, or reducing the rate, that has hit insurers whose sales force used forecasts of terminal bonuses when selling policies (notably in relation to house purchase business – see 14 USES OF LIFE ASSURANCE).

When terminal bonuses first appeared they proved very popular with the insuring public and without doubt boosted the sale of policies. Claimants under with-profits policies expected their reversionary and interim bonuses, but had a pleasant surprise when they received the 'gift' of a terminal bonus as a third tier. This honeymoon period did not last long, and soon terminal bonuses were expected and offices competed on the amounts on offer. When investment performance began to fall away, terminal bonuses were the first items insurers cut in order to save money.

Guaranteed bonuses 6.17

These must be mentioned but they are not true bonuses, as a bonus must be declared out of the surplus thrown up by the office's valuation and this can never be guaranteed in advance. Guaranteed bonuses are really increases in the sum assured (often called escalating sums assured) and are percentage additions which are pre-planned and costed in the premiums.

Chapter 7

Proposals and New Business Procedure

- **Formation of the life assurance contract**
- **Proposal forms**
- **The doctrine of utmost good faith**
- **Insurable interest**
- **The role of the intermediary**

Formation of the life assurance contract 7.1

Definition of the contract 7.2

There is no specific legal definition of a life assurance contract, beyond the classic generic definition of a contract, which is:

> 'an agreement enforceable at law made between two or more persons by which rights are acquired by one or more to certain acts or forbearance on the part of the other or others'.

A practical definition might be that a life assurance contract is one whereby one party (the insurer) undertakes for a consideration (the premium) to pay money (the sum assured) to or for the benefit of the other party (the assured) upon the happening of a specified event, where the object of the assured is to provide a sum for himself or others at some future date, or for others in the event of his death.

(**Note:** For convenience the masculine gender has been used in this definition, and this convention will be followed throughout this chapter.)

Presence of the required contractual elements 7.3

There can be no doubt that an agreement to provide life assurance meets the essential requirements of a valid contract, as the three elements:

(*a*) intention to create legal relations;

(*b*) agreement, achieved through the offer and acceptance of mutually understood terms; and (*c*) the presence of valuable consideration,

are all present. However, over the years there has been extensive legal debate as to exactly when the negotiating parties become bound in contract. The most commonly accepted sequence of events is as follows:

- the issue of prospectuses and proposal forms by the insurer constituting an invitation to treat;
- the submission of a completed proposal form by the proposer to the insurer also constituting an invitation to treat; and
- the so-called letter of acceptance from the insurer being an offer which the proposer accepts by paying the first premium.

Some legal authorities contend that the completed proposal is in law an offer and that the letter of acceptance constitutes a counter-offer which the proposer can accept by paying the first premium or reject. In practice, whichever view is taken the eventual outcome is the same. Very often insurers take the first premium as a deposit, in which case the contract will commence when the proposer agrees to the deposit being converted into an actual premium.

Contracts formed through advertisements **7.4**

Problems can arise where insurers advertise guaranteed acceptance if certain conditions are satisfied, for example, with whole life contracts sold by some form of direct marketing. Such statements would probably constitute general offers, or indeed specific offers if the material has been personalised. Provided the prospective proposer complies exactly with the terms of the advertisement – typically by completing an included application form which incorporates either a direct debit mandate or a formal undertaking to pay the premiums – he is entitled to regard himself as having accepted the offer. The only exception would be if the offer is withdrawn and (importantly) this fact is communicated to the proposer before acceptance. To avoid any areas of doubt, the insurer should make its intentions very clear when seeking to transact business in this manner.

Proposal forms **7.5**

At one time proposals were lengthy and very detailed documents. Many questions specific to named diseases were asked – one major insurer was still using a form with 52 health questions well after the Second World War. There was then a swing towards very brief proposal forms, which were found to be unhelpful for all but the most basic covers. It is now common for proposals to ask questions identifying the life proposed and seeking details of:

- occupation;
- pastimes;
- current health and physical condition;
- medical history;

- family history; and
- lifestyle.

A sample life assurance proposal form appears in APPENDIX 7A below.

Principles of proposal forms **7.6**

Over the years insurers have been subjected to criticism from the judiciary and consumer interest groups for the inclusion in proposal forms of 'sweep-up' questions such as 'Are there any other circumstances of which we should be made aware?'. It is clearly impossible for insurers to ask direct questions on every potential material fact, but the Association of British Insurers (ABI) in its *Statement of Long-Term Insurance Practice* (the Statement) lays down the following relevant principles.

> '(*c*) Those matters which insurers have commonly found to be material should be subject to clear questions in proposal forms.
>
> (*d*) Insurers should avoid asking questions which would require knowledge beyond that which the signatory could reasonably be expected to possess.'
>
> *(ABI Statement of Long-Term Insurance Practice, sections 1(c)(d))*

The Statement also makes it clear that answers to questions in the proposal form on matters of past or present fact shall not be converted into warranties (see 7.13 below), unless the answer concerns a factual matter relating to the life to be assured under a life of another contract. Specific warranties *may* be required about matters which are material to the risk.

Proposal forms invariably end with a declaration which the proposer has to sign. These declarations are nowadays worded to affirm the truth of the answers to the best of the proposer's 'knowledge and belief'. The practice of requiring the proposer to warrant the absolute truth of answers was discontinued many years ago.

Relevant legislation **7.7**

Life assurance contracts would appear at first sight to fall within the provisions of the *Disability Discrimination Act 1995* (*DDA 1995*) , as information given in answer to questions on proposal forms could be used to deal with a disabled person more harshly than someone who is able-bodied. However, *section 20* of *DDA 1995* expressly relieves insurers of any liability provided they can demonstrate that special terms imposed on a person suffering from a disability are in place purely for actuarial or underwriting reasons.

Section 24 of *DDA 1995* states that a provider of services discriminates if, for a reason which relates to the person's disability, he treats him less favourably than he treats, or would treat, others to whom the reason does not or would not apply, and he cannot show that the treatment is justified. By way of *section 20* (see above) the treatment can be justified in the case of life assurance applications.

When the *Data Protection Act 1998* was passed insurers voluntarily agreed that they would make a person's own life assurance records available to him or her without waiting for litigation under the Act.

Proposal forms today draw the signatory's attention to various rights he/she can exercise – e.g. under the *Access to Medical Reports Act 1988* (see 12 UNDERWRITING OF LIFE BUSINESS). Also, attention will be drawn to the fact that a copy of the completed proposal form and of the policy conditions will be available on request.

The doctrine of utmost good faith 7.8

In contract there is a general rule that, subject to certain exceptions – for example, where there has been a material change in circumstances since the parties commenced negotiations (*With v O'Flanagan [1936] Ch 575*) – silence is not misrepresentation and the parties need not furnish each other with information which if known might possibly affect their judgement. However, all insurance contracts fall within the exemptions as they are bound by the doctrine of utmost good faith. All material facts must be disclosed, whether asked of the proposer or not, and the proposer has a duty to disclose them voluntarily. This duty extends not only to all material facts known to him but to material facts he ought to have known if he made reasonable enquiries (*Rozanes v Bowen [1928] Ll LR 98*).

Material facts 7.9

A material fact has been defined in *section 18(2)* of the *Marine Insurance Act 1906* as:

> 'Every circumstance is material which would influence the judgment of a prudent insurer in fixing the premium, or determining whether he will take the risk.'

This definition is accepted as applying not just to marine, but to all classes of insurance. Modern academics have tended to regard this definition as perhaps too stringent in its terms, as it implies that the proposer is aware of what an underwriter regards as material, and suggestions have been made that an amendment on the lines of 'what a prudent insured would consider material...' might be more equitable between the parties. However, the statutory definition still holds good, although insurers subscribing to the ABI's *Statement of Long-Term Insurance Practice* (see 7.6 above) have sought to alleviate its harsher application.

A duty imposed by the courts 7.10

When Lord Mansfield first defined the duty of utmost good faith in *Carter v Boehm (1766) 3 Burr 1905*, and once it had been reaffirmed by the Court of Appeal in *Seaton v Burnand [1900] AC 135*, it was made clear that it was a reciprocal duty and binding on the insurer as much as the insured. Nearly all modern cases concern non-disclosure, and hence breaches of the duty, by the proposer/insured. However, the relatively recent case of *Banque Financière de la Cité SA v Westgate Insurance Co. Ltd [1991] 2 AC 249*, commonly known as the 'Gemstones' case, provided confirmation that insurers, like insureds, are very definitely obliged to observe the duty of utmost good faith in matters relating to insurance contracts.

Statement of fact **7.11**

In order for a policy to be repudiated on the grounds of non-disclosure, the inaccurate statement must be one of fact, not opinion or a matter of law. Statements of opinion which turn out not to be well-founded are not actionable if the opinion was given in good faith (*Anderson v Pacific Fire Marine Insurance Co. [1972] LR 7 CP 65*). In general, an answer to a question on a proposal form will be construed as relating to the facts themselves (*Zurich General Accident and Liability Insurance Co. v Leven [1940] SC 407*). It is irrelevant that a proposer does not consider a fact material – if it is material it must be disclosed despite his opinion (*Godfrey v Britannic Assurance Co. [1963] 2 Lloyd's Rep 515*).

Obligation to disclose **7.12**

Nobody can disclose that which he does not know, and the obligation to disclose depends on the knowledge the contracting parties possess (*Joel v Law Union and Crown Insurance Co. [1908] 2 KB 863*). The duty to disclose extends until the time the contracting parties are bound, and if there is a material change in the circumstances of the risk between the time of acceptance of the proposal and payment of the first premium the insurer can repudiate. A typical material change would be a significant deterioration in the health of the life proposed (*Looker v Law Union and Rock Insurance Co. [1928] 1 KB 554*). Nowadays most life insurers include a clause in their policies making it clear that the duty of disclosure is a continuing one right up until the office goes on risk.

Warranties **7.13**

Warranties – statements whereby the signatory states that a certain thing has been done or will be done, or whereby he affirms or negatives a particular set of facts – must be strictly and literally complied with. Failure to do so will give the insurer the right to repudiate the contract. It is not the practice of British insurers to ask proposers to warrant the absolute truth of answers to questions in the proposal form, although this may be the case with overseas offices (*Kumar v Life Assurance Co. of India [1973] 1 Lloyd's Rep 147*). Warranties are still used by British insurers as part of the underwriting process to exercise on-going control over a risk, for example:

> 'warranted no aviation other than as a fare-paying passenger on regular routes'.

Return of premiums **7.14**

If a life office avoids a contract on the grounds of non-disclosure then it is set aside *ab initio* and any sums of money paid out are *prima facie* recoverable. Premiums paid are returnable (unless the non-disclosure can be proved to be fraudulent or wilful) as the office has never been on risk. It must be noted that if an office continues, with knowledge of the true facts, to accept premiums in respect of a policy where there has been non-disclosure it cannot afterwards repudiate liability.

Misrepresentation **7.15**

It is possible that an office could take action for remedies under the *Misrepresentation Act 1967* in cases where it contends that a proposer has made a misrepresentation in the course of completing the proposal form, although such an action is unlikely unless there are particular circumstances. If it is a case of fraudulent misrepresentation there is certainly authority for an office refusing to refund premiums and even bringing an action to compel the insured to give up the policy. (This authority comes from the case of *Feise v Parkinson (1812) 4 Taunt 640*, which can also be found in *Macgillivray on Insurance Law (9th Edition)*, Sweet & Maxwell).

Insurable interest **7.16**

Prior to the passing of the *Life Assurance Act 1774* (*LAA 1774*), wagering assurances on human life were commonplace. This 'mischievous gambling', as an anonymous contemporary writer described it (going on to assign the blame for the practice to 'Scotsmen' on grounds which today are not clear!), became so pernicious that for a few years (from around 1768–9) Lloyd's of London in fact split into two organisations, one trying to run a genuine insurance market and the other offering facilities to gamble on any future uncertain event. It is known, for example that the life of the Jacobite pretender to the throne, Bonnie Prince Charles, was 'insured' in the London market for substantial sums by persons hoping to profit by his death. *LAA 1774*, which despite its name applied to all insurances other than those

> '*bona fide* made by any person or persons on ships, goods, or merchandises'
>
> *(LAA 1774, s 4)*

brought this type of speculation to an end by providing that:

(*a*) no insurance could be effected unless the person effecting the contract had an (insurable) interest* in the life assured;

(*b*) the name(s) of the person(s) interested in the policy must be inserted in the policy; and

(*c*) no greater sum should be recovered than the amount of value of such interest.

**LAA 1774* did not define insurable interest, whether by accident or design, but subsequent cases established that to constitute a lawful life assurance contract the proposer must have a financial and legal interest in the life assured, i.e. the interest must be one recognised at law and capable of valuation in monetary terms. These cases are as follows:

(i) *Anderson v Edie (1795) 2 Park Insurance (18th Edition, 1842) 1 Bos & P 315n*, confirming that a creditor could insure a debtor for the amount of the loan;

(ii) *Simcock v Scottish Imperial [1902] 10 SLT 286*, confirming that an employer could insure an employee for wages for the agreed period of notice;

(iii) *Wainwright v Bland (1835) Moo & R 481; IM & W 32*, confirming a person's unlimited interest in his own life; and

(iv) *Griffiths v Fleming [1909] 1 KB 805*, confirming a husband's unlimited insurable interest in his wife.

For many years after the passing of *LAA 1774* it was thought that life assurance contracts were contracts of indemnity. However. the case of *Dalby v India and London Life Assurance Co. (1854) 15 CB 365* established that in life assurance, provided insurable interest existed at inception, the contract would be valid even if it had ceased to exist at the time of claim.

Policies without insurable interest **7.17**

LAA 1774 provided that life assurance policies effected without insurable interest shall be 'null and void' (*LAA 1774, s 1*). Despite considerable academic debate over the years, the position is that there is nothing 'illegal' or unlawful about a life policy where insurable interest is absent – the policy will just be void and no party can take any legal action under it. Insurers can issue policies in such circumstances, but have to accept that they cannot dispute payment in court. A possible exception to this principle lies in policies which contravene the second arm of *LAA 1774*:

> '... it shall not be lawful to make any policy or policies on the life or lives of any person or persons ... without inserting in such policy or policies the person or persons' name or names interested therein...'
>
> *(LAA 1774, s 2)*

as there is legal authority for the view that such policies are illegal. However, the words of *LAA 1774* must not be construed too widely. All the parties whom it is intended shall benefit from a policy need not be named, for example, executors and beneficiaries of a policy effected for a person's own benefit need not be included.

Assignment of a policy **7.18**

Provided a policy effected on a person's own life is *bona fide* and, at the time, for his own benefit, there is nothing to prevent him from assigning it to someone else, even though at the time he had the intention of doing so. The assignment too, must be *bona fide* (*M'Farlane v Royal London Friendly Society (1886) 2 TLR 755*). However, if the insurance is really made by the beneficiary, the assignment's purpose would be to defeat *LAA 1774*, and in such circumstances the court would go behind the wording of the policy and identify the true principal in the transaction.

Policy sales **7.19**

The sale of life assurance policies is handled by a significant niche market. Policies can be put up for sale by public auction as an alternative to seeking a cash surrender value (see 5 POLICY CONDITIONS AND ENDORSEMENTS), with the title assigned to the highest bidder. There is also a 'trade-in' market, especially for endowment policies, where the company which issued the assurances, or another company, will buy them back by way of assignment and then seek buyers, to whom in turn the title will be assigned. Many insurance professionals find these practices slightly distasteful, as the subject of whether or not life assurances should be traded like tangible commodities is open to debate. However, the law permits sales as long as the assured had an insurable interest at the inception of the contract.

Examples of insurable interest in life assurance are as follows.

(*a*) A man or woman on his or her own life. Such an interest is deemed not capable of valuation and hence unlimited, although as a matter of practice a life insurer might justifiably refuse to issue a policy at a premium out of proportion to the proposer's means.

(*b*) Husband on wife or wife on husband. Again, the interest is deemed unlimited but regard would be held by a modern insurer to the size of the premium and sum assured in relation to the proposer's means.

(*c*) Debtor/creditor. A creditor (or surety) has an insurable on the life of a debtor to the extent of the debt and accrued interest (*Lindenau v Desborough (1828) 8 B & C 586*). This interest would still exist even if the debt should be statute-barred when the policy is effected. A debtor has no insurable interest in his creditor whatever the circumstances.

(*d*) An employer has an insurable interest in the life of an employee to the extent of the value of services agreed to be rendered (*Simcock v Scottish Imperial Co. 1902 10 SLT 286*). In practice a much more extensive interest will be allowed (see 14 USES OF LIFE ASSURANCE). An employee has an insurable interest in his employer to the extent of wages for the agreed period of notice, although it is unlikely that this interest will be tested today when nearly all employment is by corporate bodies.

(*e*) Business partners have an insurable interest in co-partners to the extent of the latter's share in the business.

(*f*) An insurer has an insurable interest in the lives it assures to support a reassurance.

(*g*) A surety has an insurable interest in his principal (see also debtor/creditor at (*c*) above). This relationship is now really of academic interest only.

(*h*) In industrial life assurance (see 4.10 LEGISLATION) a child, step-child, adopted child or grandchild has a very limited insurable interest in parent, step-parent, adoptive parent or grandparent.

(*j*) Companies have insurable interests in their directors (on the same lines as employer–employee relationships referred to at (*d*) above).

The role of the intermediary 7.20

It is probably easiest to distinguish between tied agents, or 'company representatives' as they have been known since the introduction of the *Financial Services Act 1986*, and independent intermediaries such as independent financial advisers or brokers. Life offices have to take responsibility for the actions of their appointed representatives (probably a more practical title than 'company representatives') and in the normal course of events a statement made to such a representative is deemed to have been made to the office, whose liability will cover both the actual authority of its agents and their ostensible (or apparent) authority. 'The knowledge of the agent is imputed to the principal', so offices are normally bound by the knowledge of their tied agents.

An independent intermediary such as a broker is deemed to be the agent of the person seeking insurance, and hence the knowledge of such an intermediary is not deemed to be the knowledge of the insurer. A life office will therefore not normally be bound by the knowledge of independent intermediaries.

Case law 7.21

Case law in this area is somewhat confusing, and attitudes have changed over the years. A relevant summary would seem to be as follows.

(*a*) If an agent falsely fills in a proposal form, inventing answers, then the insurer is not liable:

(i) *Biggar v Rock Life Assurance Co. [1902] 1 KB 516*; and

(ii) *Newsholme Bros v Road Transport & General Insurance Co. Ltd [1929] 2 KB 356.*

(*b*) If an agent is employed on the express understanding that he fills in the proposal forms, then his knowledge must be imputed to the insurer (*Stone v Reliance Mutual Insurance Society Ltd [1972] 1 LR 469*).

(*c*) Ignorance of the law is not of itself grounds on which premiums paid can be recovered, if the agent has acted innocently (*Harse v Pearl Assurance Co. [1904] 1 KB 558*).

It is relevant to conclude by considering the recommendation made by the Law Reform Committee in its 5th Report in 1957:

> 'any person who solicits or negotiates a contract of insurance shall be deemed, for the purposes of the formation of the contract, to be the agent of the insurers, and that the knowledge of such person shall be deemed to be the knowledge of the insurers'.

Appendix 7A

Life Assurance Proposal Form

CROWE LIFE

Temporary Life Assurance
Single or Joint Life

CROWE

Important - Please read this notice before completing this proposal form.
To avoid delay all questions should be answered fully. All material facts must be disclosed as failure to do so would nullify any policy issued. A material fact is one likely to influence the assessment and acceptance of this proposal by Underwriters and if there is any doubt about whether certain facts are material, those facts should be disclosed. A copy of the policy form and completed proposal form is available from your Broker on request.

PLEASE USE BLOCK CAPITALS WHEN COMPLETING THIS FORM

Section A Policy required

Type of Assurance		Single Life ☑ Joint Life 1st death ☐ Joint Life 2nd death ☐	
Period of Assurance (Max 10 years)	10	Sum to be Assured	£20,000
Premium	Yearly	Minimum Yearly Premium £50 Minimum Monthly Premium £10	

Section B The proposer (The 'Grantee')

Complete this section only if the person taking out the policy is **not** one of the Lives to be Assured and sign the Declaration in Section F upon full completion of this form.

Title (Mr/Mrs/Miss/etc)		Full surname Manyman
Full forenames	Anne	
Name of Company (if applicable)	—	
Full address	12, Nonsuch Road, Notown	Post Code C2 AB1
Proposer's relationship to the Life/Lives to be Assured	Wife	
Details of Insurable Interest	As above	

Section C Life (Lives) to be Assured

	FIRST LIFE	SECOND LIFE
Title (Mr/Mrs/Miss/etc)		
Full surname	Manyman	
Full forenames	John	
Marital status	Married	
Maiden name (if married Woman)	—	
Full address	12, Nonsuch Road, Notown Post Code C2 AB1	Post Code
Date and place of birth (For proof of age you are recommended to produce your birth certificate (and marriage certificate in the case of a married Woman) at the present time).	7/8 19 45 Age next birthday 56 Town Country Chelmsford Essex, England	19 Age next birthday Town Country
Profession or occupation (Please give precise details)	Civil Engineer	
Name and address of your doctor (If you have changed doctors in the last 6 months, please give particulars of both your old and new doctor).	Dr. A. N. Other The Surgery Notown	

 9/34 511/May 1999

(PLEASE TICK THE APPROPRIATE BOX)

Section D Personal details

	FIRST LIFE	SECOND LIFE
1. Are you suffering from any disability or illness, or receiving any medication ?	Yes [✓] No [ ]	Yes [ ] No [ ]
2. Have you been incapacitated for 10 consecutive days or more due to illness, or required treatment in a hospital or clinic within the last 5 years ?	Yes [ ] No [✓]	Yes [ ] No [ ]
3. Have you tested positive for HIV/AIDS or Hepatitis B or C, or have you been tested/treated for other sexually transmitted diseases or are you awaiting the result of such a test ? If yes, please provide details - for confidentiality these may be sent direct to the Chief Medical Officer at the head office.	Yes [ ] No [✓]	Yes [ ] No [ ]
4. Are there any hazardous circumstances which might affect this Assurance ? (e.g. travel or residence abroad, dangerous work or pastimes, aviation other than as a passenger on recognised air services).	Yes [ ] No [✓]	Yes [ ] No [ ]
5. Have you smoked any form of tobacco in the last twelve months ?	Yes [ ] No [✓]	Yes [ ] No [ ]
6. What are your height and weight ?	Height 6'1" Weight 13st	Height Weight

If you have answered Yes to any of questions 1 to 5 above, please give details below.

Question number:	Full details and dates FIRST LIFE	Question number:	Full details and dates SECOND LIFE
1	I have irritable bowel syndrome – no medications (just careful, prudent diet)		

Section E Declaration (To be signed by the Life (Lives) to be Assured)

I/We, declare that all statements made herein are true to the best of my/our knowledge and belief. I/We are aware that the Underwriters will rely upon the statements made herein and the statements made by me/us to any Medical Examiner appointed by the Underwriters when making this contract. I/We consent to Underwriters seeking medical information from any doctor who at any time has attended me/us concerning anything which affects my/our physical and mental health or seeking information from any insurance office to which a proposal has been made for the insurance on my/our lives and I/We authorise the giving of such information.

Signature (First Life) (Single Life) J. Manyman Date 21/6/2001

Signature (Second Life) Date

Section F Declaration

(To be signed by the Grantee, only if the person taking out the policy is not one of the Lives to be Assured.)

I, the person proposing to effect the policy, the Grantee, have read all the statements made herein and declare that to the best of my knowledge and belief they are true. I agree that this proposal and declaration and those statements which have been or shall be made to the Medical Examiner of the Underwriters with reference to this proposal and subscribed by the person whose life is to be Assured, shall form that basis of the contract between me and the Underwriters.

Signature A Manyman Date 21/6/2001

 9/35 511/May 1999

ACCESS TO MEDICAL REPORTS ACT 1988

Summary. Before Underwriters can apply for a medical report from your doctor, they need your consent. You should know that you have certain rights under the Act. The main points are as follows:

a. You can withhold your consent.

b. You can see the report before it is sent to the Underwriters' Senior Medical Advisor, or during the six months after that.

c. You can ask the doctor if he will amend any part of the report which you consider to be incorrect or misleading. If the doctor is not in agreement, you may append your comments.

d. The doctor can withhold from you the report, or part of it, if he thinks you would be harmed by seeing it.

If you do not say you wish to see the report, the Underwriters do not have to notify you if they apply for one. However, if before such a report is sent to them, you write to the doctor saying you wish to see it, you will then have 21 days to contact the doctor to make arrangements to see the report.

Whether or not you say you wish to see the report before it is sent to the Underwriters, the doctor must let you see a copy for up to six months after it is supplied, if you ask. If you ask the doctor for a copy of the report, he can charge you a reasonable fee to cover his costs.

Once you have seen a report before it is sent to the Underwriters, the doctor cannot submit it until he has your consent. You can write to the doctor, asking him to amend any part of the report you consider to be incorrect or misleading, and can attach to the report a statement of your views on any part where you and the doctor are not in agreement and which the doctor is not prepared to alter.

The doctor is not obliged to let you see any part of a report if, in his opinion, that would be likely to cause serious harm to your physical or mental health or that of others, or would indicate the doctor's intentions towards you, or if a disclosure would be likely to reveal information about, or the identity of, another person who has supplied information about you, unless that person has consented or the information relates to, or has been supplied by, a health professional involved in caring for you. In such cases, the doctor must notify you and you will be limited to seeing any remaining part of the report. If it is the whole report which is affected, he must not send it to Underwriters unless you give your consent.

I have been informed of my statutory rights under the Access to Medical Reports Act 1988, as explained above, in connection with the Assurance currently applied for, and hereby consent to the Underwriters seeking medical information from any doctor who at any time has attended me concerning anything which affects my physical or mental health, and I agree that a copy of this consent shall have the validity of the original.

Do you wish to see the report before it is sent to the Underwriters?
(Please delete as applicable)

1st LIFE **YES/~~NO~~** 2nd LIFE **YES/NO**

Signature (1) J. Manyman **Signature (2)** ____________

Date 21/6.2001 **Date** ____________

INSTRUCTION TO YOUR BANK TO PAY DIRECT DEBITS (MONTHLY PREMIUMS ONLY) **Please complete sections 1-**

[1] Name of account holder ____________

[2] Sort Code

[3] Account Number

[4] To the Manager

Please write the name and full postal address of your bank branch. Banks may refuse to accept instructions to pay direct debits from some types of account.

Originator's identification no. **724481**

Originator's reference no. ____________

[5] Your instruction to the bank and signature
I instruct you to pay a Direct Debit from my account at the request of CROWE LIFE. The amount is £
to be debited on or just after the of each month.
Date of first payment on or within two months of
I will inform the bank in writing if I wish to cancel this instruction. I understand that if any Direct Debit is paid which breaks the terms of this instruction, the bank will make a refund.

Signature **Date**

This Direct Debit mandate issued by
CROWE LIFE, BANKSIDE HOUSE, 107-112 LEADENHALL STREET, LONDON EC3A 4AA

Chapter 8

Reassurance of Life Policies

- **Formation of the life assurance contract**
- **Proposal forms**
- **The doctrine of utmost good faith**
- **Insurable interest**
- **The role of the intermediary**

The reinsurance/reassurance markets 8.1

The markets for general branch reinsurance and for life reassurance have basic similarities, in that there are direct insurers (ceding companies) which buy reinsurance from reinsurers. The reinsurers may then themselves seek to reinsure part of what they have reinsured by way of 'retrocession'.

However, the operation of the markets is somewhat different, and from now on this chapter will be concerned with life reassurance.

The life market 8.2

Whilst nearly all life insurers transacting direct business do also accept reinsurance, notably by way of retrocession, the life market is characterised by the number of specialist reassurers which have created a very important niche sector. They have established particularly strong reputations in the treatment of sub-standard business, and are often prepared to accept 100 per cent reassurances of risks outside the office's direct scope of retention. These specialist reassurers provide training services to companies with which they have treaties (see 8.6 below) and their underwriting manuals are comprehensive and extremely valuable (see 12 UNDERWRITING OF LIFE BUSINESS). Competition amongst life reassurers is keen and recent mergers have led to the emergence of major key players in the market, all of which are owned outside the UK.

Brokers 8.3

Brokers play a minimal role in life reassurance compared to that which they play in general branch reinsurance. Some group life and overseas business does come via brokers, but the links which life insurers and reassurers have built up over the years are quite comprehensive.

Principles and practice of reassurance 8.4

Retention 8.5

The ceding office must first calculate its retention, that is the maximum amount it can afford to pay out in the event of a life assured dying. There may well be different levels of retention, especially if a lot of non-medical business (see 12 UNDERWRITING OF LIFE BUSINESS) is being written. The approach by a newly formed office should always be cautious. The retention will be related to the capital structure of the company, but must be designed to avoid excessive fluctuations in the mortality experience. The smaller the size of the life fund, the more likely it is that 'actual' deaths will not conform to the 'expected' deaths, and one or two large claims could have serious consequences. The acquisition costs of life business are high and this causes strain on new business; indeed, for full premium business these costs often exceed the annual premium. In consequence the more that death claims can be minimised, the better.

The two main types of reassurance 8.6

There are two main types of reassurance.

(*a*) ***Facultative***. Here there are no automatic arrangements for ceding business to a reassurer, and each case is considered on its merits. Individual cover is granted and obviously this can be expensive to operate; however, substandard business which the direct office would not normally accept and 'unusual' risks (for example contingency assurances involving three or more lives) are placed on a facultative basis, as are risks over and above treaty arrangements.

(*b*) ***Treaty***. Blocks of business can be placed with a reassurer; there are automatic facilities in place for this process, which speeds up the acceptance and processing of proposals. Cover given by the reassurer is usually expressed as a multiple of 'lines', with a 'line' equating the direct office's retention. There may be further treaties arranged which can take over when the initial treaty is exhausted. If the treaty is classed as facultative/obligatory (fac/oblig), then the ceding office will retain the freedom to cede individual risks to the reassurer or elsewhere, but the reassurer is obliged, within the agreed limits, to accept the risks reassured to it.

Proportional reassurance 8.7

Most life reassurance is conducted on a proportional basis, either surplus (also known as excess of line) or quota share. Under the surplus treaty the ceding office allots any business over its set retention to the reassurer(s). Under quota share there is automatic reassurance whereby the ceding office is bound to cede a percentage of every risk written for a particular class of business, no matter how small. Usually quota share treaties contain a monetary limit (for example, 'the reassurer shall accept 50 per cent of each and every risk up to a maximum acceptance of £250,000 any one risk'). This prevents the ceding office from writing a tranche of 'bad' business and passing its poor financial risks on to the reassurers.

Non-proportional reassurance **8.8**

Non-proportional reassurance has not made anything like the progress in the life assurance sector that non-proportional reinsurance has in the general insurance sector. Life assurance lends itself to the relative simplicity of surplus and quota share reassurance, and the short-term basis of most excess of loss treaties is regarded as a major disadvantage. Insurance supervisory regulations have also constrained the supply of non-proportional reassurance. However, as direct insurers find themselves increasingly exposed to the risk of an accumulation of death claims arising from one event, there is a growing demand for excess of loss covers to guard against the risk of at least a certain number of insured lives dying within a short time (say, 48 hours) of a particular event occurring.

Cover and liability **8.9**

Cover is only against accidents and natural disasters, and a minimum number of deaths (usually at least three) is required to trigger a claim. The reassurer's liability will be based on the ultimate net loss sustained by the ceding office, but in calculating this not only must any monies received from underlying reassurances be deducted, but the mathematical reserves held by the ceding office in respect of its policies must be taken into account. The essential purpose of this type of catastrophe reassurance is to protect the ceding office against the net death strain due to multiple claims arising from one event. Limited use of excess of loss reassurance is made in connection with group life business (see 3 GROUP LIFE), although most such reassurance is on a surplus basis.

Treaty writing **8.10**

Some reassurance treaties are drawn up on a stop loss basis, whereby the reassurer accepts liability for aggregate ultimate net losses in excess of a fixed monetary amount per annum, subject to an upper limit. Others may be written as an excess of loss ratio with the reassurer's liability expressed in terms of excess claims over a percentage of expected claims. These contracts are not as common as in general branch insurance, as the loss experience on life portfolios tends to be more stable and predictable than with many classes of non-life insurance. Premium rating problems arise in particular from the reassurer's need for a substantial loading of the net premium because both the risk to be covered and the reassurer's expenses, though probably small in absolute value, are large relative to the net premium.

Note: Full technical details of the various methods of proportional and non-proportional reinsurance and reassurance can be found in *Chapter 28* –

Reinsurance of *Butterworths Tolley's Insurance Handbook, Barlow Lyde & Gilbert (2nd Edition)*, available from Butterworths Tolley, price £49. Telephone 020 8662 2000.

Risk premium reassurance 8.11

Original terms basis 8.12

Reassurance can be conducted on an original terms basis, whereby an agreed proportion of the original assurance is covered by the reassurer on the same terms as those applicable to the original policy.

As a result of covering a proportion of the sum assured, the reassurer can expect to participate in a strict proportion of several items (some of which will be costed in the premium), for example premiums, extra premiums, commissions, claims, surrenders, bonuses, options (to convert, for example). The reassurer does not participate in policy fees, overriding commission, or loadings for premium payments at less than annual intervals. Premiums are charged on a level basis for what is an increasing risk, and so reserves can accrue. Occasionally, when original terms cover is needed for with-profit cases (see 6 PROFITS, INVESTMENTS AND BONUS DISTRIBUTION), the agreement will be to reassure on a non-profit basis using the ceding office's non-profit rates. In this way the basic sum assured is covered and the additional premium charged for the bonus element in the with-profit contract is retained by the ceding company and invested to help meet the bonuses.

Original terms arrangements are easy to understand, initially easier to administer and beneficial to a new company as its high expenses are covered proportionately by the reassurer. It must be understood that original terms reassurers have to help pay claims by maturity as well as death claims.

Risk premium basis 8.13

As an alternative, life reassurance can be arranged on a risk premium basis. Here only the death risk is reassured, and the ceding office, whilst being covered for the death risk, can retain the entire investment portion of the premium together with part of the expense loading. The actual reassurance premium will fluctuate appreciably, for although the rate of premium increases each year with the increase in the age of the life assured, the sum reassured decreases due to the build-up of the policy reserve. The reassurer's liability is limited to the amount at risk in the year the life reassured dies – the ceding office's life fund is liable for maturities and surrenders. However, the ceding office, out of three potential sources of profit (mortality, investment and expenses) only shares mortality profit with the reassurer.

The following simple example, taking the first 6 years of a 15 year term, with an annual premium of £50 and £1000 endowment assurance for a male aged 30 next birthday, will illustrate the operation of risk premium reassurance.

Figure l

Ceding company: Total liability	Premium	Expenses	Total received in premiums less expenses	Interest on premium	Actual liability
£1000	£50	£50	*Nil*	*Nil*	£1000
£1000	£50	£4	£46	*Nil*	£954
£1000	£50	£4	£92	£2	£906
£1000	£50	£4	£138	£7	£855
£1000	£50	£4	£184	£13	£803
£1000	£50	£4	£230	£21	£749
			These are reserves		

Figure 2

Looked at another way, this example can be expressed as:

Ceding company's actual liability	Rate of risk premium	Reassurance premium
£1000	0.65	£0.65
£954	0.98	£0.93
£906	1.34	£1.21
£855	1.38	£1.18
£803	1.43	£1.15
£749	1.51	£1.13
(This is the amount at risk)		

In the first year the assumption has been made that the whole of the premium has been absorbed by expenses (including commission). In some short term contracts, an element of reserve will already exist in year one of the contract and hence the amount at risk will be less than the nominal sum assured.

All types of policies with a death benefit can be reassured on a risk premium basis, but traditionally whole life and endowment contracts have been reassured this way. Overseas companies seem particularly keen on making use of risk premium reassurance. Particular advantages to ceding companies are that:

- the fund grows more quickly as it receives the whole of the investment part of the premium; and
- the larger the reserves, the more that can be earned from investment.

Legal principles 8.14

The reinsurance contract 8.15

A contract of reinsurance was defined by Mansfield CJ in *Delver v Barnes (1807) 1 Taunt 48* as

> '... a new insurance effected by a new policy on the same risk which was before insured in order to indemnify the underwriters from their previous subscriptions; and both policies are to be in existence at the same time.'

It is thus shown to be a separate contract with terms which may – and often do – differ from those in the original insurance contract.

The contract between the insured and the insurer is a separate one from the contract between the insurer and the reinsurer (or reassurer). This was reiterated in the modern case of *Meadows Indemnity Company Ltd v The Insurance Corporation of Ireland Plc [1989] 2 Lloyd's Rep 298*.

Privity of contract **8.16**

Ordinarily the operation of the doctrine of privity of contract means that the insured has no claim against the reinsurer (or reassurer) in the event that the insurer does not, or cannot, pay a claim under the original policy. Some reinsurance agreements do purport to give the original insured a direct claim upon the reinsurer in respect of sums owing under the original claim in the event of the insurer's insolvency. The *Contracts (Rights of Third Parties) Act 1999* makes it possible for a third party to enforce a term in a contract which expressly confers such a right upon him or her. It is possible that facultative reinsurance contracts could be worded so as to allow the original insured to claim directly against the reinsurer in the event of an insolvency – developments must be awaited.

Reinsurance/reassurance policies must follow the law relevant to the primary policy, which has particular significance if there is an apparent conflict of laws (*Forsikringsaktieselskapet Vesta v Butcher (No 1) [1989] 1 All ER 402*).

Note: Full details of the legal principles of reinsurance agreements, and their technical applications, are contained in *Chapter 28 – Reinsurance* of *Butterworths Tolley's Insurance Handbook* (see note after 8.10 above).

Chapter 9

Reserves and Valuations

- **Backgrounds and principles**
- **Reserves**
- **Life office valuations**

Background and principles 9.1

Year-end accounting and the observance of financial rigour in internal and external procedures are part and parcel of the fabric of all commercial enterprises. However, the valuation of life funds goes beyond accountancy as so many long-term factors and influences have to be taken into account – changing trends in mortality, future lapses and surrenders of policies, expense ratios, variable investment returns etc. Only actuaries can take responsibility for the production of valuation returns, and actuarial skills are called for to interpret them and verify that they are *bona fide*.

Actuaries 9.2

As was stated in 1 ACTUARIAL PRINCIPLES, actuaries can be the employees of insurers, or can either work totally independently or for firms of consulting actuaries. Every life office must have an 'appointed actuary', who does not necessarily have to be a full-time employee. Periodically calls are made in the Houses of Parliament and in the press for all actuaries to be independent. There seems no sound reason why insurers should not employ the actuaries who work out premium tables and calculate policy reserves and surrender values, but there is a case for saying that the valuation should be handled by external independent referees. However, the formal valuation has to be submitted for careful scrutiny to the appropriate external statutory body – for many years the Department of Trade and Industry, then to the Insurance Directorate of HM Treasury (to which the relevant civil servants from the Department of Trade and Industry were moved), and now to the Financial Services Authority (FSA). The FSA is to have in place an actuarial team who will scrutinise the valuations. The degree of external scrutiny would seem sufficiently rigorous to obviate the need for all actuaries to be outside the employ of insurers, and an appointed actuary who improperly approves a valuation faces severe penalties.

Valuations 9.3

At one time, valuations were immensely labour-intensive and involved detailed and repetitive clerical work, with large numbers of clerks working from ledgers and on little else. In the relatively early days of life assurance each policy was valued individually, so it is little wonder that quinquennial valuations were the norm. Some offices moved during the 20th century to triennial valuations, aided by the introduction of business machines and the development of punch-card systems. This mechanisation of valuations was followed in the late 1950s by the advent of computerisation, and as computers became more sophisticated so much of the hard work was taken out of the valuation process, freeing staff to take on more exciting developmental work and also taking account of the widening range of contracts to be reviewed.

Offices look on annual valuations as a fact of business life, and the computer makes this process relatively easy in terms of the volume of data which can be handled. This does not stop debate within the actuarial profession on ways in which the valuation process should be used to measure solvency, and learned papers are produced every year on this subject.

As has been stated, the valuation goes beyond accountancy and measures the health of the life fund, as well as establishing solvency in the light of long-term liabilities, and surpluses for possible distribution.

Reserves 9.4

Policy reserves exist within the life fund. Offices transacting all classes of business need reserves and, *inter alia*, reserve to meet future claims and 'free reserves' which are not specifically earmarked for any one contingency. However, the calculation of life policy reserves is in the province of the actuaries and is part of the wider valuation process.

Calculation of reserve values 9.5

Reserve values can be calculated for the whole of a life office's business, and with modern computerisation this is a much simpler process than in the past. Reserve values can also be calculated for each policy; indeed cash surrender values and loans can only be paid out of the reserve.

The reasoning behind the calculation of reserves can perhaps best be understood by relating the technique used to an individual policy, although in practice actuaries will be looking at a whole class of policies when establishing the adequacy or otherwise of reserves (see *Figure 1* at 1.5 MORTALITY TABLES).

It must be remembered that 'new business strain' – for example initial expenses, commission, medical fees – will almost always prevent a policy reserve forming in the first one or even two years of a policy's currency.

Retrospective or prospective calculation **9.6**

Reserves can be calculated retrospectively or prospectively. The retrospective method looks back and calculates the reserve as the excess of accumulated net premiums over accumulated claims. The prospective method, which is much more frequently used, calculates the amount by which the discounted value of future net premiums falls short of the value of future claims, using an assumed rate of interest, 'i', which must be applied consistently throughout the process. Future net premiums, it can safely be assumed, will always be less than future claims as the insuring public, not unreasonably, look for contracts which will pay out more than they, the policyholders, pay in.

Reserves, therefore, hinge on the comparison of the present values (found at the same assumed rate of interest 'i'), of future income and future pay-outs. The pay-outs will in all probability be lump sums, or lump sum equivalents, and the income a series of regular payments in the form of premiums. The difference between these present values will constitute the reserve.

Life office valuations **9.7**

Aims of valuations **9.8**

The valuation is the process by which a life insurer will place a value on its assets and on its liabilities. The purposes are:

(*a*) to establish solvency, and to thus ensure that the office can continue trading;

(*b*) to ascertain the surplus, which is the excess of the value placed on assets over the value placed on liabilities. A 'negative surplus' – really almost a contradiction in terms – is called a 'strain. New business strain has already been mentioned at 9.5 above; and

(*c*) to determine, in conjunction with the management of the office, normally the Board of Directors, how much of the surplus can be allocated to 'divisible surplus' and devoted to bonuses for with-profit policyholders and, where appropriate, dividends to shareholders.

Solvency margins **9.9**

In the UK, as in nearly all states where insurance is transacted on a properly regulated basis, there is a statutory margin of solvency which constitutes the minimum by which the value placed on assets must exceed the value placed on liabilities. In the UK, reserves are set up on a relatively strong basis, that is with relatively large margins. However, solvency capital requirements are comparatively small and perhaps not closely related to the risks borne by the insurer.

The *Insurance Companies Regulations 1994* (*SI 1994/1516*) lay down statutory margins of solvency and set out the various requirements for the valuation of insurance company liabilities under the *Insurance Companies Act*

1982. Valuations have to be carried out at 'specific intervals'. However, the appointed actuary has a statutory duty to ensure that the long-term fund is solvent at all times, not just at the valuation dates, as far as all 'reasonable steps' can ensure. It would not be sufficient for a fund to be solvent, say, at 1 January 2000 and again at 1 January 2001 if it was not solvent at 30 June 2000.

Valuation basis **9.10**

The appointed actuary must use 'prudent bases' determined by actuarial principles in conducting a valuation. A valuation method not in general use by the profession can be employed, but it must be justified having regard to actuarial principles. The surplus revealed (or 'thrown up' to use accepted actuarial terminology) will vary according to the valuation basis selected. Mainly it will result from actual experience in mortality, interest (more correctly investment return), expenses and asset values being more favourable than assumed experience. The valuation basis does not affect the actual profit earned, but it does affect the incidence of its emergence.

Valuation methods **9.11**

As can be seen from 9.10 above, there are many views in the actuarial profession as to the most suitable valuation method. As the range of life assurance products extends, so does the propensity to extend the methods of valuing life funds. The Institute of Actuaries at Staple Inn Hall, off Chancery Lane in London, holds a number of discussion papers in this field, many of which are extremely technical in nature, for those who wish to pursue the subject in more detail. This chapter shall conclude by considering the three valuation methods that perhaps have best stood the test of time, although they are varied and adapted as necessary today as offices seek to secure a competitive edge.

Gross premium valuation **9.12**

A method for placing a value on life assurance company liabilities that explicitly values the future office premiums payable. In addition, it usually values explicitly future discretionary benefits and future expenses.

Net premium valuation **9.13**

A method for placing a value on a life assurance office's liabilities that involves valuing its contractual liabilities to date allowing for mortality and interest and deducting the value of the future net premiums. 'Zillmerisation' will smooth out the uneven incidence of expenses. 'Zillmerisation' takes its name from Zillmer, an actuary who developed procedures that dealt with unevenness in experience, typically with the effect of new business strain.

Bonus reserve valuation **9.14**

A type of gross premium valuation that allows explicitly for future bonuses under with-profit contracts.

Comments on valuation methods **9.15**

The gross premium method avoids artificiality and is perhaps best for non-profit business. The bonus reserve method was at one time primarily used for internal investigations but is now employed quite extensively. Obviously, as with reserving, the rate of interest 'i' adopted can be of crucial importance.

Chapter 10

Taxation and Life Assurance

- **Introduction**
- **Taxation of the life office**
- **Qualifying policies**
- **Taxation of the proceeds of life policies**

Introduction 10.1

As well of the use of reference works such as this, the actual legislation should also be read to give a fuller picture of the legal situation. The following thoughts are offered on this, without any intention of presumption.

(*a*) The most important thought when reading the legislation is 'what do the words actually *say*?', perhaps followed by checking whether there are any cases decided by the ultimate arbiter, the court, which will help in this. It is necessary to keep a cool head here, as one gets into all manner of trouble by importing one's own preconceptions (in reading any summary someone else's preconceptions have already been involved).

(*b*) Although it might not always be thought so, the parliamentary draftsman seeks to make the legislation as short and as precise as possible, necessarily using as a tool words, which are by nature imprecise. His concern is that, in the event of dispute, the court should agree that the meaning of the legislation is the one intended, 'and the reason that it is difficult to grasp is not that it wanders verbosely round the point but that it goes straight there with a baffling economy of words' (*Fowler's Modern English Usage*) and hopefully the reader should end up with the one meaning intended.

Taxation of the life office 10.2

A life office, whether mutual or proprietary, is liable to corporation tax on its profits and gains. The tax computation itself is complicated; a numerical example in one of the works on the subject covers eighteen pages (*Butterworths Tolley's MacLeod and Levitt: Taxation of Insurance Business*

(4th Edition), available from Butterworths Tolley, price £150).

In the most general of terms, life business is divided into two:

- basic life assurance and general (non-pension) annuity business; and
- pension business.

Basic life assurance and general (non-pension) annuity business **10.3**

Basic life assurance **10.4**

The office is liable to tax on income and chargeable gains less expenses. This is reflected in the taxation of life assurance policy proceeds, where the policy-holder is deemed to have paid income tax at the basic rate on policy proceeds. Thus if he is liable to tax at all, it will only be at the higher rate (but as will be seen below, there is always an exception).

A tax change depends on there being a 'chargeable event', which in turn depends upon whether or not the policy is a qualifying policy (see 10.8 below).

The office inevitably makes a deduction from proceeds to cover its actual or contingent liability to tax on gains, whereas the policyholder, had he held the investments personally, might well have escaped tax due to his annual exemptions. This is particularly apparent under a direct unit linked policy, where a separate deduction is shown from the value of the units on the termination statement. No matter how careful the explanations were at the outset this deduction leads to considerable discontent among the beneficiaries, and was a factor in offices turning to bond fund links, where the unit price is net of the deduction.

General annuities **10.5**

General (non-pension) annuities represent income in the hands of the recipient and are thus liable to tax at all rates. However, see 18 TAXATION IMPLICATIONS OF PENSION/ANNUITY BUSINESS regarding capital elements of annuity payments. The surrender of an annuity gives rise to a charge to tax at all rates (different from the treatment of a life policy (see 10.17 below)).

Pension business **10.6**

The pension business fund is exempt from tax on its income and realised investment profits.

Pension payments are, logically enough, regarded as income in the hands of the recipient and are fully liable to income tax accordingly (although lump sums in commutation of pension may be free from tax).

Life Assurance Premium Relief **10.7**

Life Assurance Premium Relief (LAPR) is of great antiquity, and is currently given under *section 266* and *Schedule 14* of the *Income and Corporation*

Taxes Act 1988 (*ICTA 1988*). There are three dates to consider in identifying whether LAPR may be available:

(*a*) the policy must have been issued before 14 March 1984, and must not have been varied so as to increase the benefits or extend the term since that date;

(*b*) if the policy was issued after 19 March 1968 it must be a qualifying policy (*ICTA 1988, Sch 15*) – indeed, the availability of LAPR is an indication of qualifying status (see 10.8 *et seq* below); and

(*c*) a life policy issued before 19 March 1968 should be eligible for LAPR, unless it has been varied after that date so as to increase the benefits or extend the term – after such a variation it must meet the qualification rules if it is to obtain relief (*ICTA 1988, Sch 14, para 8*) (see 10.8 *et seq* below) and it must of course comply also with (*a*) above.

LAPR is currently at 12.5 per cent (subject to upper limits under *ICTA 1988, s 274*), and is normally obtained by paying only the net premium.

LAPR is only available:

- to an individual UK resident;
- on premiums paid to a UK company;
- where the insurance is on the life of the individual or that of his or her spouse; and
- where the insurance was made by one of them.

A clawback of one year's relief is made at a whole or part surrender if there has been a previous part surrender (*ICTA 1988, s 269*).

Qualifying policies **10.8**

The qualification rules, found in *Schedule 15* of *ICTA 1988*, can be summarised as shown in the following table.

Whole life (including whole life limited premiums) (WLLP) (*ICTA 1988, Sch 15, para 1(1), (2), (5)*)	**Endowment assurance** (*ICTA 1988, Sch 15, para 2*)	**Term assurance with term of more than ten years** (*ICTA 1988, Sch 15, para 1(1), (3), (5)*)	**Term assurance with term of more than one year but less than ten years** (*ICTA 1988, Sch 15, paras 1(1), (4), (5), 10*)
	Term of at least ten years		The policy must provide that any surrender payment will not exceed the total of premiums paid
Premiums payable at yearly or shorter intervals (twelve months rule)	Twelve months rule	Twelve months rule	No twelve months rule
Premiums payable until death, or until expiry of premium-paying term of at least ten years under WLLP policy	Premiums payable until death or maturity, or lesser period of at least ten years	Premiums payable until death, or lesser period of at least ten years or three quarters of the term if less	No premium-paying term requirement
Premiums payable in any period of twelve months not greater than:			
– twice that in any such period (twice times rule)	Twice times rule	Twice times rule	No twice times rule
– one-eighth of premiums payable over ten years, or over the premium-paying term of WLLP policy	One-eighth rule over the term of the policy	One-eighth rule	No one-eighth rule
Sum assured at death at least 75% of premiums payable under the policy if death occurred at age 75	Sum assured at death at least 75% of premiums payable until maturity date: reduction of 2% for each year over 55 at inception	If: (a) no provision for surrender; or (b) term ends before age 75, no requirement as to sum assured; otherwise as whole life	Same rules as for policy for more than ten years

The policy must thus provide an adequate sum assured at death, and it may in addition provide benefits if disability occurs (*ICTA 1988, Sch 15, para 1(7), 2(1)*). Under *paras 1(7),* (8) and *2(3)* of *Schedule 15* to *ICTA 1988*, the policy may also provide:

- participation in profits;
- the right to a surrender value;
- a waiver of premium due to disability; or
- in the case of a whole life policy, an option to receive benefits in the form of an annuity.

Back-dating **10.9**

The start of the term of a qualifying policy can be back-dated for up to three months without qualification problems (*ICTA 1988, Sch 15, paras 1(8) and 2(3)*). Further back-dating is possible, but the qualification rules (for example, the one-eighth rule (see 10.8 above)) must be considered.

Variations to qualifying policies **10.10**

Qualifying policies can be varied (*ICTA 1988, Sch 15, paras 17, 18*). After variation the policy must be looked at as a new policy, starting on the date of variation (*ICTA 1988, Sch 15, para 18*). Indeed, *para 17* of *Schedule 15* to *ICTA 1988* really relates to substituted policies, and refers to the 'old policy' and the 'new policy'.

The general rules are as follows:

(*a*) if the old policy did not meet the qualifying rules, the new policy cannot be a qualifying policy (except in one specialised case relating to infants) (*ICTA 1988, Sch 15, para 17(2)(a)*);

(*b*) if the old policy qualified, and the new policy meets the qualifying rules, the new policy is a qualifying policy unless:

  (i) less than ten years have elapsed since the making of the insurance, and

  (ii) the premiums payable in any period of twelve months after variation are less than 50% of the highest total payable in any such period under the policy or under any related policy issued less than ten years before the variation (*ICTA 1988, Sch 15, para 17(2)(b)*); and

(*c*) if the old policy was a qualifying policy and the insurance was made over ten years previously, and the new policy fails only by reason of the ten years rule, the twelve months rule, the twice times rule or the one-eighth rule (see 10.8 above), then the new policy is a qualifying policy, provided that the premiums payable thereafter do not exceed the lowest level paid under the old policy (*ICTA 1988, Sch 15, para 17(2)(c)*).

Variations in accordance with options contained in the policy 10.11

Options for variation may be contained within the policy itself, and these are covered by *para 19* of *Schedule 15* to *ICTA 1988*.

For policies issued before 1 April 1976, when an option is exercised the variation rules of *para 17* and *18* of *Schedule 15* to *ICTA 1988* will apply (*ICTA 1988, Sch 15, para 19(2)*).

For policies issued on or after 1 April 1976, all options contained in the policy are pre-tested at the time the policy obtains approval as a qualifying policy, and the policy can be varied in accordance with these options without testing under *para 17* of *Schedule 15* to *ICTA 1988* (*ICTA 1988, Sch 15, para 19(3)*). Other variations will be tested at the time they are made.

The variation rules constitute something of a minefield and, as will be seen from *para 17(2)(a)* of *Schedule 15* to *ICTA 1988*, one of the most serious provisions is that if a policy is varied so as to become non-qualifying it cannot regain qualifying status.

The Inland Revenue regard some variations as being so basic as to constitute a new contract rather than the variation of an existing one.

Before making any variation at all it is certainly advisable to get confirmation from the life office that qualification will not be lost as a result.

Certification of qualifying policies 10.12

Under *paragraph 21* of *Schedule 15* to *ICTA 1988*, if the policy was issued after 5 April 1979, or has been varied since that date, the office must at the request of the policyholder issue a certificate confirming whether in its opinion the policy is, or remains, a qualifying policy.

A policy which does not have, or which has lost, qualifying status remains a perfectly valid contract, although its tax treatment will be different.

The life office issuing the policy must advise the Inland Revenue at the happening of a chargeable event under a non-qualifying policy, and will thus at all times know the qualifying status of the policy (*ICTA 1988, s 552*).

Key man policies 10.13

The object of a key man policy is to cover the estimated loss in profits which would occur following the death or disability of a key individual (see 14 USES OF LIFE ASSURANCE).

Where a term assurance is used for this purpose, premiums are normally tax deductible as expenses; proceeds, representing profits lost due to the death or disability, are taxable as trading income. Choosing not to claim relief on premiums does not result in the proceeds being free from tax.

If a whole life or endowment policy is used, however, this is normally regarded as a capital asset; premiums are not deductible and the proceeds are not trading income.

It must be borne in mind that every case is individual, and will be looked at by the Inspector of Taxes accordingly.

Pure endowments 10.14

A pure endowment policy which only pays proceeds on the survival of the life assured to the maturity date cannot be a qualifying policy, as by definition it lacks the necessary benefits payable at death.

Taxation of the proceeds of life policies 10.15

The proceeds of life policies are taxed under *sections 539* to *552* of *ICTA 1988*.

For a charge to tax to arise, a 'chargeable event' must occur and a gain must arise at the event.

It is necessary to know whether a policy is a 'qualifying policy' or not: see 10.8 *et seq* above.

Chargeable events on life policies 10.16

Chargeable events on life policies are governed by *section 540* of *ICTA 1988*. The legislation applies to policies issued after 19 March 1968, and to earlier policies varied on or after that date so as to increase the benefits secured or to extend the term (*ICTA 1988, s 539(5), (6)*). However, as shown in the table below, some specialised types of policy are outside this legislation.

Non-qualifying policies	Qualifying policies	Not caught by chargeable event legislation
Death giving rise to benefit	Death, if the policy was made paid-up within ten years after its start, or within 3/4 of the term if that is less	Loan cover policies: No chargeable event on a policy whose sole object is to cover, at the death of an individual, the balance of a loan outstanding on his residence or place of business, provided the capital is repaid by instalments at yearly or shorter intervals
Maturity	Maturity, if the policy was made paid-up within ten years after its start, or within 3/4 of the term if that is less	Policies issued in connection with a pension scheme approved under *ICTA 1988, Part XIV, Chapter I, s 590 et seq*

Non-qualifying policies	Qualifying policies	Not caught by chargeable event legislation
Full surrender	Full surrender, if made within ten years after the start, or within 3/4 of the term if less, or the policy was made paid-up within that time	Policies in respect of retirement benefit schemes (*ICTA 1988, s 621*)
'Excess' at part surrender	Excess at part surrender or part arrangement, as full surrender* **	Policies in connection with personal pension schemes (*ICTA 1988, s 630 et seq*)
Assignment for value as full surrender* **	Assignment for value as full surrender* **	
ICTA 1988, s 540(1)(a)	*ICTA 1988, s 540(1)(b)*	*ICTA 1988, s 539(2)*

* Different rules apply at a second or subsequent assignment for value (*ICTA 1988, s 544*)

** An assignment for value is not a chargeable event if made as security for a debt or on the repayment of a debt, or between spouses living together (*ICTA 1988, s 540(4)*)

A policy is deemed to start again over its remaining term if premiums are increased (*ICTA 1988, s 540(5)*)

Gain treated as income **10.17**

Any gain arising at a chargeable event will be treated as income for tax purposes (such a gain is not a 'chargeable gain', which is purely a capital gain tax term).

The policyholder will be deemed to have paid the basic rate of tax on the gain and thus may well have no further liability (although the addition of the gain may itself lift him into the higher rate band). A non-taxpayer may not reclaim the deemed tax (*ICTA 1988, s 547(5)*).

Computation of gain **10.18**

Section 541 of *ICTA 1988* sets out the computation of gain for life policies.

(*a*) **Death, maturity or full surrender:** the gain is the full *surrender value* at that time, plus the total of any previous part surrenders, less the total premiums paid and less the total of any 'excesses' (see 10.19 below) arising on previous part surrenders.

(*b*) **Assignment for value:** a similar calculation, but using the consideration received instead of the surrender value, or the market value if the assignment is between connected persons.

(*c*) **Part surrender:** the amount of any 'excess' (*ICTA 1988, s 548*) (see 10.19 below).

10.20

Example

Policy year	Premium paid	Allowance b/f	5% allowance f	Total allowance	Part surrender	Allowance c/f	Excess for year
	£	£	£	£	£	£	£
1	1000	–	50	50	0	50	0
2	0	50	50	100	0	100	0
3	0	100	50	150	120	30	0
4	0	30	50	80	125	0	45
5	0	0	50	50	75	0	25
6	0	0	50	50	0	50	0
Totals					320		70

In year 7 the policy is fully surrendered for	1100
Add total of part surrenders	320
	1420
Less total premiums paid	1000
	420
Less previous excesses	70
Gain on final surrender	350

A loan made by the office issuing the policy is regarded as a part surrender, unless the policy is a qualifying policy and interest is payable at a commercial rate (*ICTA 1988, s 548(3)*) (see 10.8 *et seq* above).

'Excesses' at part surrenders **10.19**

At a part surrender, or at a part assignment for value, allowance has to be made for the fact that part of each premium paid is being returned to the policyholder (*ICTA 1988, s 546*).

The calculation is based upon the policy year. For policies issued before 13 March 1975 the first year available is the one beginning on or after that date.

For each policy year up to 20 years after the payment of a premium an allowance is given of 5 per cent of that premium, and this allowance can be set against a part surrender or part assignment made in that policy year. Where an allowance is not used it can be carried forward indefinitely against further part surrenders under the policy.

If at a part surrender or part assignment the total of the accumulated allowances is greater than the amount withdrawn, there is no chargeable event, and any balance of allowances is carried forward. If however the withdrawal in excess of the total available allowances, there is a chargeable event and the excess is treated as a gain.

The period from the last anniversary of the issue of the policy to the termination of the policy is treated a separate year, but if this 'year' begins and ends in the same tax year it is merged with the previous policy year (*ICTA 1988, s 546(4)*).

The calculation obviously becomes much more complex in the case of a regular premium policy. (See *Example* at 10.20 above.)

Method of charging gain to tax **10.21**

A charge to income tax on the gain falls on the individual holding the rights to the policy *immediately before* the chargeable event (*ICTA 1988, s 547*). Thus, at the death of an individual who is the beneficiary under an own life policy he, and not his estate, is liable to tax.

Joint holders are allocated the gain in proportion to their rights.

If the rights to a policy issued on or after 14 March 1989 are held by a company, then the gain forms part of the company's income taxable under *Case VI* of *Schedule D* (*ICTA 1988, s 547(1)(b)*).

Top-slicing relief available to individuals **10.22**

When the chargeable events legislation was first introduced it was evident that adding the total gain arising under a policy which had run for a number of years would elevate almost any individual into the higher rates of tax (and in those days rates could be very high indeed).

Therefore, a relief, called top slicing relief, is given under *section 550* of *ICTA 1988*, which operates as set out in 10.23 below.

Top-slicing **10.23**

A	B
Add the full gain as the highest part of the individual's income, and calculate the additional higher rate tax payable as a result	(i) Divide the gain by the number of full years the policy has run;
	(ii) Add this slice to the individual's income, again as the highest part, and work out the higher rate tax thus payable; and
	(iii) Multiply this amount of tax by the number of complete years the policy has run

The relief given is A – B.

As the gain before relief is A, the gain after relief is thus A – (A – B), which algebraically equals B. From this it would appear that only B need be calculated, and this is indeed usually the case

There can however be a problem with this short-cut method. In particular, where the individual is receiving a higher personal allowance due to being aged over 65, the correct statutory calculation may reduce this allowance, effectively giving a charge to the basic rate (see the examples in APPENDIX 10A below).

At a part surrender the period over which the gain is sliced is reduced to the number of complete years since the most recent 'excess' (if any) (*ICTA 1988, s 550(5)*).

Top-slicing relief is most valuable, and may indeed result in no tax being payable if after adding the slice of the gain the individual remains within the basic rate. The relief can be of particular use where a policyholder pays high rates of tax during the life of the policy but surrenders when this is not the case, perhaps in a low-income year or after retirement.

Loss occurring at termination of policy **10.24**

Where a loss results at the termination of a policy, the amount of the loss may be deducted from the policyholder's income for the year for higher-rate tax purposes to the extent that previous part surrenders have resulted in excesses (*ICTA 1988, s 549*).

Personal portfolio bonds **10.25**

An annual charge to tax may arise in respect of personal portfolio bonds as defined in *s 553C* of *ICTA 1988*.

Appendix 10A

Top-slicing examples

These examples are based on 2001/02 rates, where the higher rate of tax starts at £29,400.

Example 1

	Full gain £	Slice of gain £	Higher rate of tax £	Relief £	Higher rate of tax payable £
Taxpayer not aged over 65					
Total income for year after allowances	26,000				
Policy gain in full	1,200				
Total income including gain	27,200		0	N/A	0
					0

Here there is no need to look at top-slicing relief, as adding the full gain does not result in any higher-rate tax liability.

Example 2

	Full gain £	Slice of gain £	Higher rate of tax £	Relief £	Higher rate of tax payable £
Taxpayer not aged over 65					
Total income for year after allowances	26,000	26,000			
Policy gain (policy has run for four years)	8,000	2,000			
Total income including full gain	34,000		828 A	828	828
Total income including top-sliced gain		28,000	0 B	0	
Relief (A–B)				828	828
Tax payable					0

In *Example 2* the top-slicing relief reduces the gain to below the higher-rate tax level; the same result can be obtained by the short-cut method of merely adding the top-sliced gain to the income. (There can be an exception to this when the taxpayer is over 65 and receiving to the higher personal allowance).

Example 3

	Full gain £	Slice of gain £	Higher rate of tax £	Relief £	Higher rate of tax payable £
Taxpayer not aged over 65					
Total income for year after allowances	26,000	26,000			
Policy gain (policy has run for four full years)	16,000	4,000			
Total income including full gain	42,000		2,268 A	2,268	2,268
Total income including top-sliced gain		30,000	108		
			4 x		
			432 B	432	
Relief (A–B)				1,836	1,836
					432

Here the relief is of value; again it will be seen that normally only the top-sliced gain, B at 10.23 above, is needed to arrive at the amount of tax payable.

Example 4

Age over 65 – personal allowance trap

	Without policy gain		With policy gain
	£		£
Total income	16,000		16,000
Policy gain			10,000
	16,000		26,000
Personal allowance 65–74	5,990	5,990	
Reduction £1 for every £2 of income over £17,000 down to normal personal allowance: £2,910/2		1,445	4,535
	10,010		21,465
Less policy gain (not taxable at basic rate)			10,000
	10,010		11,465

Tax payable	£	Rate		£	Rate	
	1,880	10%	188	1,880	10%	188
	8,130	22%	1,789	9,585	22%	2,109
	10,010		1,977	11,465		2,297

The difference is of course caused by the loss of personal allowance of 50 per cent of £2,810, bringing the increased allowance down to the standard amount.

The reasoning is that the increase in tax is not due to a charge to the basic rate of tax, it is due to a withdrawal of allowance.

Appendix 10B

Chart showing life business

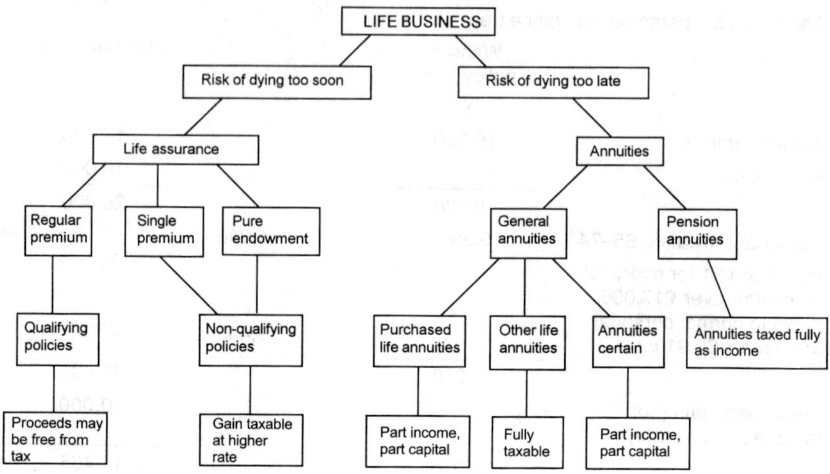

Chapter 11

Types of Policy and Policy Construction

- **The meaning of life assurance**
- **Types of life assurance**
- **Construction of life policies**

The meaning of life assurance 11.1

There is no statutory definition of the term 'life assurance' or of the related expression 'the effecting and carrying out of contracts upon human life'. However, there is a considerable amount of case law on the subject, much of it relating to the days when stamp duty was levied on life policies and disputes arose over whether the contract in question could be said to be a life policy. In addition, disputes went to law relating to questions of authorisation and whether the insurer was *intra vires*.

The contract of insurance 11.2

There are normally three elements in a contract of insurance:

- the payment of sums of money, called premiums;
- a promise by the insurer in return for the above sums to pay the insured a sum of money on the happening of a specified event; and
- the event in question should be adverse to the interests of the insured.

(*IRC v Prudential [1904] 2 KB 658*. For more on insurance contracts see 7 PROPOSALS AND NEW BUSINESS PROCEDURE.)

Indemnity 11.3

The third of the three elements in 11.2 above has been subsequently held not to apply to life assurance policies but only to policies of indemnity (*Gould v Curtis [1913] 3 KB 84*). Were it not for this ruling, endowment policies (see 11.15 below) would be disqualified from ranking as life policies, as their maturity is clearly far from 'adverse' to the policyholder's interests.

It can be seen that life policies do not follow the principles of indemnity, but are to be regarded as contingency or 'benefit' contracts. In consequence, a policy which provides an indemnity in the event of death, such as a policy to pay a certain sum if the policyholder incurs legal liability arising from the death of another, is not a policy of life assurance.

Benefits in kind **11.4**

An agreement to provide benefits in kind on the happening of the insured event is *prima facie* not a policy of insurance, subject to certain exceptions such as the provision of motor breakdown service. An arrangement which gives only a right to have a claim considered, with the other party having discretion as to whether or not to meet it, is also not to be regarded as a contract of insurance (*Medical Defence Union Ltd v Department of Trade [1980] Ch 82*).

Types of life assurance 11.5

It would seem that there are, at first glance, a multiplicity of life policies available, as the insurers compete with one another by offering a wide variety of contracts. As a marketing tool, they are given what are intended to be eye-catching and attractive names. However, in essence all life policies are variants or combinations of just three basic types of contract – term assurance, whole life and pure endowment. Some authorities would say term assurance, whole life and endowments, but an endowment policy is really a combination of a pure endowment and a term assurance – see 11.6 *et seq* below. Pension and annuity policies are to be considered separately in SECTION B: PENSIONS AND ANNUITIES.

Term assurances **11.6**

Level term assurances **11.7**

These are probably the simplest type of policy and provide for payment of the sum assured on death provided it happens before the expiry of the term. There is no payment on survival, and for young and healthy lives premiums will be very low. These policies are ideal if the motive for insurance is maximum life cover for a fixed period, and the fixed periods can be very short. Parties to High Court cases might consider insuring the life of the judge for the weeks they feel the trial is likely to last, their insurable interest (see 7 PROPOSALS AND NEW BUSINESS PROCEDURES) being the fees they would have to pay over again should the judge die and a fresh trial become necessary.

It is customary not to allow a cash surrender value of term assurances; if this was allowed lives in a good state of health would be tempted to surrender in the final days of the policy and thus exercise selection against the insurer.

Renewable term assurances **11.8**

These are as level term assurances at 11.7 above, except that the assured can effect another policy when the contract in question expires without further evidence of health. This option to renew usually ceases at age 65, after which normal underwriting criteria will apply.

Convertible term assurances **11.9**

Here there is the option available to the policyholder to convert the term assurance to a more 'attractive' type of policy, such as an endowment assurance, without any further evidence of health. This guaranteed insurability option must be exercised before a date specified in the policy, and the contract is ideal for a person of currently limited means who needs immediate life cover but whose circumstances are likely to improve in the relatively near future. As would be expected, premiums are slightly higher than with 'ordinary' term assurances.

Decreasing term assurances **11.10**

These contracts are ideal for use to secure a loan being repaid by regular instalments of capital. The sum assured will diminish over the term, often to zero at expiry. The premium will be set at a level charge for a period of years shorter than the term – this is to remove from the policyholder the temptation to cease paying in the final year(s) when cover will be low. Technically these contracts should not be offered to sub-standard (or 'impaired') lives (see 12 UNDERWRITING OF LIFE BUSINESS) in view of the high initial sum at risk in relation to the premium, but modern practice is to allow departure from this 'text-book' principle.

Increasing term assurances **11.11**

In some cases there is provision for the sum assured to be increased each year; in others the increases come at set times. There are policies available which are linked to the Retail Prices Index (RPI), subject to an annual maximum and with the proviso that if the policyholder does not opt to increase at any time then the sum assured is frozen for the future. Increasing term assurance can carry guaranteed insurability and conversion options.

Family income benefits **11.12**

Family income benefits (FIBs) are basically decreasing term assurances but aimed very much at family protection, with the sum assured paid in instalments on death. These will be instalments of a capital sum so, despite the policy's familiar name, they will not be subject to income tax in the hands of the recipient. It is now customary to allow the claimant to take a commuted cash value if required instead of the instalments. Once again, underwriting these contracts for sub-standard lives is far from easy, but is commonly done nowadays as no insurer wishes to turn away potential business if possible.

Income benefits can be written so as to increase at a pre-arranged rate. They might be index-linked but this facility is not as readily available as in the past.

Summary **11.13**

In conclusion, term assurances can be unit linked, and indexation, increasing cover and conversion options can be added to them. An interesting variation is the 'moneyback protection' policy, which is actually an endowment assurance (see 11.15 below) with a very high death benefit, and a maturity value aimed at equalling the premiums provided the units perform up to expectations.

Whole life assurances 11.14

This type of life policy was probably originally called whole *of* life, but has been known as whole life assurance since the recording of modern life assurance began. The claim is payable on the death of the life assured, whenever it should occur. The policies carry a surrender value as there is no question of selection against the insurer, and can be with or without profits, as today unit linking in its various forms is common (see 13 UNIT LINKED POLICIES).

Nowadays premiums invariably have a cessation date, the policy thereafter being in effect a paid-up policy for the full sum assured and continuing, as a rule, to participate (where appropriate) in profits. Some old policies may still be in existence without a limitation on the premium-paying period.

Endowment assurances 11.15

These policies have a high investment element and are very attractive, as they offer life cover plus the prospect of a return to the policyholder should he/she survive the set term. The claim is payable on the death of the life assured or his/her survival to the end of the policy term, whichever comes first. Nearly all endowments today are issued with participation in profits in some form or another – the modern tendency being towards unitised with-profits business (see 6 PROFITS, INVESTMENTS AND BONUS DISTRIBUTION and 13 UNIT LINKED POLICIES). The policies can be surrendered.

'Low-cost' endowments were for a time very popular and used in connection with house purchase (see 14 USES OF LIFE ASSURANCE). 'Low-start' endowments are attractive to a policyholder who sees his/her disposable income likely to rise in the not-too-distant future, as the initial premiums will be below the tabular rate but will be increased above such rate in the policy's later years to compensate.

Flexidowments 11.16

These are normally written as a number of small identical policies, but there can be one basic long-term with-profits endowment assurance. There is open-ended maturity after ten years and they can be very useful for meeting future commitments which are likely but currently uncertain.

Double endowments 11.17

These contracts provide for twice the sum assured which is payable on death to constitute the claim, should the life assured survive the term of the policy. The life assured can in a sense be said to 'back himself to survive'. Double endowments are sometimes offered as part of the underwriting process as an alternative to rating up a sub-standard life.

Pure endowments **11.18**

Here there is no death benefit, although the majority of modern policies do offer a refund of premiums if the life assured dies during the term. They are purely investment vehicles, and are not ranked as qualifying policies by the Inland Revenue (see 10 TAXATION AND LIFE ASSURANCE). During the period of life assurance premium relief, pure endowments more or less died out, and many offices removed details from their prospectus, only quoting them on demand. However, since 1984 pure endowments have made a modest 'come-back' and insurers are finding a market for well-tailored products, notably in arrangements to mitigate inheritance tax.

Policies on more than one life **11.19**

Most policies which can be written on a single life can also be written with more than one life assured, although 'joint life' business in its various forms is strongly associated with family protection, and with provision against future likely commitments such as taxation. The operative clause in the policy may provide for payment on the first death or on the last death (the latter generally known as 'joint life and survivor', although terminology varies). There must be an insurable interest (see 7 PROPOSALS AND NEW BUSINESS PROCEDURE) linking the joint lives.

Contingent assurances **11.20**

These only pay the death benefit if the specified life (the life assured) dies leaving another named person (the counter-life) surviving. If the deaths occur the other way round then there is no payment. Clearly these policies are designed to meet particular sets of circumstances. An illustration would be a man who is in receipt of a good occupational pension as long as he lives, but who is in a scheme with no widow's benefit. His death would leave his wife in financial difficulties; her death would not affect him financially. A contingent assurance with the wife as the counter-life would cover their life assurance need without 'wasting' premium taking cover which would not be required. Contingent assurances cannot be surrendered.

Universal life policies **11.21**

These must be mentioned, although they are marketed under various guises. In essence they are standard unit linked whole life policies with a range of extras (which can be added later or chosen at the outset) such as:

- option to add another life (e.g. on marriage);
- annual indexation;
- waivers of premium on disability;
- regular income options;
- income protection benefits;
- accidental death benefits (typically double); and
- critical illness cover.

'Bolt-on' options 11.22

Most policies marketed today can have 'optional extras' added to them, and some of these have already been quoted in connection with universal life policies at 11.21 above. These extras normally involve an increased premium. Examples are as follows.

- Waiver of premiums in the event of disability, or perhaps redundancy.
- Double accident benefit. Should the life assured die by accident, twice the sum assured is payable. This is standard cover in certain parts of the world (e.g. the Caribbean) – indeed, some policies even offer treble accident benefit.
- Disability benefits over and above the waiver of premiums.
- Options to increase cover with guaranteed insurability.
- Critical illness cover.
- Terminal illness (better known as accelerated death benefit).

This last option, accelerated death benefit, provides for payment of the sum assured if the life assured is certified as having a condition reducing his/her life expectancy to 12 months maximum. Early payment is not normally made in the last 18 months of a term assurance or where, with an endowment, the 12 months would run past the maturity date. If in fact the life assured survives beyond the 12 months the sum assured does not have to be repaid.

Construction of life policies 11.23

At one time life policies were quite stylish documents, often printed on high-quality tinted paper in Gothic or quasi-Gothic lettering. The language was usually quite complex and full of legal jargon. Today the policies are computer-generated, and the emphasis is on simplicity and a 'plain English' approach to the text.

Elements of life policies 11.24

Life policies should contain the following elements, although in practice these may, in certain instances, be merged together.

- **Heading**. It is customary to specify that the insurer's principal office is the place where notices as assignments should be registered.
- **Preamble**. This will lead in to the insurance and confirm that the proposal and any associated material shall be the basis of the contract.
- **Operative clause**. An important section of the policy as it sets out the circumstances in which a claim will fall due for payment.
- **Schedule**. All life policies now are scheduled policies (narrative policies in the life branch were discontinued very many years ago) and the schedule gives the details that relate the assurance to the party or

parties concerned.

- **Conditions**. These can be restrictive, privilege or explanatory (see 5 POLICY CONDITIONS AND ENDORSEMENTS).
- **Attestation**. Life policies are not sealed or signed by hand – facsimile signatures of (usually) two of the insurer's directors and/or principal officers are affixed.

Policies must set out clearly the nature and terms of the contract of insurance. General conditions will be printed in the policy form. Specific conditions are added by endorsement and override any printed general conditions. Words are given their ordinary meaning unless they have a common business or trade meaning. Any ambiguity will be construed against the insurer by the *contra proferentem* rule. The *Unfair Terms in Consumer Contracts Regulations 1994* (*SI 1994/3159*) will apply to life assurance contracts.

Endorsements **11.25**

A final point on endorsements. They can be inserted in the body of the policy or affixed as a separate wording, and in theory there is a 'hierarchy' of precedence with typed wordings overriding printed and handwriting, with 'the language of the parties' taking precedence over everything else. But in practice today handwriting and even typing are very rarely found in life assurance documentation. It is best to hold to the rule that 'special provisions take precedence over general provisions'.

Chapter 12

Underwriting of Life Business

- **Principles of underwriting**
- **Practice of underwriting**
- **Treatment of impaired lines**
- **Developments in underwriting**

Principles of underwriting 12.1

Introduction 12.2

In life assurance the level premium, once determined, cannot be altered, even though the risk of dying increases each year (see 1 ACTUARIAL PRINCIPLES). Insurers must therefore try to assess what the risk is now and also what it might be in each future year a policy will be in force. This process of assessment is known as underwriting, and entails analysing medical and other evidence relating to the history and present condition of individuals who have applied for life assurance.

Underwriting involves selection – the term used to describe the consideration given to an application for insurance to determine whether or not a policy which has been applied for should be issued. Some of the processes in selection will be explained in 12.3 below. Once the basic selection has taken place it is often necessary to discriminate within the rating bands, as lives proposed often demonstrate individual characteristics that can affect the pricing of cover.

Reasons for underwriting 12.3

The sole purpose of underwriting is to ensure that business is not acquired on unprofitable terms prejudicial to existing interests. It ensures that acceptable risks are adequately priced, and it is safe to say that as long as life assurance is voluntary, then underwriting will be necessary.

The reasons for underwriting are:

- to identify and confirm mortality assumptions;
- to maintain equity between policyholders;

- to enable an insurer to remain competitive;
- to maximise the number of persons offered cover; and
- to avoid anti-selection (i.e. selection against the insurer).

The last point above is extremely important. Experience over the years within the life assurance industry has revealed that any insurer who does not properly select will be selected against; this means that proposers whose lives are for whatever reasons impaired (e.g. by reason of health, pastimes, life-style etc.) will be attracted in disproportionate numbers to any office that does not underwrite properly. At various times insurers have sought to minimise underwriting and encourage new business by drastically reducing the information sought by their proposal forms (see 7 PROPOSALS AND NEW BUSINESS PROCEDURE), or even by seeking no information relative to selection at all – this last process being familiarly known as 'cash flow underwriting'. There is no doubt that these courses of action have stimulated sales of new policies in the short term, but the longer consequences in terms of enhanced premature claims have been grave, and in some cases disastrous.

Evolution of underwriting 12.4

Life underwriting is a complex business, and is constantly evolving. Innovative underwriters have, over the years, pioneered new techniques allowing people who were hitherto uninsurable to obtain life cover, often with relatively little extra premium. They did this because it had become apparent that certain medical conditions are much less potent in causing death, assuming there are no complicating factors, than had always been assumed. After the Second World War, the creation by specialist life reassurers of 'pools' of lives with one impairment, but otherwise free of adverse factors (for example the blood pressure pool and the diabetes pool), enabled observations to be carried out under controlled conditions which revealed that cover could safely be granted and at reasonable premiums.

'The whole is greater than the sum of the parts' 12.5

It must be remembered that a fundamental principle of good life underwriting is that 'the whole is greater than the sum of the parts'. A simple example will make this clear. Imagine that an insurer receives a proposal from a male life aged 45 who is 2 stones overweight, which is an adverse feature. He is a licensed victualler running a public house, which is occupationally also an adverse feature. His main pastime is hang-gliding, which is another adverse feature. All these adverse features will carry extra ratings on the premium, but they cannot each be considered in isolation. The man is an overweight, hang-gliding publican, and the combined extras will have to be added to an element taking this into account.

Extra mortality 12.6

It can be seen that life underwriting establishes the extent, if any, of 'extra mortality' (EM), which applies to a proposed life. The mortality table used by the insurer (see 1 ACTUARIAL PRINCIPLES) will give the average after-lifetime of a group of assured lives, as the following brief extract from a mortality table shows.

Age	Number of Persons Living	Number of Persons Dying	Rate of Mortality*
20	988,954	1,098	0.00111
40	964,767	1,811	0.00188
60	842,259	14,487	0.01720
80	301,833	34,315	0.11369

*The rate of mortality is found by dividing the number of persons dying by the number of persons living.

To the standard mortality will be added the EM factor, and this figure will be converted into a premium. It is common practice to show the standard mortality as 100 per cent and then add 'plus *X* per cent' if the life is impaired. In some cases the good features associated with a proposed life (e.g. lifelong non-smoker) may actually reduce his/her mortality expectation below the standard, and give an entitlement to a discount off the normal premium.

Practice of underwriting **12.7**

Most life insurers work via underwriting manuals, either their own or those supplied by specialist reassurers (see 8 REASSURANCE OF LIFE POLICIES). These manuals represent considerable intellectual property to their authors, who guard them jealously. 'Numerical rating', which is the allocation of percentage points of EM to underwriting factors, became commonplace in the 1950s. However, lives tend to demonstrate very individual characteristics (see 12.1 *et seq* above), and the manual should always be capable of adaptation.

Selection of lives **12.8**

In practice, the selection of lives can take many forms, for example:

- the scrutiny of proposal forms;
- reference to reports from the proposed life's own doctor, and/or to full medical examinations carried out by one of the insurer's own medical referees;
- specialist tests such as electrocardiograms and chest x-rays; and
- perusal of financial back-up reports from, *inter alia*, accountants.

Medical considerations **12.9**

Life insurers make extensive use of consultant medical officers (CMOs), most of whom work in this capacity part-time whilst following the normal duties of a medical practitioner. However, some have become so specialist in in surance matters that being a CMO is their main or sole occupation. The normal practice in the UK is for doctors to give opinions on insurance proposals and to be available for consultation by underwriters on all aspects of the applications under consideration, but not to actually do the underwriting (as many doctors do overseas, notably in continental Europe). The insurance-specific text-books of some CMOs, such as Dr. R. Brackenridge, are renowned world-wide.

All life insurers retain doctors as their medical referees to conduct medical examinations when required (see 12.10 and 12.12 below). The medical referee's report is far more detailed, and far more objective, than the private medical attendant's report which the insurer can obtain from the life proposed's doctor, but understandably considerably more expensive. Costs of medical reports, tests and examinations feature as significant items in the insurer's expenses, particularly bearing in mind that costs are frequently incurred relating to potential business which is not taken up, and hence produces no premium income. However, it is widespread practice among insurers to allow female applicants, if they so request, to have a full medical examination conducted by their own doctor.

Non-medical limits **12.10**

'Non-medical limits' are fixed by life insurers. These are the sums assured, varying with the age and circumstances of the life assured and the type of contract (see 11 TYPES OF LIFE POLICY AND POLICY CONSTRUCTION), below which no medical examination is required. These limits can be very high where a younger life who shows no adverse features on the proposal form is assured. There are usually also limits below which not even a private medical attendant's report is required unless the answers to the questions on the proposal give cause for concern. However, the insurer with conventional business always reserves the right to call for at least one form of medical report if the initial underwriting reveals features which put a prudent underwriter on enquiry.

Categories of underwriting **12.11**

Underwriting of the life proposals is carried out under the following headings.

Medical factors **12.12**

This is by far the most important factor in life underwriting and is seen as the benchmark which the other factors may adjust. This can be contrasted with personal accident insurance, when the benchmark factor tends to be occupation. As well as looking at the proposed's current medical state the underwriter will consider his/her medical history, usually going back five years, as revealed by the proposal form. All material facts must be disclosed by the proposer (see 7 PROPOSALS AND NEW BUSINESS PROCEDURE). Height/weight ratios are important. The proposed's family history will be taken into account and the premature death of parents through illness can often call for further investigation. As previously stated, the underwriter can seek more detailed examinations and tests to investigate possible problem areas, but these involve escalating expenses to the insurer and can also deter applicants from pressing on with their request for a policy.

Occupation **12.13**

Certain occupations are considered undesirable for life assurance, either because they are immediately hazardous, present long-term potential health problems or involve a questionable lifestyle. It would be extremely rare today for a person to be unable to obtain life assurance on the grounds of occupation alone, but many occupations mean that a person so employed will have to face a loading on his/her premium, or that the policy will be subject to some alternative treatment (see 12.19–12.25 below). Practice does vary between insurers, and a prospective life assured in one of the 'high risk' occupations should take specialist advice to find the most appropriate office. This should also be done in connection with pastimes and hobbies (see 12.14 below).

Pastimes and hobbies **12.14**

These are becoming much more meaningful in life assurance underwriting as increased leisure activities and the availability of various types of sports facilities draw people into a range of hazardous pursuits. Exclusions are a way of dealing with the problems presented by pastimes, but problems can arise over causation (see 12.25 below and 2 CLAIMS).

Residence/travel **12.15**

At one time large parts of the world were regarded as off-limits for Europeans wishing to obtain life assurance at ordinary rates. Nowadays political risks rather than climatic risks concern underwriters dealing with proposed lives who plan to reside in overseas countries, and these will be dealt with on a case-by-case basis. Frequent travel, especially other than by well-known carriers on recognised routes, will also be reviewed individually by the underwriter.

Lifestyle **12.16**

Alcohol consumption continues to worry underwriters, and it is well-known that certain walks of life carry a propensity to excessive drinking. Nowadays this also extends to the taking of drugs. A common problem is that many people understate their alcohol consumption when answering the relevant question on the proposal form. Sexual proclivities can also be life-threatening.

Financial factors **12.17**

Although every person has an unlimited financial interest in his/her own life (see 7 PROPOSALS AND NEW BUSINESS PROCEDURE) the insurer is bound to review the premium against the ability of the proposer to pay, and to review the sum insured against the apparent requirement for life cover. There is a possible adverse moral hazard to be considered (see 7 PROPOSALS AND NEW BUSINESS PROCEDURE) as it is not unknown for persons, having effected life assurance, to feign their death or even commit suicide. Murder for insurance monies also takes place.

Access to medical records **12.18**

It should be noted that from 1 January 1989 the *Access to Medical Records Act 1988* conferred upon individuals the right of access to any medical reports relating to their mental or physical health prepared by a medical practitioner who is or has been responsible for their clinical care. Individuals can also withhold consent to such a report being made. A report by a medical practitioner who has had no previous dealing with the individual will fall outside the provisions of the Act.

Treatment of impaired lives **12.19**

Extra premium **12.20**

Insurers 'rate up' lives which are found during the underwriting process to have a higher than average mortality risk by charging an additional premium. The percentage of EM is converted into an addition to the standard premium. This has the merit of perceived fairness; the life assured's extent of cover is unaffected and the policyholder pays for what he/she received. Equity is preserved with other policyholders.

Temporary extra premium **12.21**

In cases where the incidence of the adverse underwriting factor may be short-term, it is possible to impose a loading on the premium for only part of the currency of the policy. Once this period has run off the premium will revert to the standard rate. This method is effective when dealing with lives assured who are in a post-operative condition, or where treatment will restore a person to full health.

Variable extra premiums **12.22**

In occasional cases variable extras may be imposed; for example, racing drivers have been charged £x extra per race. This method is only employed in very special circumstances.

Debt **12.23**

As an alternative to imposing an additional premium, the insurer can reduce the size of the sum assured, leaving the premium unaffected. Debts may be constant, or reduce over the period of the policy. The purpose of the policy needs to be taken into account before this method is used, as obviously if the sum assured is designed to secure a loan, or to cover some specific eventuality, the debt could make the contract fall short of its objective. The policyholder's written agreement to the debt should always be obtained to prevent disputes should a death claim arise.

Alternative contracts **12.24**

It is possible to offer an impaired life an alternative contract to avoid having to pay an additional premium. An example would be allowing a proposer who would be rated up for a whole life assurancc to take an endowment policy at ordinary rates. The premium will be higher than for whole life assurance, and the proposed life is in effect 'backing himself/herself to survive'. Similarly a person who would be rated up for an endowment assurance might by the same thinking be offered a double endowment at ordinary rates (see 11 TYPES OF LIFE POLICY AND POLICY CONSTRUCTION).

Exclusions 12.25

These are rarely used in life assurance, as their imposition can lead to costly disputes over proximate cause (see 2 CLAIMS) in the event of a claim. However, it is certainly possible to exclude death directly resulting from an occupation or pastime, such as motor-racing or mountaineering.

Developments in underwriting 12.26

Life underwriting is by its nature highly dynamic. Risks previously considered to be uninsurable become insurable; risks previously subject to rating move to ordinary premiums. Offices will experiment with guaranteed insurability in certain areas, seeking to cut costs by reducing underwriting and relying on volume for profitability. Offices will also outsource more and more of their routine, and even some specialist, underwriting to external firms of consultants. However, the principles of prudent life underwriting set out in this chapter will remain constant.

Genetics and genetic testing are major areas of controversy, with the debate extending far beyond the confines of the insurance industry. In a sense this is a development of an existing and well-tried insurance practice, as underwriters have always considered heredity and family history very seriously. However, the use of genetic profiles of family members to assist in the rating of a life proposed, even where there have been no premature deaths, is to many people, who do not hold extremist or prejudiced views, a worrying concept with disturbing implications. How far this will develop, and the possible effect on premium rates, is as yet unsure. The Association of British Insurers (ABI) has published the *Mandatory Code of Practice on Genetic Testing and the Use of Genetic Information* for its members. This is available free of charge by writing to the ABI at 51 Gresham Street, London EC2V 7HQ. The Code is also available on their website at www.abi.org.uk.

Chapter 13

Unit Linked Policies

- **Theories and development of unit linking**
- **Operation of unit linked policies**

Theory and development of unit linking 13.1

Origins of unit linking 13.2

Originally, unit linked policies were introduced in the late 1950s as a counter-measure to the challenge offered to life offices by the emergence of unit trusts. Money which hitherto had been channelled into life assurance premiums was being moved into savings with unit trusts as members of the public sought to take advantage of the then distinctly bullish investment markets. However, before long the offices saw that another advantage of unit linking was to avoid making the type of fixed long-term commitment inherent in the formal bonus declarations fundamental to conventional with-profit business (see 6 PROFITS, INVESTMENTS AND BONUS DISTRIBUTION).

Theory of unit linking 13.3

In essence investors are offered policies directly linked to investment performance. This can be done – and in the early days very often was done – by linking the value of the policy to the units in a unit trust. As an alternative the value of the policy can be linked formally to units in a specialised unitised fund run by the life office. The values of the units will reflect the values of the assets making up the fund and will fluctuate according to the performance of these invested assets.

Principle behind unit linking 13.4

Today there is a very wide range of unit linked policies available. However, they all operate on the same principle, with the 'investment' element of the premium (which at times can be 100 per cent) used to buy units in the relevant fund at the price pertaining at the time of purchase (for more on premiums see 1 ACTUARIAL PRINCIPLES). The future value of the policy will then fluctuate with the value of the units allocated to it. Interestingly, a number of insurers over the years moved to avoiding using the word 'policy' in connection with linked business, preferring to call the contracts 'plans' or perhaps 'schemes'.

This could be taken as indicating a desire to focus prospective purchasers on the contracts being investments rather than insurance products, and indeed at times it did seem that the insurance element was there primarily as a means of securing income tax relief for the holder (see 10 TAXATION AND LIFE ASSURANCE).

As the life assured grows older the mortality risk will clearly increase (see 1 ACTUARIAL PRINCIPLES), and the amount of premium devoted to covering the mortality risk should rise as well, leaving progressively less to be set aside for investment in units.

Basics of unit linking 13.5

A brief and simplified guide to unit linking can be set out as follows:

- money is pooled and a certain number of units allocated to the plan holder;
- the future value of the plan cannot be guaranteed;
- pay-outs are determined by the market value of the units on the day of claim;
- values of units can fall as well as rise;
- past performance is an imperfect guide to future performance; and
- the higher the risk, the higher the potential returns.

Unit and investment trusts 13.6

Below is shown in tabular form the main differences between unit trusts and investment trusts.

Unit Trusts	Investment Trusts
Investors' money buys units in a trust fund. The fund buys or sells underlying securities.	Investors' money buys shares in an investment trust company, whose capital is used to buy shares
Units are bought from unit trust managements.	Shares are bought on the Stock Exchange.
The number of units can be increased or decreased.	Share capital is fixed.
The offer price is fixed by the managers and relates both to the underlying assets and to management costs.	Prices are quoted on the stock market (no costs of management are included).
Additional funds cannot be borrowed.	The trusts can borrow additional funds.
Sale of units can be advertised.	Sales of shares cannot be advertised.

Dual price structure 13.7

Many unitised funds operate on a dual price structure of offer price and bid price.

- The *offer price* is the price which the office uses to allocate units to a policy when premiums are paid. If the offer price is £1 and £100 of the premium is to be applied to purchase units, it will secure 100 units.
- The *bid price* is the price which the office will give for the units if the plan holder wishes to claim under the policy or cash the investment in. This will be lower than the offer price and this difference is known as the bid-offer spread (or gap); in practice it covers the office's expenses against the premium. There may be in addition a small monthly management charge which is deducted from the fund before the unit prices are worked out.

No bid-offer spread 13.8

Products are marketed with no bid-offer spread, notably if they are written on a single premium basis. Invariably they will carry penalties in the event of early surrender as the office must recoup its expenses, and certainly its heavy initial expenses, somehow. These products are recommended to prospective clients who have every intention of maintaining their policies to the quoted maturity or expiry date.

Types of units 13.9

Some funds contain two types of units: initial units and accumulation units. Initial units will have a higher management charge, and consequently a lower price, and are used for the early years of regular premium unit linked policies. This structure really represents a charge made by the office. Accumulation units are units added periodically after the initial allocation. Some arrangements avoid having two types of units by setting an initial period in which no units are allocated.

Operation of unit linked policies 13.10

Policies can be linked to a wide variety of funds. Indeed, it seems that any type of lawful investment can be the subject of a fund. There are specialised funds (for example, Far Eastern funds) and even somewhat exotic funds based on investment in works of art or even rare wines. The concept common to all funds is to attract the investor who does not have enough money, or enough confidence, to buy as an individual into a particular commodity or security, but who is attracted by its potential and wishes to band with other like-minded individuals and seek to make a profit.

Common types of fund **13.11**

Ignoring from now on the more unusual examples, the most common types of funds are listed below.

(*a*) **Equity funds:** the investment being in quoted ordinary shares.

(*b*) **Fixed interest funds** (or **gilt funds**)**:** the investment is in securities with a fixed rate of interest, typically UK Government issues and local authority issues.

(*c*) **Property funds:** here the investment will be real estate, usually commercial and industrial premises. There is usually provision to invest elsewhere in view of the non-liquid nature of this form of investment and the large amount of capital needed to buy further buildings.

(*d*) **Index-linked gilt funds:** similar to fixed interest funds (see (*b*) above) but with the investment in index-linked securities.

(*e*) **Building society funds:** these investments in building society deposits are becoming less common as so many societies are opting to convert to banks.

(*f*) **International funds:** investment in assets abroad (usually subject to the caveat that they are quoted on reputable foreign stock exchanges).

(*g*) **Cash funds:** the investment here is in the short-term money markets.

Managed funds **13.12**

The performance of funds will vary over time. One consequence of this has been the emergence of the managed fund, which permits the office's fund managers to invest in a mixture of whichever of their funds is felt by them to be best at any particular time. Another variation is the 'switching facility' which many offices offer to policyholders, who are allowed to follow their own judgement and switch from one fund to another. They can therefore move to a fund where prospects look better, for which service there may be a small charge.

Unitised with-profits policies **13.13**

As has been previously stated, the value of units can fall and hence a policy can fall in value. Ignoring the effect of inflation, this will not happen to a conventional with-profits policy (for details of with-profits policies see 6 PROFITS, INVESTMENTS AND BONUS DISTRIBUTION). To try and deal with this problem, offices have introduced unitised with-profits policies, with a guarantee that the unit price will not fall. Really they are with-profits contracts expressed as a unit linked policy. There may even be a guarantee that the annual bonus will not be less than a certain figure, and some such policies carry the potential to participate in terminal bonuses at a time of claim. If the fund is 'fixed-price' the unit price never varies and the annual bonus takes the form of an irrevocable allocation of extra units as this price to the policy. If the 'variable-price' system is followed the unit price only stays static until the end of the year when the annual bonus is declared. At this point the unit price rises accordingly and is guaranteed.

Single premium unit linked whole life policies **13.14**

These contracts – often called bonds – are the simplest form of unit linked policy. They are normally written as whole life contracts so that the investors can continue the contract as long as they like. When the policy is effected, the whole of the single premium is applied to purchase units in the selected fund at the offer price ruling on the day of payment. The policy can then be cashed in at any time, the surrender value being the total value of the units at the bid price on the day of surrender. The prime purpose of these contracts is investment.

If the life assured dies, the death claim value will be paid out. Many contracts allow the investor to pay in further single premiums at any time. This topping-up facility is useful since it eliminates the necessity of taking out a completely new policy. Most offices offer both single and joint life second death versions of this contract.

Withdrawals **13.15**

Almost all these policies allow the investor to take an income by making partial withdrawals each year. These withdrawals are achieved by cashing in however many units are needed to give the withdrawal amount. If the annual amount withdrawn does not exceed 5 per cent of the original investment, the policyholder will pay no income tax at that time. There may be some liability to higher rate income tax if the withdrawal rate exceeds 5 per cent or its duration exceeds 20 years.

Distribution bonds **13.16**

A number of offices offer distribution bonds. These are single premium unit linked bonds where the 'natural income' of the underlying funds (i.e. dividends, interest and rental income) is paid out, usually half-yearly, to the bondholder. This is normally done without cashing in units. The rate of income produced will vary, reflecting market conditions for the underlying funds, and thus is not guaranteed.

Regular premium unit linked whole life policies **13.17**

These policies are now the most popular type of regular premium whole life assurance. Their main advantage is their flexibility since they offer a variable mix between investment content and life cover.

Regular premium contracts **13.18**

The policies are regular premium contracts. The initial level of life cover is set for the first ten years on the basis of an assumed growth rate (often 7.5 per cent) in the fund to which the contract is linked. At the end of the ten years, the policy is reviewed to see how the actual growth rate compares with the assumed growth rate. This determines whether the value of the units allocated at the time will be enough to maintain the sum assured.

Sum assured **13.19**

The earliest policies had a fixed relationship between the premium and the sum assured. However, most current versions allow policyholders to choose their own sum assured, within certain limits, for any given premium. Policyholders may then have the right to adjust their sum assured up or down according to their circumstances, again within certain limits. Obviously, the more premium that goes into life cover, the less is invested in units. The attraction of this type of plan is that the level of life cover is extremely flexible, enabling a high degree of protection to be given in the early years and then reducing it to give high levels of investment later in life, when protection for the family is no longer the main aim.

In order to maintain the qualifying status of the policy (see 10 TAXATION AND LIFE ASSURANCE), the minimum sum assured is set no lower than the Inland Revenue minimum: 75 per cent of premiums payable up to the age of 75.

Cancellation of units **13.20**

The cost of the life cover is met by the monthly cancellation of units. The amount cancelled is based on the difference between the sum assured and the value of the units, and is calculated with reference to the latest mortality tables. Enough units are cancelled each month to pay for that month's life cover. The policyholder can thus benefit from future improvements in mortality statistics. A further advantage is that, as the value of the units builds up, the cost of the life cover can reduce rather than increase as it would on a conventional policy. Once the value of the units overtakes the sum assured, deductions for life cover will cease. These contracts are used for family protection and inheritance tax funding. They are available on a single life, joint life first death or joint life second death basis.

Unit linked endowments **13.21**

A great deal of regular premium unit linked savings plans are written as endowment assurances, either long-term or for ten years with an option to extend. Plans are frequently made up of a 'cluster' of small, individual policies; these can be treated separately and have the advantage of considerable flexibility.

Qualifying policies **13.22**

The contracts are written with sufficient life cover to ensure that, coupled with the minimum ten year period, they rank as qualifying policies (see 10 TAXATION AND LIFE ASSURANCE). On death during the term, the amount payable will be either the guaranteed sum assured or the bid value of the units, whichever is the higher.

Allocation percentage **13.23**

A specific proportion of each premium is applied to buy units. This allocation percentage will reduce as the life assured grows older and the mortality charge increases, but overall more and more units will be purchased as the policy progresses so its value should not stop rising. Units will be bought at the offer price ruling on the day of payment. Proposals should be properly underwritten in view of the life cover, though it is probably fair to say that nearly all plan holders are primarily looking on their contracts as investment vehicles.

Maturity value **13.24**

The maturity value will be the bid value of the units. This concept will also apply to surrender values, but offices reduce the relevant bid value by a discontinuance charge or 'surrender penalty' in the earlier years of the policy's term (generally the first ten years). This deduction is to cover the various management charges.

Chapter 14

Uses of Life Assurance

Introduction 14.1

The basic purposes of life assurance remain family protection and investment; it provides cover against the twin risks of dying too soon or living too long (see 1 ACTUARIAL PRINCIPLES). However, over the years life assurance has evolved into being applied for a variety of special purposes, either in response to public demand or as the result of shrewd marketing. The various types of policy were considered in 11 TYPES OF POLICY AND POLICY CONSTRUCTION; this chapter will address how the types of policy can be adapted and tailored to meet specific needs.

Key man policies 14.2

These policies have their basis in the insurable interest which arises out of the employer-employee relationship (*Simcock v Scottish Imperial Co. [1902] 10 SLT 286*). The extent of this interest was held to be the value of the employee's services for the agreed period of notice – see 7 PROPOSALS AND NEW BUSINESS PROCEDURE. For some years it had been generally agreed that limiting the financial interest in this way was not relevant to a changing business climate, and on 27 July 1944 the then Chancellor of the Exchequer, Sir John Anderson answered a question in the House of Commons by stating that insurances by employers on employees could be dealt with as detailed in 14.3–14.9 below.

Premiums **14.3**

Premiums paid are to be treated as admissible deductions provided that:

- the sole relationship is that of employer and employee;
- the insurance is intended to meet the loss of profits resulting from the loss of the employee's services; and
- it is an annual or short term assurance.

Sum assured **14.4**

The sum assured must be 'reasonable', having regard to the matters stated above. This means that the rigid limits arising out of *Simcock v Scottish Imperial* (see 14.2 above) need no longer apply. The Inland Revenue have taken the view that most employees can effectively be replaced within five years at the most, and so the sum assured should not reflect loss of profits for more than that time period. To secure deduction under the *Income and Corporation Taxes Act 1988* (*ICTA 1988*) (as subsequently amended), the expense represented by the premiums must be incurred wholly and exclusively for business purposes and must be a revenue, not a capital, expense.

It should be noted that if the employee whose life is being assured has a 'significant' proprietary interest in the employing company – a good rule of thumb figure is 5 per cent – the Inland Revenue may not allow relief, as it can be argued that the policy has been effected for the life assured's own advantage.

Trading receipts **14.5**

The policy proceeds will be treated as a trading receipt (that is, as income) in the hands of the employer; this is the corollary of the premiums being allowed as an expense for corporation tax purposes. It is possible for companies worried about a high tax burden in the year of claim to arrange for payment to be made in instalments, and, as each case is considered on its merits, early discussion with the relevant inspector of taxes is recommended to secure advance clearance (always subject to the proviso that the inspector's clearance can be subsequently withdrawn by the Inland Revenue). Just because premiums have been disallowed as a charge against taxation, it does not mean that the policy proceeds will not be treated as a trading receipt.

Length of assurance **14.6**

It is possible for an employee to continue to be of essential importance right up until retirement, and so a term assurance of considerable duration, or even a whole life policy, might be the correct option. This is probably more likely to be the case with a small family business. However, key man policies are usually for terms of around five years or less, and certainly rarely more than ten. It is unlikely that the premiums on a whole life policy would be treated as a revenue expense.

'Key person' 14.7

The term 'key man' includes both sexes. For a time there was an attempt to market these plans as 'key person' policies, or some similar non gender-specific title, but this move seems not to have taken root and today the phrase 'key man' can be taken as covering men and women.

Financial interest 14.8

Determining the extent of the financial interest in a key man policy can be difficult. Consideration should be given to the following factors, with the underlying proviso that the sum assured must be 'reasonable' (see 14.4 above):

- how much the recruitment and training of a suitable replacement would cost;
- how much profit can be traced to the key employee (for example, what would the loss in turnover and profitability be should the employee die); and
- the salary which the key employee receives (often cover can most satisfactorily be expressed as a multiple of salary, perhaps somewhere between five and ten times).

Contractual relationship only 14.9

Nowadays key man business is often written on individuals who are in a contractual relationship with the proposer but who are not true 'employees' in the legal sense. An impresario, for example, may need to insure the life of an entertainer who is under contract to perform a series of concerts, and whose death during the term of the contract would cause considerable costs in terms of cancellation charges, as well as irrecoverable advance expenses and loss of anticipated profits. Some offices prefer to stay only with *bona fide* employer/employee business, but with more and more people working under contracts the situation is very fluid.

Educational policies 14.10

Provision for the cost of privately educating children can be made through:

- income;
- investment of a capital sum or sums;
- borrowing (which should be a last resort); or
- a combination of all three.

Life assurance has an important role across all three of the above methods of provision. For example, the policies can safeguard the income element should the payer die prematurely; the premiums can be paid for policies, the proceeds of which will actually fund the school fees; and loans can be sought from existing assurances.

The flexibility of the investment will always be important, for example can the scheme be terminated and does it allow for a change of school. In addition, the taxation position must be taken fully into account (see 14.13 below).

Choice of provision **14.11**

The choice of assurance provision will be determined by, amongst others, the following factors:

- the number of children to be educated;
- the imminence of entry into the desired school;
- the likely cost of fees;
- who may be providing the funds;
- the current availability of funds; and
- likely extra expenses.

Investment vehicles **14.12**

There are two investment vehicles specifically designed for school fees planning. The first is the educational trust. These are registered charities to which the donor (usually the parent) transfers capital which is used to purchase a deferred annuity (see 19 TYPES OF ANNUITY) on the life of the child to fund schooling. This type of operation is very flexible as there is no need to nominate a particular school in advance. The second vehicle is the composition fee scheme, where the school (which is likely to enjoy charitable status) takes a discounted lump sum in lieu of school fees. Once again, a deferred annuity on the child's life will fund his or her education.

The major drawback of these schemes is the lack of flexibility, and not all schools will redirect the annuity payments if the child fails to attend.

Tax exemption **14.13**

A parent making use of either of the schemes discussed at 14.12 above can enjoy exemption from inheritance tax on the capital transfer, provided that the right to terminate the plan is waived from the outset. If the person is not the parent then exemption (other than the annual exemption) is not possible unless the transfer can be successfully claimed as normal expenditure.

Protection of school fees **14.14**

Life assurance can be employed to protect school fees being paid out of their income by the parent, or quite often by the grandparent. The premature death of the payer could cause the child to be forced to leave the school, often with an adverse effect on his or her educational progress. A decreasing term assurance timed to coincide with the duration and scale of payment of the school fees is the obvious choice, but as fees tend to rise steadily, at least a level term assurance ought to be considered. Some schools, not wishing to lose pupils and aware of the trauma that changes of school can bring about, do their utmost to ensure that fees being paid out of income are protected by life assurance.

Advance planning **14.15**

The advance planning of future school fees can be done via an endowment assurance policy written on a with-profits or unit linked basis. The proceeds, provided that the Inland Revenue qualification rules are met, will be tax-free. As payment is made on the death or survival until the end of the term of the life assured (normally the parent), and as the term will be fixed to run until the child starts at the private school, the desired education is guaranteed. Arrangements can be made for the proceeds to be paid in instalments, often direct to the school, and timed to coincide with school terms. An alternative is to invest in a series of endowment assurances, the maturity dates of which are designed again to coincide with the dates at which fees will need to be paid.

Other options **14.16**

A parent should look at all the options available, and it must be stressed that in many cases it will be the grandparents or even other relatives who will express an interest in funding a child's future education in the private sector. Deferred annuities commencing when the fees are required will always be a possibility, although these are probably not to be recommended unless annuity rates are attractive.

House purchase business 14.17

Endowment mortgages (see 14.20 below) are now unpopular, and many life offices have effectively withdrawn from this area of business as a result of worries about adverse publicity and considerable public disenchantment. Undoubtedly this has been caused by practices in the 1970s and 1980s in particular, which ranged at best from over-optimistic marketing to at worse something akin to mis-selling. The concept of utilising life assurance to aid the purchaser of property (the term 'house' in the title is of course generic to all types of residence) remains perfectly sound, but in the past forecasts which could not be achieved left many mortgagors financially embarrassed, and it will be very many years before confidence is restored. People buying property are usually working to tight budgets, and thus are unfortunately vulnerable to schemes which have an attractive face value. Life assurance salespersons seized their opportunity with the encouragement of their employers, and in the 1990s things started to go very wrong.

To understand house purchase and its role in the life market, it is essential to separate the two distinct uses of policies in this context: mortgage protection and house purchase.

Mortgage protection **14.18**

Here the life policy is not an instrument for the purchase of property, but is used to secure a purchase already made, or being made, in the event of the purchaser's death. The assumption is that a loan has been secured from a lender, typically a building society or other appropriate financial institution, and the purchaser's worry is that the property may have to be disposed of should he die prematurely, leaving a family homeless or certainly in difficult circumstances. Some reputable lenders insist contractually that their borrowers effect life assurance to protect mortgage loans, as although the ultimate security will always be the property, such lenders do not want to be responsible for evicting families by foreclosure or by exercising their power of sale. If the protective policy is assigned to the lender then the loan is paid off 'painlessly' should the borrower die. The mortgage will be repaid by instalments of capital and interest; the life policy will only come into play in the event of the mortgagor's death.

Decreasing term assurance **14.19**

A decreasing term assurance (see 11 TYPES OF LIFE POLICY AND POLICY CONSTRUCTION) is the conventionally recommended policy; the assured pays for no more cover than he needs and the sum assured will reduce as the loan is repaid, in the end declining to zero. However, problems may be experienced keeping the cover matched to the outstanding loan as borrowers often extend, or even reduce the terms, and changes in interest rates can influence repayments. A level term assurance for the amount and duration of the full loan has much to recommend it therefore, and will still be relatively inexpensive for a young life. If the mortgage term is significantly lengthy a young borrower ought to consider making use of a whole life policy (see 11 TYPES OF POLICY AND POLICY CONSTRUCTION), as if he/she survives then there will be life cover available either at a low premium (relating to the age when the policy was effected) or as a paid-up policy with no further premiums due.

House purchase **14.20**

Full-cost endowments **14.21**

House purchase can be done by the full-cost endowment method, although this is expensive in real terms, especially at a time when most people are hard-pressed financially. A mortgage is obtained from a financial institution in the usual way, with the security for the loan being the property. Some life offices will act as mortgagees, lending the money and thus keeping the whole transaction 'in house', although in many cases this facility is only available to their own staff. The offices do not want too much of their investment portfolio tied up in private property. Occasionally offices have, or more likely had, an annual quota of lending on property which was a facility only open to applications from policyholders of specific classes of assurance and with minimum periods completed on the office's books.

Interest will be paid on the mortgage loan, but there will be no repayments of capital. Instead the mortgagor will pay premiums under an endowment assurance for an amount and term equal to the mortgage. The policy will be assigned to the mortgagee and the proceeds will be available to repay the loan on death or maturity, whichever comes first. Some of the more wealthy borrowers were encouraged to effect the policy on a with-profit basis, thus giving them the 'sweetener' of the prospect of something for themselves or their family at time of claim.

It is fair to say that some building societies in particular lacked enthusiasm for this type of plan as they felt they were missing out on the enhanced cash flow which repayments of capital would ensure them (although there were agency agreements that brought them commission). When Life Assurance Premium Relief (LAPR) came into operation prior to March 1984 the great attraction for borrowers was the tax relief their premiums would attract, relief which was not available on capital repayments. With the introduction of Mortgage Interest Relief At Source (MIRAS), even the most entrenched societies concluded that endowment mortgages had a great deal to recommend them, and applications flooded in to the life offices. However, the problem of cost to the borrowers remained, and most business was written on the low-cost endowment basis which had begun in the late 1960s/early 1970s (see 14.22 below).

Low-cost endowments **14.22**

Low-cost endowments were offered to encourage financially-stretched property buyers to opt for life assurance as their preferred purchase method. The sum assured under the endowment would be significantly less than the amount of the mortgage, but the contract would be written with-profits in the expectation that by the end of the term the bonuses would make up the balance (hopefully more than make it up). The possible shortfall in the event of the mortgagor dying would be covered with a decreasing term assurance, linked to the endowment and with a sum assured which reduced in tandem with the increase in the endowment policy bonuses. Bearing in mind that these contracts were until March 1984 being issued with the attraction of LAPR, they were immensely popular and large numbers are still in existence.

Clearly the efficiency of low-cost endowments hinges on the insurer's success in forecasting the future bonuses. Forecasting reversionary bonuses is an inexct science, but forecasting future terminal bonuses (see 6 PROFITS, INVESTMENTS AND BONUS DISTRIBUTION) and taking them into account, as well as calculating the balance of the two sums assured, became commonplace early on in the operations of low-cost endowments. This was done at a time when bonus rates were generally high, terminal bonuses were making very significant additions to claim payments, and property prices seemed on an ever-rising spiral.

With hindsight it is easy to see that future possible terminal bonuses should never have been brought in to the equation. Bonus rates fell, insurers cut terminal bonuses or even passed up on annual declarations, and during the 1990s property values levelled off and in some areas fell significantly. Borrowers found themselves with 'negative equity' in their properties, having mortgages for larger sums than their residences were now worth. Then came the hammer blow of finding that poor bonus returns, notably on terminal bonuses, meant that the low-cost endowments produced insufficient sums to pay off mortgages at the time of claim. Consumer interest groups have been active on behalf of those suffering in this way, and life insurers have received unwelcome publicity.

The abolition of LAPR hit the life assurance house purchase market hard, but the failure of low-cost endowments to deliver their issuers' promises has been disastrous.

Partnership and business protection policies 14.23

There are far fewer partnerships today than in the 19th and early 20th century. Other than in professions where incorporation is not an option, most business people favour forming private companies as the advantages seem to outweigh the administrative requirements (for example the registration fee and the filing of documents at Companies House), which in any event are now relatively straightforward. In England, unlike in Scotland, a partnership is not a separate legal entity, and unless the partnership agreement provides otherwise there will be automatic dissolution on the death of a partner (*Partnership Act 1890, s 33*). Any capital belonging to the deceased partner will become part of his estate and will be lost to the firm. As well as causing financial problems to the surviving partners, the deceased partner's spouse may be left with an unwanted business interest. Very similar considerations apply to private companies; they do not dissolve on the death of a director or shareholder, but the latter's shares may pass to someone with no interest in the company.

For convenience the rest of this section will refer to 'partners', but the considerations will apply to both private companies and partnerships; specific comments will be made about companies where appropriate. Most schemes have taxation implications which are subject to on-going variation and often case-by-case consideration, so professional advice should be sought at the time that policies are effected if taxation is likely to be a major factor.

Insurable interest 14.24

The relationship of partner or director does not of itself give rise to an insurable interest. However, the view has long been taken that partners have an insurable interest in the life of a co-partner if the articles of partnership provide that on such a co-partner's death they shall purchase, from his/her legal representatives, the appropriate share of goodwill or other partnership assets. Offices will normally issue policies for the full amount of any such partnership obligation. Hence it can safely be said that 'a partner has an interest in the life of a co-partner to the extent of the latter's share in the business' (*Chapters 2 and 3, Life Assurance (Chartered Insurance Institute coursebook 735), Chris Marshall*). Similar principles apply to co-directors of a private limited company where there is a binding 'buy-and-sell' agreement or a 'cross-option' arrangement, requiring the shares of a deceased or retiring director to be offered for purchase to the remaining directors, or enabling one party to require the other(s) to purchase or sell shares. Such an agreement would create the pecuniary liability, as between the directors, upon which an insurable interest would be based.

Joint life (first death) policies **14.25**

With joint life policies, one policy covers all the partners and pays out when the first one dies. This scheme is really only suitable for a two-person partnership where the shares in the business are equal. If business interests are unequal the scheme is not appropriate, not least because changes in the organisation cannot be accommodated.

Individual trust policies for each partner separately **14.26**

Individual trust policies allow each partner to effect an own life policy in trust for the benefit of each of the other partners. There is no flexibility and the multiplicity of policies make it unsuitable for large partnerships. At one time discretionary trusts were used, but tax changes since 1976 have made these unattractive.

Automatic accrual **14.27**

Provided the business interests in the partnership are equal, an automatic accrual scheme can be very effective and has the merit of simplicity. The partnership agreement will provide for the deceased partner's interest in the goodwill and his capital account to pass automatically to the other partners. Each partner will take out a whole life policy on his own life to compensate his estate for the value of the interest which has passed to the co-partners. However, if there is to be automatic accrual on retirement as well, an endorsement assurance might be better.

Own life policies cross-assigned **14.28**

Own life policies cross-assigned were at one time the most popular method of arranging partnership assurances. However, complications arising if the make-up of the partnership changes, and the likely capital gains tax liability on any gain under a policy, have changed attitudes. Each partner takes out a policy on his own life, pays the premiums, and assigns the policy in favour of his partners.

Life of another policies **14.29**

A life of another policy is a very straightforward scheme, with each partner insuring the lives of each of his other partners with a sum assured to cover his interest in the particular partner's business interest. However, if there is a wide disparity in the partners' ages it may be hard – and rather invidious – for younger partners to afford the premiums. There is no flexibility and policies may be left remaining on the lives of individuals who have ceased to be partners.

Individual trust policies for other partners **14.30**

An individual trust policy is perhaps the best all-round scheme in current circumstances. Each partner effects just one policy on his own life in trust for the other partners, provided such partners remain partners at a set date after the life assured's death. The extent of the partners' interests and the wording of the trust document need to be handled very carefully, and as usual the taxation implications should be referred for professional advice. Variations of this type of plan are available to company directors under the general title of 'Directors' Share Protection Schemes for Small Companies'.

Life of another policies on shareholders 14.31

A final area of interest to company directors is the possibility of a company (which is a legal entity under the *Companies Act 1985*, as amended by the *Companies Act 1989*) effecting life of another policies on certain of its shareholders. Since 1982 private limited companies have been allowed to buy their own shares, so to help them conduct this transaction on the death of a shareholder it could be a prudent move to insure, if not all shareholders, certainly those with significant holdings. It seems unlikely that the existence of insurable interest would be challenged.

Children's policies 14.32

Insurable interest 14.33

In England there is no automatic insurable interest (see 7 PROPOSALS AND NEW BUSINESS PROCEDURE) in parent on child policies, although the position is different in Scotland. Up until the *Industrial Assurance and Friendly Societies Act 1948* there was a limited insurable interest in the industrial branch (4 INDUSTRIAL LIFE ASSURANCE), where the maximum sum assured was £10. This was designed to help with funeral expenses. Some of these policies are still in existence. It is known that in the more distant past children were murdered for the insurance money – one woman was executed for several such crimes in the mid-19th century. Parents can effect pure endowments on their children, as there is no life cover involved.

Life assurance contracts 14.34

Under English law, life assurance contracts with minors are likely to be treated as voidable, and in Scotland, even though contractual capacity starts at 16, it seems possible for insurance contracts to be repudiated up to age 18. In the 19th century it was held that an accident insurance policy was 'beneficial' to a minor and hence binding (*Clements v London and North-Western Railway [1894] 2 QB 482*), and it is possible that in some circumstances this ruling could apply to a life policy. There is also the argument that, given the appropriate financial and social circumstances, a life assurance policy could be regarded as a 'necessary'. However, the likelihood remains that a minor could propose for and effect a life assurance policy and avoid it at 18, or within a reasonable time thereafter (*Ritchie v Salvation Army Association Society Ltd [1930] IAC Rep 31*).

Competency 14.35

There is also the problem of whether a minor knows what he or she is doing when effecting a policy. Due to recent mis-selling controversies this has become very important. Offices will need to be satisfied that the child is of sufficient age and understanding. In the days of LAPR the Inland Revenue took the view that no child of 'tender age', which they assessed as being less than twelve, could lawfully take out a policy; some insurers as a result issued assurance contracts to children as young as twelve. It is very unlikely that, in view of the modern requirements for best advice, offices will now do this.

The above paragraph shows how difficult it is to issue policies to children. The volume of such policies has never been significant and is likely to diminish. Friendly Societies do issue baby bonds purchased for someone under 18 by a lump sum, which is subject to a strict ceiling. These bonds must cover investment for a period of at least ten years. Some offices will grant to grandparents single premium bonds with the bond in absolute trust for the grandchild whose life is assured, and with whom the entire beneficial interest in the policy will lie.

Child's deferred assurances 14.36

The aim of these contracts is thoroughly wholesome and in many ways to be encouraged; namely, to give a young person an attractive and advantageous life policy at age 18. There is invariably guaranteed insurability and the young person gets a policy without evidence of health (although in reality very few 18-year olds would have trouble getting a policy other than at standard rates). The problems always arise at the conversion date of 18, with the parent wanting the young person to take a life policy and the potential beneficiary of the conversion wanting instead to take a cash sum. This conflict invariably draws in the insurer, and it is for this reason that, whilst some offices write this type of business successfully, others will not transact it at all.

During the time of LAPR the initial policy was almost always an endowment on the life of the parent, timed to mature when the named child reached 18. Nowadays pure endowments on the child can be used. If the endowment option is followed and the parent dies, the proceeds can be held until the child is 18 and then the conversion proceeded with in the usual way. Provided both parent and child are in accord and sign jointly, the policy is converted to one on the child, owned by the child, and paid for by premiums considerably discounted to take into account the sum the parent will already have paid in over the years. The resulting policy will be at most advantageous rates and will constitute an excellent 18th birthday gift. It is customary, but not axiomatic, for the original policy on the parent's life to be put in trust for the child.

Tax planning 14.37

Life assurance has always been closely linked to taxation (see 10 TAXATION AND LIFE ASSURANCE), but in certain areas policies can be specifically tailored to help meet (and perhaps partially defeat) tax bills. Mostly over the years these policies have been aimed at 'death duties' under their varying names – estate duty, capital transfer tax, inheritance tax. Some schemes were esoteric in the extreme and quickly abandoned, and it must be remembered that following the cases of *WT Ramsay Ltd v Inland Revenue Commissioners [1979] 3 All ER 213* and *Furniss v Dawson [1982] STC 267*, the courts will follow the principle that where there is a pre-ordained series of transactions or a single composite transaction which include steps which have no commercial (or business) purpose apart from the avoidance of liability to tax, the steps inserted for no commercial purpose may be ignored. In consequence, professional advice should be obtained before embarking on any plan to mitigate tax through the use of life assurance, not least because the regulations, such as *ICTA 1988* (as subsequently amended), change with often bewildering speed.

Uses of life policies for taxation 14.38

Life policies can be utilised as follows:

- a policy, typically whole life (see 11 TYPES OF LIFE POLICY AND POLICY CONSTRUCTION), can provide funds to meet tax liabilities on the life assured's death and can be made payable direct to the Inland Revenue;
- life policies can be designed to protect and preserve an estate planning programme should the estate owner die prematurely;
- a qualifying policy (see 10 TAXATION AND LIFE ASSURANCE) written under trust will provide funds free of income tax and capital gains tax to the recipient, and should be free of inheritance tax;
- a person wishing to divest himself/herself of capital over a number of years can do so easily by paying premiums within the 'annual exemption' under a life policy written in trust (see 10 TAXATION AND LIFE ASSURANCE);
- payment of claims under trust policies can generally be made without waiting for a grant of representation (see 2 CLAIMS) and there may be protection against creditors (especially if the *Married Women's Property Act 1882* is used); and
- decreasing term assurances (or level term assurances) (see 14.19 above) can be used to protect the value of gifts made during the donor's lifetime (gifts *inter vivos)* for the seven year period after the gift in which they might become at least in part chargeable transfers.

Miscellaneous uses of life assurance 14.39

Home income plans 14.40

The concept of home income plans is basically quite sound, but the image of some plans has suffered due to mis-selling and the targeting of vulnerable people. There is definitely a market consisting of elderly people who own unencumbered properties worth considerable sums, but who have low incomes and live in what can be described as 'genteel poverty'. Plans vary, but the concept is that the owner can mortgage the property and use the loan to buy an immediate annuity which will service the interest on the debt and provide an income during the person's life. If there is a spouse involved, a life assurance policy can be arranged to provide additional protection even in circumstances when life cover would not normally be available. Clearly the advantage is the immediate realisation of a lot of the equity in the property; the major disadvantage is that at least the greater part of an asset which people had hoped to pass to their children will now go to the mortgagee on the mortgagor's death. However, most children would prefer to see their parents living out their days in relative comfort and forego to at least some degree their eventual inheritance.

Issue risk policies **14.41**

Issue risk policies are not really life assurance, but rather are contingency policies, although some offices do seem to place them in their life funds. They are used when trusts are being broken up, for whatever reason, and cover against the risk of another child being born who would be entitled to benefit from the trust property.

Securing loans **14.42**

The creditor/debtor relationship can be used to give an insurable interest to a lender on the life of a person taking out a loan. This has already been discussed in connection with house purchase business (see 14.17 above) but any creditor can make use of life assurance to secure his/her loan, as it is quite unlikely that the estate of a borrower who dies prematurely will have adequate funds to make full repayment.

Section B:
Pensions and Annuities

Chapter 15

Occupational Pensions and Group Schemes

- **Background and development**
- **An overview of regulations and requirements**
- **Types of pension schemes**
- **Special arrangements**

Background and development 15.1

Concerns over the welfare of the nation's older citizens are not new. The *Poor Laws 1597* and *1601* recognised the need to make some provision for the aged and the many localised schemes were finally centralised by the *Poor Law Amendment Act 1834*. There was a considerable stigma attached to being on 'parish relief' and 'paupers' suffered disgrace and social ostracism.

Pensions 'for all' 15.2

Pensions 'for all' were introduced by the *Old Age Pensions Act 1908*, but the benefits were limited to those over 70 and with an income less than a specified amount. This means testing was even extended in 1911 when a person's capital reserves were also taken into account in determining the entitlement to an old age pension. These early state pensions were paid out of taxation – the idea of a National Insurance Scheme and of a universal right to pension benefits was to follow later.

Occupational pension schemes 15.3

Occupational pension schemes actually have a surprisingly long history. In 1712 staff of HM Customs and Excise were awarded a staff pension scheme, although the exact details are hard to establish. In 1834 the Civil Service set up a non-contributory pension scheme for its permanent employees, and in 1898 school teachers were granted occupational pensions. Other public servants followed, such as police officers, and members of the Fire Service in 1925.

Early pension schemes **15.4**

Early pension schemes were not confined to workers in the public sector. At the end of the 18th century, the staff of the Bank of England (which was then in private hands) and the East India Company enjoyed staff superannuation benefits, and in 1842 the Gas, Light and Coke Company conferred a pension scheme on its clerical/administrative staff. Later, in 1870, this company very unusually for the time, admitted its manual workers to the pension scheme. Other pioneers of employee pensions were Prudential Assurance (1872), Lever Brothers (1904) and Rowntree (1906).

Most of the occupational schemes up to the First World War based benefits on $\frac{1}{80}$ of final salary for each year worked and allowed retiring members to take a tax-free cash lump sum of three times annual pension. As early as 1853 the cost of deferred annuities to pay staff pensions was allowed as an expense against taxation – it is possible that there was some abuse of this concession as in 1918 the relief was altered to be only available on new annuities if they formed part of a *bona fide* pension scheme.

Paternalism **15.5**

Well into the 20th century a strong element of paternalism could be found associated with the establishment of pension schemes for employees. Undoubtedly many employers meant well and had a genuine concern for the well-being of ex-employees in old age, but there is no denying that the pension scheme – in particular a non-contributory scheme – gave members few if any rights should they leave the firm and often acted as a 'tie' preventing mobility of labour and forcing men and women to stay in jobs which were unfulfilling. The fear of 'losing one's pension' was very strong, and workers as a result spent unhappy years doing jobs they actively disliked. One of the great steps forward in the world of occupational pensions was the passing of the *Social Security Act 1973* which preserved benefits under occupational schemes for those who left their employment, subject to certain qualifying criteria, before normal pensionable age. This will be examined in more detail in 15.10 below.

Funding **15.6**

The funding of early pension schemes seems to have been less than scientific, but the advantages of having a specialist provider who was independent of the firm were spotted by the more far-sighted employers. The first insurance company to act as a pensions provider was the Metropolitan Life of New York, and its UK activities were taken over by Legal and General.

Sadly, history shows cases of pension funds being 'raided' by unscrupulous or desperate employers, or of simply failing to meet obligations due to poor financial management. Many early schemes were very sketchy in construction, with no proper funding and benefits being paid 'out of the till' – invariably a recipe for eventual disaster. Probably most observers thought these scandals were behind us by the last decade of the 20th century and then the 'Maxwell affair' showed that it was still possible for pension funds to fall victim to predators from within. Under the *Pensions Act 1995* there is now a requirement for all occupational schemes to have member-nominated trustees. Employers were given two years to opt out subject to their alternative arrangements gaining statutory approval.

The future 15.7

There are still many non-contributory pension schemes in force, but changing social attitudes and alterations to the business environment mean that the future is almost certain to lie with contributory schemes of various sorts. Another factor is the mobility of human resources today and the tendency of firms to 'outsource' operations and make use of staff on fixed-term contracts rather than open-ended contracts of employment. The present generation of workers will look to carry their pension benefits with them and take 'ownership' of the same as well as the responsibilities that come with it.

An overview of regulations and requirements 15.8

To be value for money an occupational pension scheme has to satisfy the requirements of the Inland Revenue. Any scheme not approved would suffer such financial penalties as to be worthless. This section is largely concerned with the Inland Revenue regulations (typically under the successive annual *Finance Acts*, but sometimes by way of specific legislation such as the *Social Security Act 1973*), although it must be kept in mind that the 'rules' change virtually every year, and in most cases there is scope for relaxation of rigidity and for some degree of flexibility.

Insured schemes 15.9

The basic choice facing any organisation setting up an occupational pension scheme is between running the scheme itself (a self-administered scheme) or placing it with an external provider, almost always an insurer. Self-administered schemes involve recruiting specialist staff and taking on heavy technical administrative and investment responsibilities. Out-sourcing to a provider makes business sense and generally appeals to the members of the scheme. There is also the subtle but significant advantage that an external provider, such as an insurer, makes a very useful 'whipping-boy' for unpopular decisions. It is distinctly convenient for the employers to have an insurance company to blame when the staff are unhappy with some aspect(s) of their pension scheme and/or its administration!

A halfway-house between the self-administered and insured scheme is the operation of the managed fund. Here the pension fund is managed by an insurer but the firm employing the scheme members retains considerable control and, in association with its employee representatives, has more flexibility over the actual pension arrangements.

Contributions 15.10

The contributions of both scheme members and their employers are chargeable against tax, provided they meet the criteria laid down from time to time by the relevant statutes and applied by the Inland Revenue. The major decision an employer has to make is whether the scheme is to be contributory or non-contributory. Non-contributory schemes were very popular with employees, for fairly obvious reasons, until quite recently and there are many still in existence. However the modern tendency is to set up pension schemes on a contributory basis. This removes the feeling of 'paternalism' (see 15.5 above) and gives employees a direct involvement in their pensions. It also often makes for better funded pensions.

Retirement ages 15.11

Under *Schedule 6* to the *Finance Act 1989* retirement must be after age 50 – in general terms between 50 and 70, although in special circumstances consideration will be given to late retirements, unusual though these may be in today's climate. With male scheme members 50 is the minimum age for early retirement, but with female members retirement at 45 can be allowed as long as the lady is within ten years of 'normal retirement age'. For many years 60 was taken as the normal retirement age for females and 65 for males – there is now a strong move for equalisation of retirement ages for both sexes in all areas of pensions, and EU judgments (for example *Marshall v Southampton AHA [1984] IRLR 353* and *R v Secretary of State for Social Security ex parte Equal Opportunities Commission [1992] 3 All ER 577*) have indicated that the right of women to work through to the same age as their male colleagues will be respected. Many schemes now adopt a common retirement age, often 62 or 63, and provide for retirement at 60 as a right with no sacrifice of benefit. Disability retirement, if genuine, can be at any age.

It is intended that equalisation of retirement ages becomes a fact across the European Union by 2020 and thus *Article 119* (formerly *Article 141*) of the *Treaty on European Union* and *Directive 76/207/EEC* will be fully implemented.

Transferability on leaving service 15.12

As stated above, the *Social Security Act 1973* provided for preserved pension benefits for those who belonged to occupational pension schemes and left their employment prior to the attainment of normal pensionable age. Benefits are now preserved under the terms of the *Social Security Act 1986*. At one time a person only qualified for preservation of pension rights if he/she had completed five years service and was aged at least 26, but the age limit was removed by way of the *Social Security Act 1985*. The present qualifying period is two years of service.

On leaving pensionable service an ex-employee can:

- take a deferred pension and/or a deferred lump sum from the scheme itself;

- take a transfer value to another scheme or to a personal pension scheme; or
- take a deferred annuity or lump sum benefit from a life office or a Friendly Society.

Note: Compulsory membership of an occupational pension scheme has been unlawful since the *Social Security Act 1986* (*Social Security Act 1986, Part I*).

Benefits **15.13**

Despite many variations over recent years, only schemes with a maximum potential benefit of ⅔ of an employee's final salary will receive Inland Revenue approval. Traditionally this would be arrived at in terms of 1/60 for every year's service with a ceiling of 40/60. In consequence many schemes with a retirement age of 65 did not admit employees until they had attained the age of 25.

An exception to the two thirds rule can be found concerning late retirements. Employees who extend their service can get a pension up to 45/60 of final salary, and the lump sum can be increased by up to 15/80 of the same amount, assessed at the rate of 3/80 per year.

In recognition that businesses were moving into an era of shorter service, earlier retirement, and higher rewards over fewer years, from 1987 onwards 3/80 of final salary for each year worked was allowed, always subject to the ⅔ 'cap' as stated above. Nowadays some schemes allow 1/30 of final salary for each year worked, giving a retiring employee a pension of 20/30 (i.e. ⅔ again) after 20 years service.

Lump sum **15.14**

A tax-free lump sum cash benefit at retirement is allowed up to a maximum of 120/80 of final remuneration (that is 150 per cent of final remuneration).

Maximums **15.15**

Finally, it is worth noting that there is a maximum set on the amount of final salary or final remuneration (this latter term is now more widely used) which can be allowed for the calculation of benefits under occupational schemes. At present it is restricted to £100,000 'or such other sum as the Treasury might permit'.

Types of pension schemes **15.16**

In essence occupational pension schemes divide into final salary schemes (see 15.17 below) and money purchase schemes (see 15.20 below). Under final salary schemes the benefit is known in advance but not the cost. With money purchase schemes the cost will be known but not the eventual benefit. It can therefore be said that final salary schemes are 'defined benefit' and money purchase schemes are 'defined contribution'. Final salary schemes involve an open-ended commitment.

Final salary schemes **15.17**

Having made the initial basic division it is possible to sub-divide final salary schemes into true final salary and average final salary.

True final salary schemes **15.18**

True final salary schemes are simple to understand and were the traditional occupational group pension up to and beyond the Second World War. They work well if the employing firm follows a conventional incremental and hierarchical staff salary structure and is totally ethical in its approach, especially in its dealings with the pension provider. However, it no longer follows in today's commercial world that a person's final year at work will be their 'best' in terms of reward. From the employee's perspective it may well be better to take into account other years in assessing pension benefits. Earnings can now decline as an employee slows down a little with age, or accepts a reduced role within the organisation.

A problem detected by some insurers providing occupational pensions, especially in the 1950s and 1960s, was that firms artificially promoted employees who were very close to retirement. Consequently their final salary was quite out of line with their career earnings, but produced a most generous pension.

Both the above potential difficulties can be resolved by using average rather than final salaries.

Average final salary schemes **15.19**

When average final salary schemes were first introduced it was usual to take the salary average over the last three or five years of the retiree's working life. Some quite complex formulae have now emerged, but in general average salary schemes take either:

- the basic salary in a single year plus fluctuating emoluments averaged out over (usually) three years; or
- the average total emoluments over three years ending in the last ten years before retirement.

Money purchase schemes **15.20**

Originally money purchase schemes were associated with shop floor workers, especially those whose earnings were not incremental and whose gross wages would almost certainly decline with age as their energy and desire for high piece work and bonus-driven rewards ran down. Contributions are based on earnings, each year's contributions securing £x pension, and at retirement the accumulated pension can be identified. Contributions accumulate in a specific fund for each member.

Money purchase schemes are generally attractive to younger members. They have high portability, which appeals to a generation which expects to change employers several times during their career, either voluntarily or involuntarily, but it is the members who carry the investment risk.

Hybrid schemes 15.21

Variations of these schemes come on the market with regularity as providers seek to secure a competitive edge. One typical hybrid scheme is a final salary scheme, but with a money purchase underpin, and with the employee getting the higher figure at retirement. Another is a money purchase scheme with a final salary underpin – this gives a minimum proportion of final salary guarantee should the money purchase computation not reach this figure. These hybrid schemes have much to recommend them in terms of allowing for the benefits of good investment performance whilst at the same time reducing the investment risk.

Special arrangements 15.22

Hancock annuities 15.23

Hancock annuities take their name from a party to the case of *Hancock v General Reversionary and Investment Company Ltd [1918] 7 TC 358*, and are a means of providing a pension for an employee – usually at senior level – who has joined a firm late in life and would have only a few years of service which would count for the normal occupational scheme. A single premium is paid by the employer and is tax deductible as long as the pension is:

- purchased after the employee has retired;
- non-commutable; and
- non-assignable.

A legal commitment to provide a pension must have been made before the employee's retirement, for example by Board minute, and the actual pension must:

(*a*) correspond with that which was promised; and

(*b*) fall within the normal approvable limits on benefits.

Executive pension plans 15.24

Executive pension plans (EPPs) are designed as special benefits for 'top executives' and have their origins in the 'Top Hat' schemes popular in the 1950s and 1960s. They can be created for selected single individuals (along the lines of the 'Top Hat' schemes) or for groups of selected individuals, and provide either the recipient's only pension or a 'top-up' to their existing pension benefits. All the selected employees can go into one EPP.

EPPs are aimed at controlling directors or other key executives, but they may not be used for controlling directors of investment companies – that is to say, those companies so registered for tax purposes.

The employer *must* contribute to an EPP. Employees *can* contribute (subject to normal approvable limits), and in this way EPPs differ from the old-style 'Top Hat' schemes which had to be non-contributory, although there could be salary sacrifice 'as long as the one was not consequential upon the other' – a degree of artificiality which seemed to add nothing to the validity of the plan.

Note: Pension mortgage arrangements – schemes whereby loans are granted against the tax-free sum due at retirement and secured by house property – can be set up under EPPs.

Small self-administered schemes (SSASs) 15.25

These enjoy considerable tax advantages, notably on investment income. Basically there must be fewer than twelve members, with at lease one member 'connected' with either another member, with an employer or with a trustee. They must have a pension trustee who is not a scheme member, although it seems possible that a trustee corporation could act as a custodian trustee instead.

Occasionally the Inland Revenue may make it a requirement for approval that the membership exceeds twelve if it feels that one or two low-paid employees have been added to a scheme aimed at a few family directors purely to act as make-weights.

A significant advantage is that on the death before retirement of a director, a tax-free sum of up to four times annual salary can be payable.

Anyone interested in setting up a SSAS must have regard to the *Retirement Benefit Schemes (Restrictions on Discretionary Approval) (Small Self-Administered Schemes) Regulations 1991* (*SI 1991/1614*).

Additional voluntary contributions and free standing additional voluntary contributions 15.26

It is possible for scheme members to pay additional voluntary contributions (AVCs) into their scheme to enhance their pension, or to pay free standing additional voluntary contributions (FSAVCs) to another pension provider – typically an insurer – again with a view to supplementing their pension. The benefits obtained by these extra contributions do not have to be taken at the same time as the main pension, as long as they are received between the normal minimum and maximum retirement ages.

Total contributions to the main pension and to the AVCs and FSAVCs must not exceed the normal maximum of 15 per cent of net relevant earnings.

Chapter 16

Personal Pensions

- **Individual pensions**
- **Personal pensions**
- **An overview of pensions in the current market**

Individual pensions 16.1

Individual pensions were given effect by the *Finance Act 1956* (incorporated into the *Income and Corporation Taxes Act 1988* (*ICTA 1988*)). One of the great attractions of individual pensions was that under the *Finance Act 1971* part of the pension could be commuted for a tax-free lump sum. The *Finance Act 1976* extended the maximum retirement age to 75. Another attraction was the wide interpretation of the term 'relevant earnings' on which contributions could be based, although any remuneration received as a controlling director of an investment company (as construed under *Schedule 16* to the *Finance Act 1972*) had to be excluded.

As from July 1988 these pensions came to an end, although there was a great scramble in the final days to get plans through before the cut-off. However many thousands are still in existence.

Permissible contracts 16.2

The types of contract permissible under the pre-July 1988 regulations (*Finance Act 1956* and subsequent amendments) are:

- retirement annuities (written under *section 226* of the *Income and Corporation Taxes Act 1970* (*ICTA 1970*));
- dependant's annuities (written under *section 226A(1)(a)* of *ICTA 1970*);
- life assurances (written under *section 226A(1)(b)* of *ICTA 1970*).

These assurances were term assurances payable on death before age 75, but significantly the lump sum could be payable by instalments.

Annuities **16.3**

Annuities could be written with an 'open market' option under the *Finance Act 1978*. This gave the recipient the right to commute the annuity for cash to buy an annuity from another provider if the latter offered better terms. Part of the annuity could – and where appropriate still can – be commuted for a cash sum which must not exceed three times the annuity. The annuity could be guaranteed for up to ten years and could carry a dependant's benefit as long as the latter did not exceed the basic annuity.

Retirement ages **16.4**

Retirement ages were set at 60–75 with certain exceptions – boxers, jockeys, deep sea divers and, rather oddly, TV newscasters could retire at 50, and airline pilots, professional singers and deep sea trawler skippers at 55. Eligible classes of people were:

- the self-employed;
- members of business or professional partnerships;
- directors and employees who were not members of an occupational scheme; and
- employees in occupational schemes with additional income from non-pensionable employment (the 'two-job person').

Tax relief **16.5**

Details of the tax relief available can be found in 18 TAXATION IMPLICATIONS OF PENSION/ANNUITY BUSINESS. Unused relief can be carried forward for six years under the *Finance Act 1980*. Pensions are taxed as earned income, but it is possible for the annuity to be paid without the deduction of tax if income is below the level set from time to time by the Inland Revenue. The annuitant has to account for any Higher Rate tax but can recover any tax in excess of his/her basic liability.

It must be mentioned that special arrangements apply to doctors and dentists. Some can be in the NHS Superannuation scheme but most are technically self-employed on *Case 1, Schedule D* (this Case is under the *Income Tax Act 1803* (*43 Geo. 3c 1022*)). The Inland Revenue allows special dispensation and each case is dealt with on its own merits.

Personal pensions **16.6**

Personal pensions were introduced from July 1988 by *ICTA 1988*, and superseded the 'old style' retirement annuities. They are essentially money purchase schemes and need to be approved by the Board of Inland Revenue. Model rules have been published by the Pensions Schemes Office, which has now been merged into the IR Savings, Pensions, Share Schemes business stream of the Inland Revenue and should certainly be perused by anyone thinking of effecting a personal pension. *Model Rules: For Personal Pensions Schemes Including Stakeholder Pension Schemes* are available on the Inland Revenue website at www.inlandrevenue.gov.uk/pdfs/modelrules.pdf.

Employer contributions 16.7

An employer can contribute to a personal pension, always subject to the overall limits set out at 16.9 below. Personal pension schemes are private contracts between a provider and an individual and must provide for the benefits to be drawn between ages 50 and 75.

Group personal pensions 16.8

Group personal pension schemes can be written as bulk arrangements for groups of employees, but each employee must receive an individual pension policy. 'Appropriate' personal pension schemes are schemes that an individual can join instead of the State Earnings Related Pension Scheme (SERPS) or his/her employer's contracted-out scheme, and are qualified to receive minimum contributions from the Department of Social Security.

Contributions based on net relevant earnings 16.9

Contributions are based, subject to an earnings cap which varies from time to time, on 'net relevant earnings'. The allowable percentages are:

Age range	Percentage
16–35	17.5%
36–45	20.0%
46–50	25.0%
51–55	30.0%
55–60	35.0%
61–74	40.0%

Up to 5 per cent of net relevant earnings can be used to secure a lump sum on death and up to 25 per cent as a premium devoted to a disability policy, both within the overall maxima as set out in the table above.

Sources of contributions 16.10

Contributions to personal pension schemes can come from:

- members;
- employers of members; or
- from the Secretary of State under *Part I* of the *Social Security Act 1986.*

Benefits 16.11

Benefits are restricted under *ICTA 1988* (*ICTA 1988, Part XIV, Ch IV*) to:

- payment of an annuity;
- payment of a lump sum to the annuitant;
- a dependant's annuity; or
- a lump sum on death.

Up to 25 per cent of the accumulated fund can be taken as a lump sum.

Authorised providers 16.12

Contributions have to be invested with 'authorised providers'. These include insurance companies, Friendly Societies, building societies, banks and unit trusts. Providers may, if they wish, allow persons to specify, within limits, their investment portfolios.

Open market option 16.13

Annuities bought by the administrator of a personal pension fund carry an open market option (see 16.3 above) in that they must be bought from a provider of the member's choice. This option must be exercised before the vesting date.

Drawdown 16.14

Of great importance is the availability of personal pensions drawdown, allowed by the *Pensions Act 1995*. The taking of pensions in annuity form can be deferred and withdrawals instead made direct from the fund – this is particularly advantageous when annuity rates are low. This drawdown facility does not apply to a retirement annuity policy unless it is first transferred to a personal pension.

An overview of pensions in the current market 16.15

The pensions mis-selling scandal 16.16

When compulsory membership of a firm's occupational pension scheme was outlawed by the *Social Security Act 1986* (see 15 OCCUPATIONAL PENSIONS/GROUP SCHEMES) few people could have foreseen the consequences. As soon as personal pensions were introduced in July 1988 unscrupulous, poorly trained but avaricious salespersons descended upon financially unsophisticated people in perfectly sound occupational schemes and persuaded them to switch to personal pensions, often on very disadvantageous terms. This 'mis-selling' become a scandal of significant proportions that has cost the insurance industry dear in terms both of money (quite massive amounts of compensation have had to be paid) and of reputation.

With only a few exceptions the salesforce concerned have left the industry, as have most of their management, either voluntarily or involuntarily, but the damage will take decades to completely repair. Nurses, schoolteachers and public services employees seem to have been particularly vulnerable groups. High rates of commission tempted salesmen and women to push personal pensions at individuals who should never have even considered leaving their occupational schemes. Today's requirements for all those selling pension and investment products, *inter alia*, to have demanding professional qualifications should prevent any recurrence of the abuses of the late 1980s and 1990s. but the reputation of the industry has been tarnished and it will take a lot to restore it in the eyes of the public.

The repercussions of the tribulations of the Maxwell Group pensions will be felt for a long time yet. Robert Maxwell may have been a 'one off' but the fact that controls in place at the time were ineffective in preventing his pillaging the pension fund sent shockwaves across industry and commerce. Thanks to steps taken after the magnitude of Maxwell's defaults become apparent, an event such as this could never happen today, but many members of schemes remain uneasy.

Stakeholder pensions 16.17

The present thrust is towards stakeholder pensions, covered in detail in 17 STAKEHOLDER PENSIONS. Governments keep on trying to achieve some sort of ideal world of pensions and never quite getting there. One hopes that stakeholder will 'take off' successfully, but already the detailed administrative requirements are causing concern and the rewards may not be sufficient to attract either providers or intermediaries. The underlying concept behind personal pensions of 'portability' – of everyone carrying his or her pension with them through life – is basically faultless, but attempting to introduce it instantly by breaking up perfectly good and well-established occupational schemes spoilt a fundamentally sound idea and damaged the whole pensions industry.

Pensioners by definition are elderly people who do not look for problems and concerns in their finances. They want the stability and security for which they have made sacrifices throughout their working lives. Every time a pension provider expresses doubts over whether it can meet guarantees, let alone meet forecasts on which prospective pensioners relied, the industry loses credibility. A period of stability is now essential to bring belief back to all sectors of the market, and it is hoped that stakeholder pensions schemes will achieve this.

Chapter 17

Stakeholder Pensions

- **Introduction and background**
- **The establishment of stakeholder pensions**
- **Stakeholder pensions – the employer's perspective**
- **Stakeholder pensions – the employee's perspective**
- **Stakeholder pensions – the insurer's perspective**
- **Conclusions**

Introduction and background 17.1

The need to provide for one's retirement has always been paramount. In the past the privilege of retirement benefits was only offered to those working for large institutions or public bodies, and often only as part of an employment package. The benefits packages were frequently non-contributory.

The development of pensions for all workers 17.2

The *Finance Act 1956* established the concept of pensions for the ordinary working man, and heralded the advent of the self-employed retirement annuity. Originally it was felt that the 'old-age pension' provided by the Government would suffice, and those not fortunate enough to benefit from a company pension would have their benefits topped up by the State Assistance. This ultimately led to the introduction of graduated contributions to supplement the basic State Pension, and this scheme was replaced by the State Earnings Related Pension Scheme (SERPS) in 1978. Over the years, pensions have become more sophisticated and the introduction of executive pensions has enabled company directors to provide for retirement.

Tax relief 17.3

Tax relief has always been allowed at the highest rate of tax payable on pension contributions, and this has been a major attraction for those wishing to invest. In addition, a tax-free cash amount equivalent to approximately 25 per cent of the pension fund at retirement has been a further attractive proposition. The tax-free cash stems from the original intention of the Government to provide civil servants with a facility to purchase a property on their return from abroad, and the scheme evolved from there.

Personal pensions **17.4**

In 1988, the advent of personal pensions took place. An option was available to contract out of the Government's SERPS scheme, and contributions to personal pension schemes could be backdated to April 1987. This facility was not extended to the basic State Pension which is still available to all who have contributed. The aim of personal pensions was to enlarge the marketplace, and to allow individuals much more freedom of choice as to whether or not to contract out of company pension schemes. In many instances previously, it had been mandatory to join a company pension as a condition of employment, but this condition was removed. Existing pensions could be transferred into personal pensions, enabling members leaving the service of an employer to have a portable pension. However, this did lead to the pensions mis-selling scandal, more details of which can be found at 17.7 below.

The establishment of stakeholder pensions 17.5

The need for a new type of pension 17.6

Subject to minor amendments, the Government pensions system remained very similar until 1997 when, on election, the new Labour Government announced its intention to carry out a radical shake up of the Welfare State including State Pensions. The reason for this was the realisation that no government could sustain the continuing drain of paying pensions to a population living longer and working less without a massive hike in National Insurance contributions, which would in turn be perceived as an increased tax.

A lack of confidence in personal pensions **17.7**

The pensions mis-selling scandal in the late 1980s to mid-1990s involved people either being mis-sold personal pensions or being given inappropriate advice to transfer from good company schemes to personal schemes. The industry had to compensate thousands of people who were victims of this, and confidence in personal pensions fell to an all-time low by 1997. Another strand of the mis-selling scandal arose from people being persuaded not to join good company schemes, but to take out a personal pension instead, thereby forgoing the employer contributions. High projection rates of return led to inappropriate pensions being sold with the on-going consequences that when investment returns fell, it was not possible to achieve results equivalent to company schemes.

Personal pensions were perceived to be expensive as they tended to contain a series of charges that in many cases ate up the first year's premium (the worst scenario being where the charges consumed the first five years' premiums). Some of the more well known insurance companies improved their terms in what was known as 'fair deal pensions', but even these were perceived to be over-priced.

Certain groups less likely to have pensions **17.8**

Under Frank Field, the then Minister of State for Social Security, a Green Paper entitled *A New Contract for Welfare, Partnership in Pensions* was produced for consultation with all interested parties. This looked at ways of widening the appeal of pensions in order to encourage more people to look into providing a pension for themselves. It recognised that the income group between £9,000–£18,000 per annum as well as part-time workers were less pensioned, and that the new proposed pension should be targeted at those groups. The aim was to make people want to have a 'stake' in providing for their own retirement, hence the formulation of the name 'stakeholder pension'. The consultation was followed by six detailed consultation papers examining all aspects of the stakeholder pension (available on the Department of Social Security website at www.dss.gov.uk/publications/dss/1999/stakepen/).

Legislation governing stakeholder pensions **17.9**

The *Welfare Reform and Pensions Act 1999* established the framework for stakeholder pensions. The first set of regulations in this area, the *Stakeholder Pension Schemes Regulations* (*SI 2000/1403*), came into force in 2000: *Parts 1–3* on 1 October 2000 and *Part 4* on 8 October 2000. Since then the *Stakeholder Pension Schemes (Amendment) Regulations* (*SI 2001/104*) and the *Stakeholder Pension Schemes (Amendment) (No 2) Regulations* (*SI 2001/934*) have also come into force.

What is a stakeholder pension? **17.10**

Stakeholder pensions are a charge-capped product with only a single annual management charge of a maximum of 1 per cent permitted. No other charges are allowed, and the product must be transparent in transferability, flexibility, and free of penalties. This permits the product to be portable and more attractive to those who wish to purchase a pension. Tax relief at the basic rate is deducted at the source in both employed and self-employed pensions (a departure from personal pensions where the self-employed paid gross premiums), and the minimum premium is set at £20 per month gross, or a £20 single premium. Access to stakeholder schemes is either through an employer-based scheme, where salary deduction is mandatory, or a personal scheme, where premiums are normally paid by Direct Debit.

Currently the law provides that every employer with five or more employees, who can be either full or part-time, must register for stakeholder pensions. The cut-off point by which all employers must have registered is 8 October 2001, and has been incorporated into the legislation. Those not registering for stakeholder schemes by that date face a penalty of up to £50,000.

Access to stakeholder schemes **17.11**

Access to an employer-based stakeholder scheme must be provided to employees after three months of employment. There is no compulsion for the employer or the employee to contribute to the scheme, so in essence, it is only mandatory to set up a designated scheme capable of receiving contributions.

Exemption from schemes **17.12**

Employers with less than five employees, or who ordinarily provide a company pension scheme by way of group personal pension (GPP), money purchase or final salary schemes (which must all conform to certain minimum criteria) may apply for exemption. In these instances, the law requires a minimum employer contribution. The exemptions to GPP are to be reviewed after three years.

Currently, the minimum contribution to gain exemption from stakeholder pensions under a GPP scheme is a 3 per cent employer contribution, which must at least be matched by the employee. In addition, schemes taken out before 8 October 2001 can insist on a larger employee contribution, particularly where the employer contribution is greater than 3 per cent. The *Welfare Reform and Pensions Act 1999*, and *Regulation 22(4)* of the *Stakeholder Pensions Regulations* (*SI 2000/1403*) indicate that as of 8 October 2001 an employer can no longer make it a condition that the employee must pay more than 3 per cent.

Final salary schemes are costed differently as the employer contribution is based entirely on the requirement to obtain the percentage of final salary laid down in the scheme and this is then supplemented by an employee contribution in most instances.

Stakeholder employer contributions are not normally linked to a percentage of salary but are for a monetary amount.

Contributions **17.13**

A major departure from personal pensions is that contributions will no longer be salary-based (up to a total of £3,600 per annum). This basically means that anyone can contribute, irrespective of their level of income. This will particularly be an encouragement for part-timers to pay into a pension, where previously they were very restricted because of their income levels. In addition, stakeholder pensions will provide for a facility to continue contributions up to five years after leaving employment which will encourage certain people, such as those taking a career break, to continue with contributions even though there is no income eligibility.

Providers **17.14**

Providers of stakeholder pensions will primarily be insurance companies, although other bodies may apply to run the schemes, (for example, banks, building societies, and unit trust companies). Individual pension accounts run through investment trust companies will also feature in stakeholder pensions.

Other benefits **17.15**

Other benefits, such as death benefit or waiver of premium, may run alongside stakeholder pensions. Premium waivers will no longer be eligible for income tax relief – a departure from the situation under personal pensions. Retirement ages may be between 50 and 75 with similar 25 per cent tax-free cash options as personal pensions (see 17.3 above).

Stakeholder pensions – the employer's perspective 17.16

The Occupational Pensions Regulatory Authority (Opra) will be responsible for making sure employers meet their responsibilities. Most employers who are affected by the new legislation will regard the newly imposed obligations as further bureaucracy. Already employers act as unpaid tax-collectors for income tax and National Insurance contributions, and the legal requirement of having to set up a stakeholder pension scheme will not be welcome. In order to achieve the aim of providing greater accessibility to pensions, the workplace seemed to be the most suitable option for the Government to take. Overtures made to large bodies such as trade unions or federations of workers to sponsor schemes in the workplace also put more pressure on employers to offer stakeholder pensions with employer contributions. Smaller firms may find the administration of stakeholder schemes cumbersome, with perhaps deduction and pay over of premiums being alien to their normal working practices. These problems might be more prominent in areas where employees are still paid in cash in the wage-packet.

Some employers will recognise stakeholders as a starting point for providing a new benefits package. Experience has shown that employees greatly value indirect benefits such as pensions, healthcare, and death benefit provision.

Most employers will be resilient, accept the situation, and deal with the stakeholder installation using one of the avenues available to them:

- financial advisers;
- direct dealing; or
- the 'decision trees' provided by the Government (available from the Opra website at www.stakeholder.opra.gov.uk/decisontree/).

Some larger employers may use gateways through bodies such as trade unions to set up the scheme (for example Friends Provident and AEUW), so that all union members in the firm can use the sponsored scheme. It is possible that in the future compulsory employer contributions may come, as the stakeholder pensions scheme tends to mirror the Australian pattern in many ways. This scheme is similar to our stakeholder pensions, but contributions are now mandatory with employers having to contribute around 9 per cent of the employee's salary to the pension fund. Because of the very tight charging structure, the number of providers has fallen to two, of which AMP is the largest.

Stakeholder pensions – the employee's perspective 17.17

For many employees, the option to join a pension scheme will be a new departure. Many will already have personal pensions and will be suspicious of joining something new, especially if it means cancelling or stopping payments on an existing plan. To enable an employee to join, the scheme will have to be measurably better, although there would be an option for an employee to continue with existing personal contributions into an old scheme, as well as joining the stakeholder if they could afford it. Bearing in mind there is no tie-in to income with contributions of up to £3,600, some better-off employees may wish to pay as much as they can afford. It is also possible to set up a stakeholder pension for one's wife or children, so that the 'cradle to grave' concept of providing support is gradually shifted away from the Government to the individual.

Another departure from the previous regime is that even employees in a company final salary scheme or money purchase scheme can have a stakeholder pension and contribute up to £3,600 on top of the contributions to the company scheme. The main restriction here is that any employee earning over £30,000 per annum will be excluded from the arrangement, although if any year out of the previous five years is below £30,000, this can be used as the benchmark. This will call into question the comparison between the additional voluntary contributions (AVC) contracts, where people top up company pensions, and the stakeholder scheme. It would appear to be a major benefit to use the stakeholder pension since there is a tax-free cash option which is not available with AVC contracts. In these days of low annuity rates, this is obviously a valuable option providing access to what may be essential cashat retirement.

Employees are often suspicious of financial packages offered to them, and stakeholders will be no exception. They should, however, be encouraged to accept stakeholder pensions as an integral part of employment, particularly where an employer contribution is offered. The long-term benefit of a pension scheme with low charges cannot be over-emphasised.

Stakeholder pensions – the insurer's perspective 17.18

Most leading insurance companies are very innovative, and capable of handling the changes in legislation handed down by respective governments. The last 20 years have seen the abolition of life assurance tax relief, many different pension regimes, qualifying and non-qualifying policies and much more. The objective of the Government to shift the burden of old age retirement provision from the State to the individual has led to major changes in recent pensions legislation. The perceived high-charging personal pensions were not acceptable to the current Government. The pensions mis-selling scandal (see 17.7 above) severely impacted on the confidence in company pensions and provided a platform for the revolution in pension scheme provisions and charges. Insurance companies were given an ultimatum to come up with a product which was transparent in charges, flexible, penalty free, and providing real value for money, hence the creation of stakeholder pensions.

Most personal pensions had a number of charge components such as bid-offer spread (the difference between the buying and selling price of 5 per cent), policy fee, capital units and annual management charges. This meant, in many instances, that the first year or two's premiums were eaten up in costs and if the purchaser ceased payments, particularly in these early years, only a small fund remained and continued to be eroded by charges.

Some companies introduced 'fair deal pensions' with no penalties for flexibility, but even these with high initial values still incorporated a series of charges. The Government insisted that insurers move to a single charge. The annual management charge of 1 per cent of the fund was imposed, although insurers insisted that this left little or no room for profits, providing payment for advice and general administration to cover legal requirements of trusteeship, etc. Insurers would have preferred an annual management charge of, say, 1.5 per cent per annum so that paying financial advisers would still be feasible. However, this was ruled out, so the majority of insurers have now come up with very innovative contracts within the 1 per cent fund charge. In many instances this will result in a limited fund choice including a 'default' fund which may be a tracker or a with-profits fund. Many companies have already stated they will not make available with profits funds because of the financial requirements imposed. It is important to have a low-risk fund available and the with profits fund is ideal since it offers the possibility of greater returns than, say, a cash fund with only a slightly higher risk factor. The inevitable effect of the changes has been to minimise commissions paid to advisers to the extent that many have withdrawn from the market or are now charging fees for advice. The consequence of this is that there will be less provision for advice, but the Government has insisted that because of the new simple structure of a stakeholder pension, most purchasers should be able to use a 'decision tree'.

The reality is that very few people understand the concept of pensions, even the simplest products, and therefore need advice. Many people will also need to discuss other pensions which they may have at the time of taking out a stakeholder, and the lack of advice could result in a further pensions scandal at some time in the future. Time will ultimately tell whether or not the need for advice will be as paramount as it has been in the past.

Around 15–20 insurers have indicated they will enter the stakeholder arena. Most are aware that the break-even point for stakeholder could be at least 10 years, so the financial strength of insurers is paramount. It is also widely recognised that a critical mass of at least 500,000 policyholders will be needed to operate stakeholder pension schemes profitably.

Informed sources say that the market will eventually crystallise to probably around five providers, and even finally reduce below this level. This assumes that there will be no further major changes in legislation which will affect the companies. One such example of what could occur is the loss of basic rate tax-relief on contributions by members, which would then lead to the questioning of what advantages existed in a pension as opposed to other investments.

Conclusions **17.19**

Whether or not stakeholder pensions will be successful will be determined by the take-up rate. Without critical mass, providers operating on thin margins will only remain in the arena if there is some likelihood of profit for themselves in the future. Financial strength will also play a major part in subsidising the costs of acquiring stakeholder pension business. Many providers may withdraw after an initial foray into the market, and ultimately the numbers providing stakeholder pensions may fall to a handful. If the Australian pattern is followed (see 17.16 above), we could be left with as few as two providers, and faced with the prospect of compulsory contributions by both employers and employees.

The failure of stakeholder pension schemes will present future governments with a growing problem and could lead to substantial changes in current State Pension arrangements.

Another factor which will dictate the success of stakeholder pensions will be a stable period of little or no change in the regulations governing the schemes. Too often in the past, frequent changes have complicated pensions and made them incomprehensible to the average person. As stakeholder schemes are designed for a new non-pensioned mass market, it is essential that they retain their simplicity and stability.

Chapter 18

Taxation Implications of Pension/Annuity Business

- **Pension schemes**
- **Personal pensions**
- **General (non-pension) annuities**
- **Occupational pension schemes**
- **Exempt approved schemes**
- **Free standing additional voluntary contributions schemes**

Pension schemes **18.1**

The legislation dealing with pension schemes inevitably changes almost year by year, resulting in there being many important dates governing this area. Indeed, many changes came into effect in April 2001. As a consequence there are people who still contribute to, or receive benefits from, schemes to which the current rules do not apply, or apply only in modified form, and it is quite possible for someone to be receiving a pension from one or more schemes and contributing to another under different rules. Queries must therefore be looked at very much on an individual basis, which may not be a simple matter.

It has also to be said that practically every statement made regarding pension schemes is subject to qualification in some way. For example, final remuneration, a central and apparently simple concept, takes several paragraphs of Inland Revenue notes to explain.

The favourable tax treatment of a pension scheme depends upon its having and maintaining Inland Revenue approval, which will probably include some element of discretionary approval. Each scheme may thus to some extent be unique.

In considering a particular case the rules of the relevant pension scheme will govern what may be done, and may not provide all the benefits that the legislation offers. It will thus be necessary to see the relevant documentation to see what the scheme does not allow, just as much as what it does.

Inland Revenue guidance 18.2

The Inland Revenue issues guidance notes, which are also available on their website at www.inlandrevenue.gov.uk/pensionschemes/guidance.htm. The guidance relating to pensions includes the following.

IR 12	–	Occupational pension schemes
IR 12 Supplement	–	Free standing additional voluntary contribution schemes
IR 76	–	Personal pension schemes

Personal pensions 18.3

Retirement annuities 18.4

Provisions for the self-employed, and for those employees not in an occupational scheme, were introduced in the *Finance Act 1956*. After consolidations the relevant legislation now appears as *sections 618* to *629* of the *Income and Corporation Taxes Act 1988* (*ICTA 1988*).

The contracts specified by *sections 618* to *629* of *ICTA 1988* could be sold until 1 July 1988, on which date they were superseded by personal pension plans (see 18.5 below). However, there are many existing contracts which may run on for years.

Personal pension schemes 18.5

Personal pension schemes are governed by *sections 630* to *655* of *ICTA 1988*. The Inland Revenue has issued *IR 76: Personal Pension Schemes Guidance Notes (including Stakeholder Pension Schemes)*, which describes the practice of the Inland Revenue in approving schemes under *ICTA 1988*. *IR 76* is available on the Inland Revenue website at www.inlandrevenue.gov.uk/pensionschemes/ir76.htm.

Many changes took effect from 6 April 2001, and transitional provisions have allowed earlier schemes to be varied to comply with the new rules (*Finance Act 2000, Sch 13, Part II*).

An individual may open a number of schemes provided that the overall contribution limits are not exceeded.

Pension providers 18.6

Under *section 632* of *ICTA 1988*, a personal pension scheme must be approved by the Inland Revenue, and approval will only be given to authorised pension providers (*IR 76, para 2.1, Glossary*), among which are companies issuing insurance policies or annuity contracts.

Benefits 18.7

The only benefits which can be provided under *section 633* of *ICTA 1988* are:

(*a*) an annuity or income withdrawals payable to the member;

(*b*) a lump sum payable to the member at pension date;

(*c*) an annuity or income withdrawals payable to the member's widow, widower or dependants following the death of the member;

(*d*) a lump sum payable by an insurer on the death of a member before age 75; and

(*e*) on the death of the member before any annuity has been, or is to be purchased, a return of contributions, together with interest at a reasonable rate (or the sale price of units under a unit trust scheme) (*IR 76, para 2.10*).

A scheme must be approved by the Inland Revenue, who may apply restrictions (*ICTA 1988, ss 638, 638A*).

Contributions to schemes **18.8**

Contributions to personal pension schemes may be made by the individual or his employer. Historically, personal pension schemes have only been available to those not within pensionable employment, and have been based upon net relevant earnings (see 18.12 below).

However, from 6 April 2001 the availability of personal pension schemes has been extended to include the following:

(*a*) an individual who has no net relevant earnings and who is not in pensionable employment may contribute up to the earnings threshold (see 18.9 below); and

(*b*) an employee whose emoluments from his employment do not exceed £30,000 in a tax year may make contributions up to the earnings threshold in respect of that year and for the following five years, even if he is a member of an occupational scheme (*ICTA 1988, s 632B*) – this is subject to residence requirements, and also to restrictions on controlling directors.

Contributions may only be made in respect of individuals aged under 75. This is stated in a backwards fashion by *sections 634* and *638(7A)* of *ICTA 1988*, and explained by *IR 76, para 3.7.*

Transfer payments from other approved schemes, including occupational schemes, may be made into a personal pension scheme (*IR 76, para 3.9*).

A guardian may take out a plan on behalf of a minor (*IR 76, para 3.11*).

Earnings threshold **18.9**

The earnings threshold for personal pension schemes is set by *section 630(1)* of *ICTA 1988*. From 6 April 2001, if the individual is a member of an occupational scheme then the total contributions up to the earnings threshold of

£3,600 may be made even if there are no earnings, or earnings within the limits mentioned above. Contributions can thus be made by unpaid or voluntary workers, or by those not working at all. Contributions for this purpose are in gross terms but, as will be seen at 18.23 below, the member may actually make payments net of tax at the basic rate.

Contributions above the earnings threshold **18.10**

An individual may make contributions which are higher than the earnings threshold provided he has net relevant earnings, which are defined by reference to relevant earnings (see 18.11 below).

Relevant earnings **18.11**

Relevant earnings are governed by *section 644* of *ICTA 1988*, and consist broadly of income taxable:

(*a*) under *Schedule D* (*ICTA 1988, s 18*) in respect of income from a trade, profession or vocation;

(*b*) under *Schedule E* (*ICTA 1988, s 19*) provided that the individual is not a member of an occupational scheme in respect of that source of income (*ICTA 1988, s 644(2)(a), (3)* and *(6F)(b)*), although there are circumstances (set out by *sections 632B* and *645* of *ICTA 1988*) in which a member of an occupational scheme may contribute (*IR 76, para 3.16*); and

(*c*) in respect of certain property and patent income.

Restrictions relating to directors of investment companies and controlling directors of companies are set out by *section 644(5)* and *(6F)* of *ICTA 1988*.

Net relevant earnings **18.12**

Net relevant earnings are relevant earnings less certain deductions which reduce income for tax purposes (*ICTA 1988, s 646*).

Basis year **18.13**

In calculating the contribution which can be made in a tax year, a member may pick as the basis year (under *section 632A* of *ICTA 1988*) their net relevant earnings for:

(*a*) the current tax year; or

(*b*) any of the previous five tax years in which he had relevant earnings (although he need not have been a member of the personal pension scheme in those years),

and may use this amount as the basis of his maximum contribution for the current tax year of payment, subject to the overall limits below and taking his age as at 6 April in the tax year (*IR 76, para 4.10*).

The net relevant earnings for the basis year may be used not only for the current year but also for the following five years, unless the member decides to change to a later year (*ICTA 1988, s 646B*; *IR 76, para 4.11*).

Higher-level contributions **18.14**

Higher level contributions are set out by *section 640* of *ICTA 1988*. Subject to the allowable maximum mentioned below, contributions may be made as follows:

Age at 6 April	NRE%
<35	17.5
36–45	20
46–50	25
51–55	30
56–60	35
>60	40

Allowable maximum **18.15**

Irrespective of a member's actual earnings, the amount which can be regarded as net relevant earnings in a year of assessment is subject to an upper limit (earnings cap) (*ICTA 1988, s 640A*); for 2001/02 the allowable maximum is £95,400. There are additional rules in respect of concurrent employments (*IR 76, para 4.7*).

Effect of employer's contributions **18.16**

If the member's employer contributes to the plan the amount the member can contribute is reduced accordingly under *section 640(4)* of *ICTA 1988*.

Cessation of earnings **18.17**

Under *section 646D* of *ICTA 1988*, where an individual:

(*a*) has no relevant earnings in a tax year beginning after 5 April 2001 (the break year);

(*b*) had relevant earnings in the previous tax year (the cessation year); and

(*c*) was eligible to pay higher-level contributions under the scheme in one or more of the six years preceding the break year (the reference years),

then he may make contributions based upon any of the reference years for the remainder of the break year and for the following five years (or, if earlier, until he again has relevant earnings or becomes a member of an occupational scheme). These are known as the qualifying post-cessation years. During these years his maximum contribution is based upon his age at the beginning of the tax year of payment (*IR 76, para 4.12*).

After that he will, if appropriate, be able to contribute up to the earnings threshold.

Carry-back of contributions and carry-forward of relief **18.18**

The carry-back of contributions is set out by *section 641* of *ICTA 1988*, and the carry-forward of relief by *section 642* of *ICTA 1988*. Up to and including 2000/01, considerable flexibility was available for a member to treat contributions as made in earlier years and to carry unused relief forward.

From 6 April 2001, however, the rules have been changed so as to be in line with stakeholder pensions (see 17 STAKEHOLDER PENSIONS), and this flexibility has been almost completely removed.

In restricted circumstances it is possible to combine carry-back and carry forward in respect of contributions made before 31 January 2002 (*IR 76, para 6.41*).

Election to treat contributions as paid in the previous tax year **18.19**

Section 641A of *ICTA 1988* provides a facility enabling a member of a personal pension scheme (but not an employer) to elect at or before the time of payment that a contribution made between 6 April and the following 31 January should be treated as being made in the previous tax year (*IR 76, para 6.30*).

Payment of contributions **18.20**

Contributions may be paid by the individual, his employer or the National Insurance Contributions Office (*IR 76, para 4.1*).

A group personal pension scheme is merely a collection of individual arrangements although, for convenience, actual payment may be made by the employer in respect of all members.

Waiver of contributions **18.21**

As regards personal pension schemes commencing on or after April 2001, it is not possible for the scheme to include waiver of premium benefits; this must be done by a separate contract (*IR 76, para 4.21*). However, such provisions in earlier contracts may continue.

Term assurance cover **18.22**

In respect of schemes beginning on or after 6 April 2001, up to 10 per cent of the contributions paid to personal pension schemes (*ICTA 1988, s 640(3)*) in a year may in addition be applied to premiums under a term assurance contract

(*ICTA 1988, s 637*). The 10 per cent is part of the earnings threshold or the relevant percentage, not an addition (*ICTA 1988, s 640(3A)*; *IR 76, para 4.14*).

Before 6 April 2001 different rules applied under *section 640* of *ICTA 1988*; in particular, the maximum contribution was 5 per cent of net relevant earnings.

Income tax relief on member's contributions **18.23**

The individual may make contributions net of income tax at the basic rate for the year when the payment is made (*ICTA 1988, s 639*); the scheme administrator must accept the reduced amount and reclaim the tax from the Inland Revenue. A person paying contributions up to the earnings threshold may thus get tax relief even if he has no income.

Contributions may be deducted in full from income for the year of assessment in which they are made. A claim must be made to the Inland Revenue in respect of relief for higher-rate tax.

Employer's contributions **18.24**

The contributions made by an employer are not emoluments of the employment (*ICTA 1988, s 643(1)*).

The employer's contributions must be made gross and his ordinary contributions should be deductible from profits under the general rules of *Schedule D* (*ICTA 1988, s 18*). However, unlike with occupational schemes, there is no specific right to such a deduction (*IR 76, paras 4.35, 5.12*).

Taxation of the personal pension scheme fund **18.25**

The personal pension scheme fund is exempt from taxation on income, with the exception of UK dividends (*ICTA 1988, s 643(2)*), and chargeable gains (*Taxation of Chargeable Gains Act 1992, s 271(1)(h)*).

Annuity payable to member **18.26**

The contract will specify a pension date on which the annuity under the contract becomes payable (*ICTA 1988, s 634*). From 6 April 2001 the rules of the scheme:

- may allow flexibility as to the pension date (*IR 76, para 8.4*);
- may allow more than one pension date; and
- may take annuities at different times and income drawdowns at different times (*ICTA 1988, s 638ZA*).

The annuity must be paid by an authorised insurance company which is selected by the member. This company is not necessarily the one which has administered the scheme (*ICTA 1988, s 634(1)*).

Start date of annuity **18.27**

The annuity may not start before the member attains the age of 50 or after he attains 75. A person may however take the annuity before age 50 if he is in an occupation where it is customary to retire earlier. The Inland Revenue issues a list giving examples of occupations and ages (*IR 76, para 8.7, App 10*).

Length of annuity **18.28**

The annuity must be for life, but may be for a term certain of up to ten years. It must not be capable of assignment, except that it may be assigned in respect of any remaining term certain in the distribution of an estate (*ICTA 1988, s 634(4), (5), (6)*).

Type of annuity **18.29**

The annuity may be level, variable, escalating or index-linked (*IR 76, para 9.3*). There is of course no maximum annuity level as in an employed scheme, since there is a limit on contributions. There may be further restrictions in respect of protected rights under the *Pension Schemes Act 1993*.

Income withdrawals on deferment of annuity **18.30**

A member may defer the purchase of an annuity under *section 634A* of *ICTA 1988*, and until purchase may withdraw certain sums in cash from his fund. Withdrawals can only be made between the ages of 50 (or earlier where retirement may be earlier, as at 18.27 above, or in the case of disability) and 75.

The amount withdrawn in each successive period of twelve months must be between 35 per cent and 100 per cent of the annual amount of annuity which would have been purchasable at the pension date or, if the withdrawals continue so long, at each third anniversary of that date. The right to the income withdrawals must not be assignable.

Taxation of annuity payments and income withdrawals **18.31**

Income payments from the plan are regarded as earned income of the recipient under *section 643* of *ICTA 1988*, and are taxable under *Schedule E* (*ICTA 1988, s 19*). Pay As You Earn (PAYE) schemes will be operated by the pension provider.

An exception to this is that the payment of an annuity for the remainder of a guaranteed term following the death of the member will be treated as unearned income (*ICTA 1988, s 643(4)*).

Lump sum at retirement **18.32**

An election to take a lump sum must be made on or before the pension date (*ICTA 1988, s 635(1)*), and the sum must be payable on the pension date (*ICTA 1988, s 635(2)*).

The maximum sum available is calculated by deducting from the total fund available the value of protected rights under the *Pension Schemes Act 1993*, and taking 25 per cent of the remainder.

This is however an area where the start date of the personal pension scheme may affect the rules, and different rules again apply to schemes with more than one pension date (*ICTA 1988, s 638ZA(4)*).

The lump sum is free from tax.

Death benefits **18.33**

Life assurance contracts **18.34**

Any death benefit under a term assurance must be payable before the member attains the age of 75, and must be payable by an authorised insurance company (*ICTA 1988, s 637*).

The death benefit is free from tax.

Benefits on death before pension date **18.35**

In the simplest case where the member has no survivors, the benefits at death will be:

(*a*) as a maximum, a return of contributions with reasonable interest or bonuses; in the case of a unit trust linked plan the repayment may be the bid value of the units (*ICTA 1988, s 637(A)*); and

(*b*) any term assurance payment.

These benefits are free from tax. In practice things will almost certainly be more complicated (see *IR 76, paras 10.2–9, 10.37–41*).

Annuities on death after pension date **18.36**

Here again there are many variables (*ICTA 1988, s 636*; *IR 76, paras 10.10–35*).

Any annuities must be payable to the surviving spouse of the member or to a dependant, and must be paid by an insurance company chosen individually by the beneficiary or beneficiaries.

The aggregate annuities must not exceed:

(*a*) the annuity being paid to the member; or

(*b*) if the member is not yet receiving an annuity, the highest annuity which would have been payable, ignoring any entitlement to commute part for a lump sum, had it been purchased on the day before his death.

The purchase of annuity payable to the surviving spouse may be deferred until he or she attains 60 or until the end of a guaranteed period of the deceased's annuity (*ICTA 1988, s 636(5)*).

The annuity must be payable for life (*ICTA 1988, s 636(4)*), although it may have a guaranteed term of up to ten years (*ICTA 1988, s 636(9)*). There are also certain other possibilities (*ICTA 1988, s 636(5)–(9)*). It must not be capable of being surrendered (or assigned (except in respect of any unexpired guaranteed term) (*ICTA 1988, s 636(10)*).

Income withdrawals after death of member **18.37**

The purchase of an annuity may be deferred in a similar way as that of the member (*ICTA 1988, s 636*), and income may be withdrawn from the fund (although not in a case where purchase has been deferred under *section 636(5)* of *ICTA 1988*.

General (non-pension) annuities 18.38

Purchased life annuities 18.39

An annuity purchased from a life office and calculated by reference to human life will probably fall within the definition of a purchased life annuity set out by *sections 656* to *658* of *ICTA 1988*.

If so, part of each annuity payment will be treated as a repayment of purchase money, such that the full sum will be returned over the expectation of life of the individual concerned (or over the period to the earlier end of the annuity payment term). Only the remaining income element will be liable to income tax.

The annuity may commence immediately or there may be a period of deferment before payments start. There may be a guaranteed period of payment.

The life office normally agrees purchased life annuity treatment with the Inland Revenue at the outset, as a matter of routine.

Purchased life annuity treatment is not available in all cases; in particular, not to an annuity purchased under a direction in a will, or under an approved pension arrangement (*ICTA 1988, s 657(2)*). However, a lump sum taken at retirement from a pension scheme may be used to buy a purchased life annuity.

Tax on annuity payments **18.40**

The office will deduct income tax from the income element, and this will cover the recipient's basic rate liability.

Chargeable events on purchased life annuity contracts **18.41**

The same rules apply to chargeable events on life annuity contracts as for life policies (*ICTA 1988, s 542*). However, there are the following differences:

(*a*) at full surrender, whether taking a cash option or receiving a capital sum at death, the gain is calculated as being the amount received plus the total of any previous part surrenders, less:

(i) the purchase cost less total capital elements already returned in annuity payments, and

(ii) any excesses at previous part surrenders (ICTA 1988, s 543(1)(a)); and

(*b*) at an assignment, the same calculation but using the consideration received (*ICTA 1988, s 543(1)(b)*).

Rates of tax on chargeable events under life annuity contracts **18.42**

A gain on a chargeable event under a life annuity contract made after 26 March 1974 is liable to income tax at basic and, if applicable, higher rates of tax (*ICTA 1988, s 547(5A)(6)*).

Different rules apply to an annuity contract if before 26 June 1982 the contract was assigned for value. In this case, a capital gains tax charge arises (*ICTA 1988, s 542(3)*).

Other life annuities **18.43**

If an annuity dependent upon human life cannot meet the purchased life annuity rules, then the total annuity payment is liable to tax as income.

Annuities not dependant on human life – 'annuities certain' **18.44**

Where an annuity is payable for a term certain, payments are divided into capital and income elements, with only the latter being liable to income tax, provided that payments are made to the original purchaser.

Occupational pension schemes **18.45**

Salary-based schemes **18.46**

Benefits from salary-based pension schemes may be calculated by reference to:

- final remuneration;
- average remuneration over a period of employment; or
- a combination of the two.

The scheme may be contributory, with both the employer and the employee making contributions, or it may be non-contributory with the employer completely funding the scheme.

These schemes were satisfactory in times when:

(*a*) people worked for the same employer all their lives and thus built up a full pension; and (*b*) wages and salaries did not increase much, or increased mainly on a known scale, enabling the employer to build up the fund at a controlled rate.

These conditions can no longer be said to apply. Employers with final salary schemes are faced with increasing and unquantifiable liabilities as pensioners live longer, particularly if there is an element of index-linking of pensions under the scheme. Employees now move from one employment to another, willingly or not, and may end up having several small pensions based on a succession of earlier, probably lower, levels of emolument, or taking transfer values, rarely noticeably generous, from one employer's fund to another.

Money purchase schemes 18.47

Employers may thus turn to money purchase schemes, where contributions are made each year based upon emoluments and an identifiable fund built up for each employee. At retirement the fund which has been built up is used to purchase an annuity for the employee.

The employer thus knows that his liability is fully funded at all times, and the employee can take the current value of his fund with him as he changes jobs.

A money purchase scheme may be self-administered or insured.

Additional voluntary contributions 18.48

An employee may make additional voluntary contributions (AVCs) so as to increase his pension benefits, perhaps with a view to funding an earlier retirement, either to the company's scheme or to a free standing scheme offered by a pension provider (see 18.70 below on free standing additional voluntary contributions).

Exempt approved schemes 18.49

The tax legislation is somewhat basic, and most schemes depend on approvals given under Inland Revenue discretion.

The normal vehicle for an employed scheme is the exempt approved scheme (*ICTA 1988, ss 590–612*).

Creating an exempt approved scheme 18.50

Retirement benefits scheme **18.51**

The starting point is the retirement benefits scheme, defined under *section 590* of *ICTA 1988* as one established solely for the purpose of providing relevant benefits in respect of service as an employee, payable to him or to his dependants. Relevant benefits are in turn defined under *section 612(1)* of *ICTA 1988* as including any pension, lump sum or like benefit to be given on retirement or death, or on change in the nature of the employment.

A retirement benefits scheme must meet all the requirements of *section 590(2)* of *ICTA 1988*. These conditions include:

(*a*) that the scheme is *bona fide* established for the sole purpose of providing relevant benefits in respect of service as an employee;

(*b*) that those benefits do not include any benefits payable to a person other than:

(i) the employee or a scheme member's ex-spouse,

(ii) a widow, widower, child or dependant of the employee or of a scheme member, or

(iii) the personal representatives of the employee or of a scheme member's ex-spouse;

(*c*) that the scheme is recognised by the employer and the employees; and

(*d*) that the employer is a contributor to the scheme.

Approved scheme **18.52**

If the scheme also meets all the requirements of *section 590(3)* of *ICTA 1988* then the Inland Revenue will agree that it is an approved scheme. The Inland Revenue may at its discretion agree that a scheme which does not meet one of more of the prescribed conditions is an approved scheme (*ICTA 1988, s 591*).

Special circumstances **18.53**

An approved scheme which is set up under irrevocable trusts, or is otherwise accepted by the Inland Revenue taking into account special circumstances, will be granted the status of an exempt approved scheme (*ICTA 1988, s 592(1)*).

Benefits of exempt approved status **18.54**

Exempt approved status gives the following benefits:

(*a*) the fund is free from tax on income from investments held in connection with the scheme (except in respect of dividends paid by UK companies) (*ICTA 1988, s 592(2)(3)*) and on chargeable gains (*Taxation of Chargeable Gains Act 1992, s 271(1)(g)*);

(*b*) the employer's contributions are deductible from profits (*ICTA 1988, s 592(4)–(6)*);

(*c*) the employee's contributions are allowable against *Schedule E* income (*ICTA 1988, s 592(7)–(8A)*);

(*d*) pension payments are taxable under *Schedule E* as earned income (*ICTA 1988, s 597*); and

(*e*) part of the benefits may be taken as a lump sum at retirement, free from tax, in accordance with the scheme rules, with an appropriate reduction in pension (*ICTA 1988, s 590(3)(d)(da)*).

Contributions **18.55**

Employer **18.56**

The employer *must* contribute to the scheme, and his ordinary annual contributions are deductible from profits (*IR 12, para 5.1*); the Inland Revenue may require any special contributions to be relieved over a period of years (*IR 12, para 5.5*).

Employee **18.57**

Tax relief on an employee's contributions will be given on contributions, including AVCs, of up to 15 per cent of remuneration (defined as income charged to tax under *Schedule E Case I* or *Case II* (*IR 12, Glossary*) (*ICTA 1988, s 592(8)*), and the scheme rules will normally preclude any higher contribution (*IR 12, para 4.4*). The Inland Revenue has power to allow a higher rate in a particular case (*ICTA 1988, s 592(8)*).

Unless the member joined a scheme before 17 March 1987, or a pre-14 March 1989 scheme prior to 1 June 1989 (*IR 12, Appendix 3*), there is a permitted maximum (earnings cap) of remuneration for this purpose; for 2001/02 this is £95,400 (*ICTA 1988, s 592(8B)–(8E)*), and the maximum permitted contribution is thus £14,310.

Relief for employees' contributions (apart from those to free standing additional voluntary contributions – see 18.70 below) is given through PAYE (*IR 12, para 4.3*).

Pension date **18.58**

The scheme will specify a normal retirement date between 50 and 75, and the pension must start at retirement (*IR 12, para 6.1*). The normal retirement date may vary between classes of employee (*IR 12, para 6.6*).

AVC benefits, free standing or in the main scheme, may start at a different time from the main pension, but still between the ages of 50 and 75 (*IR 12, para 6.1*).

Earlier retirement dates may be agreed for certain professions – there are no stated ages as under personal pension plans (see 18.3 above) and each case is treated on its merits (*IR 12, para 6.7*).

A pension due to incapacity may be payable at any age (*IR 12, para 6.2*).

Pension benefits **18.59**

The maximum pension payable is 2/3 of final remuneration, whether the scheme is final salary or money purchase (*IR 12, paras 7.2–7.4*; see also *7.8*).

Final remuneration,is defined for the purposes of an exempt approved scheme (*IR 12, Glossary*) and is of course defined in the individual scheme.

The earnings cap applies to benefits as it does to contributions; in these circumstances the maximum pension for 2001/02 is £63,600. The rules of the scheme may provide for benefits on retirement to be purchased on the open market (*IR 12, para 6.12*).

The pension must not start before actual retirement or leaving of service, and must be for life, although it may be guaranteed for up to 10 years (*IR 12, para 7.32*).

The scheme may provide for pension benefits to be increased to counteract inflation, although in practice there will probably be some limit on this (*IR 12, para 9.4*).

Lump sum benefit at retirement **18.60**

Part of the pension benefit may be commuted for a lump sum, which must be taken at the time the pension benefits begin (*IR 12, para 8.2*). The amount which can be paid depends upon the rules of the scheme, the length of service and when the employee joined the scheme; the maximum possible is one and a half times final remuneration (which is subject to the earnings cap if applicable) (*IR 12, para 8.5*).

AVCs cannot be commuted, but can be taken into account in computing the lump sum although not if drawdown of income has been taken under the free standing additional voluntary contributions (*IR 12, para 8.3*).

Serious ill-health **18.61**

The Inland Revenue may permit the whole benefit of the scheme to be commuted for a lump sum if the member is unlikely to survive for more than twelve months (*IR 12, para 8.17*).

Death-in-service benefits **18.62**

Death-in-service benefits may be paid as a lump sum – an amount may be paid of up to four times final remuneration, as defined for this specific purpose (*IR 12, para 11.1*, 2).

Death after retirement **18.63**

When death occurs after retirement, a pension may be paid to a widow, widower or dependant; they may receive up to 2/3 of the pension payable to the employee at retirement, increased in line with the Retail Price Index (*IR 12, para 12.2*).

Leaving pensionable service **18.64**

An employee leaving pensionable service has the following options (*IR 12, para 10.2*):

(*a*) a deferred pension from the former employer's scheme;

(*b*) a transfer of benefits to the scheme of a subsequent employer, or to a personal pension scheme; or

(*c*) the purchase of a deferred annuity from an insurance company or a friendly society.

Other pension arrangements **18.65**

It is of course possible for pensions to be paid without any approval or indeed without any funding; obviously the tax position will be less favourable and will depend on the particular circumstances.

Non-exempt approved scheme **18.66**

An approved scheme which is not an exempt approved scheme does not have exemption from tax on income and gains, but the employer's contributions do not give rise to a taxable benefit to the employee (*IR 12, para 2.1*).

Single premium payment **18.67**

A single premium payment to purchase an immediate annuity, if approved by the Inland Revenue and subject to a trust, can be an exempt approved scheme under *paragraph 2.2* of *IR 12* in the following cases:

(*a*) when the purchase is after retirement (known as a Hancock annuity);

(*b*) for the widow, widower or dependant of a deceased employee; or

(*c*) under a scheme set up for an individual shortly before retirement.

Payment of pensions **18.68**

Under a final salary scheme, pension payments are paid directly from the scheme; under a money purchase scheme, or an open market option, the employee's fund is used to buy an annuity from an insurance company, which makes the payments.

Pension payments are taxable under *Schedule E* (*ICTA 1988, s 19*), and are thus paid under PAYE (*ICTA 1988, s 203*).

Scheme rules paramount **18.69**

As will be seen from the above, occupational schemes can vary widely from one to another. To arrive at any decision in an individual case it will probably be necessary to find exactly what the rules of the particular scheme actually permit; the trustee or administrator will be able to provide relevant information.

Free standing additional voluntary contribution schemes **18.70**

Free standing additional voluntary contribution schemes (FSAVCs) are available solely to employees to top up benefits being accrued under their employer's scheme, and the employer may not contribute (*IR 12 (Supp), para 1.2*).

Scheme approval and establishment **18.71**

Approval of a scheme is given by Inland Revenue discretion under *section 591(2)(h)* of *ICTA 1988* (*IR 12 (Supp), para 1.4*).

An FSAVC scheme may only be established by a person authorised under *Chapter III, Part 1* of the *Financial Services Act 1988* who may be, among other bodies, an insurance company (*IR 12 (Supp), para 2.1*).

There must be a named administrator, and the scheme must be under an irrevocable trust. The scheme must state that its sole purpose is to provide relevant benefits (*IR 12 (Supp), paras 2.3–2.5*).

Contributions and benefits **18.72**

An employee may contribute to only one FSAVC in respect of each employment in any tax year (*IR 12 (Supp), para 3.2*). However this does not prevent payment of AVCs into the employer's scheme in addition. The contributions limit is similar to, and includes contributions to, the main employed scheme (*IR 12 (Supp), para 4.2*).

Where the employee leaves the employment contributions may be continued to the FSAVC upon his joining a new employer's scheme (*IR 12 (Supp), para 4.9*).

Contributions are paid net of tax at the basic rate; relief for higher-rate tax has to be claimed (*IR 12 (Supp), para 15.1*).

Headroom checks are made to ensure that over-funding does not take place, aggregating benefits from all schemes (*IR 12 (Supp), para 4.3 et seq*).

Pension payments normally begin at the same time as the employer's pension (*IR 12 (Supp), para 5.1*), but the member may elect to receive benefits at any age between 50 and 75 if permitted to do so by the rules of the scheme (*IR 12 (Supp), para 5.3*).

Benefits are payable for life, and may have a guarantee of up to ten years. There may be pension benefits for a widow, widower or dependant (*IR 12 (Supp), para 6.1*). The total benefits from the employer's scheme and all FSAVCs relating to service with the same employer must not exceed Inland Revenue maxima (*IR 12 (Supp), para 6.2*).

Under *paragraph 8.1* of *IR 12 (Supp)*, the pension may be increased by no more than the greater of:

- 3 per cent per year; or
- the rise in the cost of living index.

If the scheme permits, benefits may be taken by income withdrawal under similar rules to those relating to personal pension schemes under *section 634A* of *ICTA 1988*, rather than by purchase of an annuity (*IR 12 (Supp), para 5.6*).

Benefits must be on a money purchase basis, except for death benefits (*IR 12 (Supp), para 2.7*).

Any benefits taken before normal retirement date must be in the form of income withdrawal; when the employer's scheme commences to pay benefits an annuity must be purchased with the balance of the FSAVC fund, unless the FSAVC has a drawdown facility (*IR 12 (Supp), para 5.6*) in which case drawdown may continue to age 75 (*IR 12 (Supp), para 6.3*).

No lump sum benefits are available apart from commutation in respect of triviality or ill-health, as under approved employed schemes (*IR 12 (Supp), para 7.4*).

Death benefits follow broadly those under the main scheme (*IR 12 (Supp), para 5.5*).

Chapter 19

Types of Annuity

- **The concept of the annuity**
- **Pension annuities**
- **Purchased life annuities**

The concept of the annuity 19.1

As the name suggests, the annuity was originally an annual payment, but nowadays annuities are usually paid at more frequent intervals, for example quarterly or monthly. References to annuities can be found in earlier life assurance records, and it would seem that they were often associated with remittance men – 'ne'er-do-wells' packed off to the Colonies with a modest annuity, or 'remittance', which lasted as long as they made no attempt to return to Great Britain.

Lack of underwriting 19.2

There is no underwriting of annuity business. Indeed, looked at purely objectively, the worse the physical risk, the better it is for the office granting the annuity as the annuitant is unlikely to live long and hence will receive relatively little in terms of pay-out under the contract. Anyone applying for an annuity is treated as an acceptable mortality risk, and some offices will even give favourable annuity rates for impaired lives.

Annuity rates 19.3

Annuity rates vary with the effect of interest rate fluctuations and market forces generally. At times an annuity can represent an attractive method of investing a lump sum so as to ensure a steady income. Guaranteeing future annuity rates can be a means of bringing in business, but the practice can also be dangerous and has caused offices to run into financial difficulties.

Pension annuities 19.4

The topic of pension annuities is covered thoroughly in 16 PERSONAL PENSIONS and 18 TAXATION IMPLICATIONS OF PENSION/ANNUITY BUSINESS. However, for convenience, it can be recapitulated here that this particular type of annuity benefits the annuitant in that, subject to Inland Revenue approval, contributions can be charged against tax under the *Finance Act 1956* – they enjoy tax relief. The opposite side of the coin is that benefits, when received, are taxed as income.

Pension annuities can be traced back to the Self-Employed Retirement Annuities (SERAs) created in 1956 to enable the self-employed to make provision for their old age and enjoy the same tax advantages as their employed counterparts.

Purchased life annuities 19.5

Annuities due 19.6

It is possible for annuities to be payable in advance, rather like having one's salary paid on the first of the month. Such annuities are relatively rare but when they do occur they are called annuities due and characterised by the symbol 'ä'.

Immediate annuities 19.7

The majority of purchased life annuities – in effect this encompasses all annuities which do not qualify as pension annuities – are immediate annuities. Despite the use of the word immediate, if annuities of this type are not classified as annuities due, they are payable in arrears. They can be with proportion (or apportionable), in which case, should the annuitant die between payment dates, their estate will receive the proportion of the annuity instalment represented by the period of time survived since the last payment divided by the total period before the next payment. Therefore if the annuity is payable by quarterly instalments and the annuitant dies six weeks after a payment has been made, the estate will receive 6/13 x quarterly instalments in full settlement. Alternatively annuities can be without proportion (or non-apportionable). Sometimes such annuities are called curtate annuities. Here if the annuitant dies between instalment dates no balance is payable – the annuity is treated as having ceased at the last payment date. It is extremely important for the definition to be made quite clear when the annuity is effected.

Deferred annuities 19.8

Annuities do not have to be immediate. Many deferred annuities are effected where the annuity will commence at a specified future date and the contract does not meet the criteria of a pension annuity. Such annuities can be apportionable or non-apportionable. Clearly a cause for concern is the position should the annuitant die before the 'vesting date' (the date when the payment of the annuity commences). Payment of extra consideration can purchase the provision for a refund of purchase price in the event of premature death. Deferred annuities can be bought by a lump sum or by regular instalments – effectively, by premiums.

Guaranteed annuity **19.9**

A potential drawback in effecting an annuity is the concern that the annuitant might die early on in the term. This can be countered by opting for a guaranteed annuity, whereby payment is guaranteed for a certain number of years and thereafter will continue as long as the annuitant lives. Should the annuitant die during the guarantee period then the instalments will be paid to his/her legal representative in the absence of an express nomination. Obviously an extra sum will be added to the purchase price to secure the guarantee.

Temporary annuities **19.10**

For people with different needs temporary annuities are available – these run for an agreed period provided the annuitant is still alive, but then cease when the term has expired.

Joint annuities **19.11**

In common with life assurance policies, annuities can be on more than one person.

Joint life annuities **19.12**

A joint life annuity will cease as soon as one of the named lives dies.

Joint life last survivor annuities **19.13**

In contrast to joint life annuities, joint life last survivor annuities continue until the last life has died.

Contingent reversionary annuities **19.14**

Of particular interest are contingent reversionary annuities, which commence to run if a named party to the contract dies leaving the other party surviving. If the latter party dies first, then nothing is due. These arrangements are ideal for situations where, say, one spouse has a pension but there is no built-in provision for a dependant's pension should they die. As there is always the possibility that the sequence of deaths will be such that no pay-out ever falls due, the consideration for this type of contract can be significantly lower than if another form of annuity is selected.

Benefits of purchased life annuities **19.15**

Up until 1956 the benefits of purchased life annuities were taxed as income. Under the *Finance Act 1956*, a major change took place in that year, when the then Chancellor of the Exchequer allowed each payment of annuity to be artificially 'split' by an actuarial formula into an instalment of interest and an instalment consisting of the repayment of capital. Only the interest element was subject to income tax when in the hand of the recipient. Although the money devoted to buying purchased life annuities could not, and still cannot, be charged against tax, the concession given to the treatment of annuity benefits made these contracts quite attractive and greatly boosted sales.

Annuities certain **19.16**

Annuities certain must be mentioned. These are somewhat anomalous in that they do not depend on human life and hence are not truly purchased life annuities, although it seems the accepted practice for offices to include them with their other annuity business. They are written to run for a fixed period regardless of whether the annuitant is alive or dead, but then cease, again regardless of whether the annuitant is alive or dead. It will be seen that they are quite different from guaranteed annuities, which continue after the guarantee period as long as the annuitant survives.

Tax treatment **19.17**

The tax treatment of annuities certain retains the anomalous element associated with these contracts. As stated above, they are not purchased life annuities – if anything they are straight investment/savings contracts on a repayment basis – but so far the Inland Revenue seem content to allow benefit instalments to be 'split' on the same lines as true purchased life annuities. Probably there are not enough annuities certain in existence to force the issue and the 'loss' of taxation regarded as too minimal to be of significance.

Certificates of continued existence **19.18**

It is customary for insurers to ask periodically for annuitants to provide certificates of continued existence. This is a reasonable precaution to prevent payments from being made after the legal recipient has died, but for some reason it is not uncommon for annuitants to find these certificates rather offensive. Insurers cannot dispense with them, but do everything possible to reduce the sense of intrusion (or worse) that their arrival on the doormat sometimes produces.

Section C:
Health and Related Insurances

Chapter 20

Critical Illness Insurance

- **Overview of critical illness insurance**
- **Types of policy**
- **Medical conditions**
- **Benefits**
- **ABI model critical illness definitions**
- **Exclusions**

Overview of critical illness insurance 20.1

Principles 20.2

Critical illness insurance is, in effect, very similar to conventional life assurance, the main difference being that the sum assured is payable not on death but on suffering a specified critical illness or condition (see 20.20 *et seq* below). Policies pay out upon:

- the diagnosis of a specified condition, for example a heart attack;
- undergoing a specified procedure, for example a coronary artery by-pass graft; or
- admittance to an official waiting list for an organ transplant.

A cash lump sum assured is payable, regardless of the severity of the condition and of the outcome of any medical treatment (unless the claimant dies within any initial waiting period).

History and development 20.3

Critical illness assurance is much newer than life assurance, and owes its success partly to the fact that most people now survive conditions which would have proved fatal to previous generations.

Present critical illness insurance can trace its roots to South Africa, where the product – then known as dread disease insurance – proved popular for people who suffered serious illness but who had to pay for their treatment. Even before that, however, policies had existed which paid out a lump sum upon the diagnosis of cancer, although these products never proved very popular in the UK, partly because they were often marketed on fear.

Critical illness insurance was introduced to the UK and the first policies sold in 1985 by Cannon Lincoln (now Lincoln). A year or so later the large direct salesforce companies Abbey Life and Allied Dunbar began to market the plans. Initially, the products were not popular, and it was only when the first claims began to arise that their popularity increased. People saw that it was possible, for example, to suffer a serious illness, recover, and then receive a cash lump sum to help rebuild their life.

Throughout the 1990s critical illness policies continued to grow in popularity, and now over three-quarters of a million new policies are sold each year.

Types of policy 20.4

Critical illness insurance policies may be written on a term or a whole life (in effect, open-ended) basis (see 11 TYPES OF POLICY AND POLICY CONSTRUCTION).

As with life assurance, policies may be without-profits, with-profits (see 6 PROFITS, INVESTMENTS AND BONUS DISTRIBUTION), unit linked (see 13 UNIT LINKED POLICIES) or unitised with-profit. The investment-linked route is often used with a periodic review mechanism, whereby factors such as claims experience and investment returns will determine whether the premium or sum assured will be subject to alteration at each review. This rather complex mechanism is adopted as, in theory, it can enable the insurer to offer cheaper premiums without incurring too high a risk if the assumptions it has built into its pricing turn out to have been too optimistic. However, the trend is towards more policies with guaranteed rates, which generally prove more popular with consumers.

Critical illness insurance is available in a number of guises, and the main ones are set out at 20.5–20.11 below.

Standalone cover 20.5

A standalone critical illness policy, as the term implies, is a simple critical illness policy only. There is no death sum assured and the claimant must usually survive for a period of 14–30 days (as specified in the policy conditions) after making the claim before the sum assured will be payable.

Accelerated cover 20.6

Accelerated or rider cover is the most popular way to buy critical illness insurance. It is also the cheapest way to buy it. That is because the insurer will only have to pay out the sum assured once. On whole life and endowment policies, the risk premium will be based on the sum assured less any cash value built up within the policy. In other words, it should always be cheaper to add critical illness cover to an existing policy than to take out separate cover.

There are various ways in which accelerated plans can be written and these are set out at 20.7–20.9 below.

Whole life 20.7

With whole life policies, the sum assured is payable on death or on suffering a specified critical condition at any time.

Endowment 20.8

With endowment policies, the sum assured is payable on maturity or on prior death or on suffering a specified critical condition.

Term 20.9

In term policies the sum assured is payable on death or on suffering a specified critical condition during the term of the policy only.

Children's cover 20.10

Children's cover is often in-built. Typically the policy pays out the lower of half the sum assured or £15–20,000 if a child under age 18 suffers from one of the listed conditions. However the list of conditions is often shortened for children's cover.

Short term cover 20.11

Critical illness insurance is also available as general insurance. Such policies are often annually renewable and have the advantage that premiums are usually much lower initially as the risk to be insured effectively lasts only one year. After the one year period has elapsed, the insurer may continue to offer cover on the same or different terms, but as the insured is a year older the premium is likely to be higher.

Such policies have greatest value where cover may be required for a short term only, or where the term needed is not known but is expected to be relatively short.

To avoid the disadvantages of being annually renewable, some policies may be written still as general insurance but for a period of two years or more. Only short-term policy premiums will be subject to insurance premium tax.

Hybrid critical illness/long term care insurance 20.12

Some critical illness policies are marketed as providing an in-built element of long term care insurance cover. In practice this simply means that the sum assured is payable if the insured is no longer able to maintain their independence. A range of definitions may be used to determine exactly when the benefit should be payable. For example, one definition of loss of independent existence is:

> 'Confirmation by a consultant physician of loss of independent existence resulting in a permanent inability to perform at least three of the following activities of daily living either with or without the use of mechanical equipment, special devices or other aids and adaptions in use for disabled persons. For the purpose of this benefit the word 'permanent' shall mean beyond the hope of recovery with current medical knowledge and technology.
>
> The activities of daily living are:
>
> - ***Transfer and mobility:*** The ability to move from one room to an adjoining room or from one side of a room to another or to get in and out of a bed or chair without requiring physical assistance from another person.
> - ***Continence:*** The ability to voluntarily control bowel and bladder functions such as to maintain personal hygiene.
> - ***Dressing:*** Putting on and taking off all necessary items of clothing without requiring assistance of another person.
> - ***Toileting:*** Getting to and from the toilet, transferring on and off the toilet and associated personal hygiene.
> - ***Eating:*** All tasks of getting food into the body once it has been prepared.'
>
> *Source: Liverpool Victoria Life Company, 2001.*

It should be noted that such policies pay out a cash lump sum, whereas long term care fees are usually payable weekly or monthly.

Such policies are therefore likely to only be a partial solution for those looking for long term care cover.

Trusts 20.13

As with life assurance, it is possible to set up a critical illness policy under trust. This is often done where the policy is being used for business purposes, when a flexible interest in possession trust would be used.

Types of group policy 20.14

Group schemes 20.15

Although most critical illness policies are sold to individuals, group schemes are fast growing in popularity too, albeit from a small base. Benefits are similar, with premiums usually paid by the employer and benefits paid to the employee.

In some cases, key man critical illness may be set up to pay benefit to the employer if a key employee suffers a critical illness (see 14 USES OF LIFE ASSURANCE).

Flex schemes **20.16**

Flex schemes, or flexible benefits schemes, allow employees to choose from a menu of benefits to create a package of employee benefits which best suits their personal needs. The constituent insurance covers will however follow the norm for that product type.

Employees may be given a choice of how much cover as well as what type to have; they may be able to add spouse, partner or children's cover and to change cover periodically. In many cases, changes will be subject to fresh underwriting.

Claims **20.17**

Overseas claims **20.18**

Many policies impose geographical limits on where claims may be accepted from. Generally this includes all EU countries plus most major English-speaking countries. The list will vary however from insurer to insurer. Generally, insurers impose restrictions to accept medical evidence only from those countries where there is a record of such evidence being reliable.

The effect of greater screening on claims **20.19**

In 2001, an Association of British Insurers (ABI) working party expressed concern over the effect of introducing more screening for prostate cancer. There is a high prevalence of this disease in older men but much of it remains non-life threatening. Widescale scanning could lead to many more positive diagnoses for prostate cancer, increasing claims experience by up to 40 per cent. At the time of writing the ABI was consulting with its members to determine how great a threat this would be and what, if any, action should be taken. Possible options include charging higher premiums, restricting benefit payout on prostate cancer only at later stages or restricting cover to the under 50s.

Medical conditions **20.20**

Core conditions **20.21**

All critical illness policies are likely to pay out on the following seven conditions:

- cancer;
- coronary artery by-pass graft or surgery;
- heart attack;
- kidney failure;
- major organ transplant;
- multiple sclerosis; and
- stroke.

These are termed the core conditions.

Comprehensive conditions **20.22**

In addition, many policies will also pay out on suffering one of a number of other serious conditions. Such comprehensive policies may include any or all of:

- Alzheimer's disease;
- angioplasty;
- aorta surgery;
- aplastic anaemia;
- bacterial meningitis;
- benign brain tumour;
- brain damage;
- major burns (usually third degree burns over 20 per cent or more of the body's surface);
- cancer, excluding some skin cancers, pre-cancerous conditions and kaposi sarcoma (if AIDS-related);
- CJD (Creutzfeldt-Jakob disease);
- coma (minimum 96 hours);
- coronary artery by-pass surgery/graft;
- diabetes mellitus (usually from age 45);
- heart attack;
- heart valve replacement or repair;
- Human Immunodeficiency Virus (HIV) or Acquired Immune Deficiency Syndrome (AIDS) (usually only for medical/emergency professions and where contracted from a blood transfusion or needle-stick injury);
- Hodgkin's disease;
- irreversible disability or loss of independent existence (usually measured on failing activities of daily living (ADLs));
- kidney failure (end stage);
- liver failure (end stage);
- loss of hearing;
- loss of limbs;
- loss of sight;
- loss of speech;
- major bacterial illnesses;
- major organ transplant (or admission to the UK official waiting list);

- motor neurone disease;
- multiple sclerosis;
- paralysis/paraplegia;
- Parkinson's disease;
- permanent and total disability (on an own occupation or any occupation basis);
- pre-senile dementia;
- rheumatoid arthritis;
- stroke; and
- terminal illness (where death is expected within twelve months).

New conditions **20.23**

The trend has been to continue to add new conditions to the lists set out at 20.21 and 20.22 above, although the rate of doing so has now slowed. Policies may also pay out a (usually) smaller benefit on suffering a serious injury or on long term hospitalisation.

Definitions **20.24**

Each condition covered will have a precise definition set out in the policy conditions, and many insurers will also include a 'plain English' translation. The former will be couched in medical language, while the latter will explain in layman's language what is and what is not covered. For example, one insurer's plain English definition of a heart attack is:

> 'When someone has a heart attack, part of the heart muscle dies because the blood supply has been restricted to that part of the heart. This is often accompanied by chest pain which is acute (severe or short term) o continues, on and off, for some time.
>
> To confirm the diagnosis, a doctor will usually test the patient's heart using a machine called an electrocardiograph (ECG). This tells the doctor whether there have been any changes in the heart's function and, in turn, whether it is likely that the patient has suffered a heart attack.
>
> While the ECG can show changes in the heart, it cannot identify when they happened. To do this, the doctor may use a blood sample. This can show that markers are present in the blood (in the form of enzymes) at a much higher level than is normally expected. This indicates that the heart muscle has been damaged and that a heart attack has recently taken place.
>
> Some heart attacks can be "silent", where the patient suffers a heart attack but does not have significant chest pain. ECG readings, as part of an annual medical check-up for example, can detect silent heart attacks. We will pay claims for a silent heart attack if the patient can show that the ECG readings have changed since taking out the insurance.

> Angina can be confused with a heart attack. Although there may be considerable chest pain, this normally comes with physical exertion and will ease on rest. With angina, no part of the heart muscle dies and no marker enzymes can be seen, so we would not pay a claim.'
>
> *Source: Skandia Protect, Skandia Life, 2001*

Contrast this with the policy definitions set out at 20.29–20.31 below. Not every insurer includes such explanatory notes nor notes to the same detail, but it is important to note that insurers will usually only pay a claim which meets their definition precisely. In some cases, an insured might be told that they 'probably' had a heart attack; the insurer would only pay out if the specified medical tests were carried out and if the result was as set out in the policy definition.

Definition disputes **20.25**

As stated in 20.24 above, a policy will only pay out if the precise definition of that condition has been met. In some cases, this can lead to disputes, especially on policies that cover permanent and total disability. It should be noted that different treatments of the same condition may also be excluded. For example, a policy may pay for a coronary artery by-pass graft but not an angioplasty; may pay for an angioplasty only if more than one blood vessel is treated; or may not pay for laser treatment at all.

Benefits **20.26**

Policies pay out a tax-free cash lump sum. This may be used for any purpose and is not repayable if the condition turns out to be a relatively minor form. For example, an individual who suffers a heart attack and returns to work a few days later having not been hospitalised, other than for tests, would receive the same benefit as someone who had received treatment as an intensive care patient and remained in hospital for some weeks.

Soft benefits **20.27**

Life insurers generally are looking to add value to their products by providing a range of 'soft' benefits. These typically include telephone helplines and counselling services, usually provided as a no-cost addition to the plan's main benefit.

Increase in benefits **20.28**

Many policies include the right to increase benefits in the event of a certain event arising and/or in line with an inflation index – usually the Retail Prices Index (RPI) or the Average Earnings Index (AEI). The specified events may include:

- the birth or adoption of a child;
- marriage;

- a major promotion at work; or
- a new or increased mortgage (for home improvements only),

when the sum assured may be increased without fresh medical evidence for typically 25–50 per cent of the sum assured up to a total increase over the policy term of 50 per cent of the sum assured.

ABI model critical illness definitions **20.29**

The ABI has set out model critical illness definitions which its members must adopt, although they may adopt a super-equivalent definition if preferred, that is one that provides wider cover than the model. It is likely that in future the ABI will extend this list as other conditions become more widely adopted by insurers.

The core conditions **20.30**

(*a*) **Cancer**

A malignant tumour characterised by the uncontrolled growth and spread of malignant cells and invasion of tissue. The term 'cancer' includes leukaemia and Hodgkin's disease, but the following are excluded:

(i) all tumours which are histologically described as pre-malignant, as non-invasive or as cancer *in situ*;

(ii) all forms of lymphoma in the presence of any HIV;

(iii) kaposi sarcoma in the presence of any HIV; and

(iv) any skin cancer other than malignant melanoma.

(*b*) **Coronary artery by-pass surgery**

The undergoing of open heart surgery on the advice of a consultant cardiologist to correct the narrowing or blockage of one or more coronary arteries with by-pass grafts, but excluding balloon angioplasty, laser relief or any other procedures.

(*c*) **Heart attack**

The death of a portion of the heart muscle as a result of inadequate blood supply as evidenced by an episode of typical chest pain, new ECG changes and by the elevation of cardiac enzymes. The evidence must be consistent with the diagnosis of heart attack.

(*d*) **Kidney failure**

End stage renal failure presenting as chronic irreversible failure of both kidneys to function, as a result of which either regular renal dialysis or renal transplant is initiated.

(*e*) **Major organ transplant**

The actual undergoing as a recipient of, or inclusion on an official UK waiting list for, a transplant of a heart, liver, lung, pancreas or bone marrow.

(*f*) **Multiple sclerosis**

A definite diagnosis by a consultant neurologist of multiple sclerosis which satisfies the following criteria:

(i) there must be current impairment of motor or sensory function, which must have persisted for a continuous period of at least six months; and

(ii) the diagnosis must be confirmed by diagnostic techniques current at the time of the claim.

(*g*) **Stroke**

A cerebrovascular accident resulting in permanent neurological damage. Transient ischaemic attacks are specifically excluded.

The additional conditions **20.31**

(*a*) **Aorta graft surgery**

Undergoing surgery for disease of the aorta needing excision and surgical replacement of a portion of the diseased aorta with a graft. For this definition, aorta means the thoracic and abdominal aorta, but not its branches.

(*b*) **Benign brain tumour**

A non-malignant tumour in the brain resulting in permanent deficit to the neurological system. Tumours or lesions in the pituitary gland are not covered.

(*c*) **Blindness**

Total permanent and irreversible loss of all sight in both eyes.

(*d*) **Coma**

A state of unconsciousness with no reaction to external stimuli or internal needs, persisting continuously with the use of life support systems for a period of at least 96 hours and resulting in permanent neurological deficit. Coma secondary to alcohol or drug misuse is not covered.

(*e*) **Deafness**

Total permanent and irreversible loss of hearing in both ears.

(*f*) **Heart valve replacement or repair**

Undergoing open heart surgery from medical necessity to replace or repair one or more heart valves.

(*g*) **Loss of limbs**

The permanent physical severance of two or more limbs from above the *[elbow/wrist]* or *[knee/ankle]* joint.

(*h*) **Loss of speech**

Total permanent end, irreversible loss of the ability to speak as a result of physical injury or disease.

(*j*) **Motor neurone disease *[before age x]***

Confirmation by a consultant neurologist of a definite diagnosis of motor neurone disease *[before age x]*.

(*k*) **Paralysis/paraplegia**

Total irreversible loss of muscle function or sensation to the whole of any two limbs as a result of injury or disease. The disability must be permanent and supported by appropriate neurological evidence.

(*l*) **Parkinson's disease *[before age x]***

Confirmation by a consultant neurologist of a definite diagnosis of Parkinson's disease *[before age x]*. Parkinson's disease secondary to alcohol or drug misuse is not covered.

(*m*) **Terminal illness**

Advanced or rapidly progressing incurable illness where, in the opinion of an attending consultant and our Chief Medical Officer, the life expectancy is no greater than twelve months *[AIDS is specifically excluded and not covered under this definition]*.

(*n*) **Third degree burns**

Third degree burns covering at least 20 per cent of the body surface area.

Note: '*Age x*' means that some insurers will only provide this benefit above or below a certain age at claim.

Exclusions **20.32**

The ABI has also developed a standard set of exclusions that its members may adopt. However, these are not compulsory and more or fewer conditions may be included. Exclusions will normally start with a preamble such as 'We will not pay a critical illness claim if it is caused directly or indirectly from any of the following'. Example conditions include the following.

- ***Aviation:*** Taking part in any flying activity, other than as a passenger in a commercially licensed aircraft.
- ***Criminal acts:*** Taking part in a criminal act.
- ***Drug abuse:*** Alcohol or solvent abuse, or the taking of drugs except under the direction of a registered medical practitioner.
- ***Failure to follow medical advice:*** Unreasonable failure to seek or follow medical advice.
- ***Hazardous sports and pastimes:*** Taking part in, or practising for, boxing, caving, climbing, horse racing, jet skiing, martial arts, mountaineering, off-piste skiing, pot-holing, power-boat racing, underwater diving, yacht racing or any race, trial or timed motor sport.
- ***HIV/AIDS:*** Infection with HIV or conditions due to AIDS.
- ***Living abroad:*** Living outside of the EU for more than 13 consecutive weeks in any 12 months.
- ***Self-inflicted injury:*** Intentional self-inflicted injury.
- ***War and civil commotion:*** War, invasion, hostilities (whether war is declared or not), civil war, rebellion, revolution or taking part in a riot or civil commotion.

Source: ABI Critical Illness Exclusions, Association of British Insurers, 2001

Chapter 21

Income Protection Insurance

- **Overview of income protection insurance**
- **Types of policy**
- **Benefits**
- **Claims**
- **Disability definitions**
- **Exclusions**

Overview of income protection insurance 21.1

Income protection insurance is the generic term for what was previously known as permanent health insurance (PHI) or long-term disability (LTD) insurance. If the insured is unable to work because of illness or disability after an initial deferred or waiting period of being off work, policies pay out a regular weekly or monthly benefit, usually up to retirement age. Policies must have a minimum term of five years.

Such policies were first developed in the late 19th century and the basic concept has remained broadly the same since then.

Types of policy 21.2

Standard policies 21.3

Standard policies usually will pay benefit continuously until:

- the claimant returns to work;
- the claimant dies;
- the claimant retires; or
- until the end of the policy term.

Holloway plans 21.4

Holloway plans are a combination of income protection and regular savings, and were first developed by George Holloway MP in the 1870s. Such plans remain in existence, usually written by Friendly Societies (see 4 INDUSTRIAL LIFE ASSURANCE), as a means of combining protection and savings. They provide protection up to retirement age at which time the proceeds of the savings element are paid out tax free.

Unit linked and with-profits plans **21.5**

Some plans offer unit linking or a with-profits link in conjunction with a policy review system (see 13 UNIT LINKED POLICIES for details of unit linking and 6 PROFITS, INVESTMENTS AND BONUS DISTRIBUTION for details of with-profits business). This is often done as a means of minimising the premium. Such plans may offer a small cash value (the value of the units held or profits declared) if the policy is surrendered after on average one to two years.

Budget policies **21.6**

Budget policies generally have a fixed maximum payment term of two to five years. By excluding very long-term claims, insurers can offer significantly reduced premiums.

Short term policies **21.7**

Some creditor insurances are, confusingly, also marketed as 'income protection'. Although such plans provide a similar benefit initially, payments are usually restricted to one or two years only.

Non-assignability and trusts **21.8**

Income protection is one of the few long-term policies that is not assignable to a third party. The policy conditions will usually make this clear. Nor can income protection policies be set up under trust.

Group policies **21.9**

Group policies pay benefit to the employer, not to the employee. Tax will not be paid on the benefit where it is paid on to the employee, who will themselves pay tax and National Insurance contributions (NICs) on it as a continuation of their earned income.

Technical guides **21.10**

Group Risk Development (GRiD) a group of group risk insurers, reinsurers and intermediaries, is developing the concept of technical guides, which explain the key features of a product in a common format – as happens with individual products that are regulated by the Financial Services Authority (FSA).

By mid-2001, such guides were just beginning to be issued by insurers, but it will probably be some months before all insurers adopt the concept.

Flex schemes 21.11

Flex schemes, or flexible benefits schemes, allow employees to choose from a menu of benefits to create a package of employee benefits which best suits their personal needs. The constituent insurance covers will however follow the norm for that product type.

Employees may be given a choice of how much cover as well as what type to have; they may be able to add spouse, partner or children's cover and to change cover periodically. In many cases, changes will be subject to fresh underwriting.

Third party rights 21.12

The *Contracts (Rights of Third Parties) Act 1999* gives third parties such as individual employees rights under contracts made by others, such as their employer, and which affect them. However, it may be made a condition of the contract that the terms of the Act do not apply.

In practice, most group income protection insurers will grant rights to employees so far as claims under a policy are concerned. This means that, in the event of a dispute, the claimant can deal direct with the insurer rather than having to go through their employer, who, on cost grounds alone, may have an incentive to wish a claim not to succeed as this might affect the premium they pay in future.

Benefits 21.13

Standard individual policies pay out typically up to 50–60 per cent of pre-disability income (or up to 75 per cent less a single person's state long-term incapacity benefit) after a deferred period of either 1, 3, 6, 12 or 24 months (or their weekly equivalent). In addition there is likely to be a maximum overall benefit, of say £150,000 a year.

The maximum benefit will include any other income to which the claimant may be entitled, for example continuing income from their employer or benefits from any other policies.

Lump sum payments 21.14

Some policies will pay a lump sum in the event of permanent and total disability.

In the event of a claim, the insurer may be prepared to consider paying a commuted lump sum instead of a regular income. This is not usually included as a right within the policy conditions, but if approached, the insurer may be prepared to offer terms, based on the likelihood of the insured being unable to work again and on their life expectancy.

Rehabilitation and proportionate benefit 21.15

Most policies include rehabilitation and proportionate benefit. The former is where the insured returns to their normal job but is paid less (usually because they are not able to do the full job they did previously). Proportionate benefit is where the insured returns to another, but lower paid, job. For both benefits, the insurer will pay some benefit, usually in proportion to the income being received.

Linked claims **21.16**

Sometimes an insured who was off work returns, but then has to take more time off. Provided that the underlying cause is the same, and the second claim is (usually) within six months of the first, they are regarded as the same claim and a new deferred period is avoided.

Housepersons and those taking a career break **21.17**

It is usually a requirement that the insured is working immediately before disability in order for the benefit to be payable. For housepersons, those taking a career break or anyone who is temporarily unemployed, this could mean that benefit would not be payable, regardless of the reason for their disability. Many insurers will now therefore offer houseperson or career break cover. Typically this will have a lower maximum annual benefit (say £15,000 a year), and the insurers will apply one of the tests detailed at 21.30–21.33 below, rather than the usual own occupation definition (see 21.27 below).

Soft benefits **21.18**

Insurers are increasingly looking to add 'soft' benefits, such as telephone helplines and counselling services.

Extra benefits **21.19**

In some cases, insurers may be prepared, on an *ex gratia* basis, to provide other benefits. For example, an insurer may pay for rehabilitation treatment or for an operation to be carried out privately where the NHS waiting list is such that otherwise the insured would be off work for some time awaiting treatment. Such proactive claims management is becoming more popular, although it is as yet rarely featured in insurers' marketing material, let alone in their policy documentation. The incentive for the insurer to make such *ex gratia* benefits available is that ultimately the insurer's claims costs may reduce. However, it is rare for an insurer to be able to quantify in advance exactly what if any savings might be made, so there is an act of faith to some extent in providing such benefits.

Rates reviews **21.20**

As with other long-term protection policies, premium rates and benefits may be subject to periodic review when premiums or benefits may go up or down. Otherwise, rates and benefits will be guaranteed throughout the policy term.

Non-aggregation 21.21

Insurers always limit the maximum benefit under their policy to take account of any other income that the insured may receive – particularly where that income comes from another income protection policy. Already existing investment or pension income will be ignored though.

Claims 21.22

Claims proof and evidence 21.23

Insurers will clearly require evidence that an insured is unable to work before paying benefit. Usually, this is straightforward and provided unequivocally by the insured's medical practitioner or specialist consultant. However, in some cases the medical evidence may be ambiguous or there may be reasons to believe that the insured is not being honest about their disability.

In such cases, so as to prevent possible fraud, insurers may adopt a range of techniques designed to help determine whether the claim is genuine. This might include:

- requiring the claimant to visit an independent medical assessor or expert appointed, and usually paid for, by the insurer;
- making enquiries about any other activities being pursued by the insured; and
- using the services of professional investigators.

The onus is on the insurer to prove that their investigations are reasonable and do not infringe the claimant's human rights. With the passing of the *Human Rights Act 1998*, it is likely that case law will develop in this area to determine what is a breach of human rights and what is not.

Claims management 21.24

'Proactive claims management' is a buzz phrase being used more by insurers of late. It means that the insurer looks beyond their contractual obligations under the contract in order to provide both a more valuable benefit to the policyholder and ultimately to reduce its claim costs.

The insurer does this by looking at ways to help ill or disabled claimants return to work more quickly than might otherwise be the case. For example, an insurer might agree to pay for private treatment or an operation, to fund physiotherapy or to work with an employer to help adapt a claimant's work station or job role so that the individual can return to an active role; however, they will not necessarily return to the role that they had previously.

This can be a double-edged sword. In rare cases, the insurer, or the claims management organisation that they sub-contract, might recommend a course of action that would be damaging to the claimant. There have been examples of over-zealous claims counsellors who have recommended a course of action which has subsequently been criticised by the claimant's medical adviser. Generally, however, insurers argue that their role is to help people to maximise their potential, and that cost saving must not be the sole reason to adopt such proactive action.

Most disputes are likely to arise on conditions that are difficult to 'prove' absolutely, such as back conditions and conditions which are difficult to diagnose, such as ME. Permanent and total disability can also be difficult to prove unless there is clear clinical evidence supporting the diagnosis, which must be made by a recognised expert.

Claims in payment (group only) **21.25**

A growing concern for employers and trade unions has been the situation of what happens when a scheme is switched to a new insurer. It is likely that the 'old' insurer will no longer have a responsibility (or the motivation) to continue the claim. However, the 'new' insurer will also be reluctant to take on previous responsibilities – especially as anecdotal evidence suggests that once a claimant has been off work for six months, they are increasingly unlikely to ever return to their previous job.

However, Group Risk Development (GRID) (see 21.10 above) is addressing this issue with a view to establishing a code of practice that would be adopted by the industry.

Disability definitions **21.26**

The main definitions adopted are as set out at 21.27–21.33 below (although the precise wording will vary from insurer to insurer).

Own occupation **21.27**

The guidance note published by the Association of British Insurers (ABI) on the definition of incapacity states that the insured is:

> 'totally unable through sickness or accident to follow their own occupation or one to which they are suited by reason of training or experience and is not following any other occupation for profit or reward.'

This definition is set out in its *Statement of Practice for Income Protection Insurance*, published August 2000 (the Statement is available free of charge by writing to the ABI at 51 Gresham Street, London EC2V 7HQ, or on their website at www.abi.org.uk).

The definition may be refined by stating that the insured is 'unable to carry out the material and substantial duties or main tasks and duties of their occupation', and/or that they 'must not be carrying on any other occupation for profit or reward'. Otherwise, benefit would not be payable if the insured were to carry out part-time unpaid charitable work for example. Such refinements help avoid arguments about whether a policy should pay if, for example, an accountant is unable to drive a car, even though they typically only make one or two business trips by car a year.

Own or suited **21.28**

In some cases, the definition may change from 'own occupation' to 'own or suited' after the claim has been paid for a specified period – usually one or two years.

Own or suited definitions are the ones most commonly used, although insurers will often adopt other definitions for specific occupations. For example, an own occupation definition would be expensive for a surgeon who requires full use of each of his or her fingers to perform operations. A relatively minor accident could prevent them from carrying out their job as a surgeon. However, the individual may be able to teach or do some other occupation, and a definition which reflects this could be offered at a much more attractive premium.

Any occupation **21.29**

'Any occupation' is the strictest definition, and means that the policy will not pay if the insured is able to do any occupation whatsoever.

Activities of daily living **21.30**

In this definition the insured is unable to carry out $\frac{2}{3}$ or more of typically $\frac{5}{6}$ activities of daily living (ADLs). For further details of ADL definitions, see 22 LONG-TERM CARE INSURANCE.

Activities of daily working **21.31**

Here the insured is unable to carry out $\frac{2}{3}$ or more of typically $\frac{5}{8}$ activities of daily working (ADWs).

Typical ADWs may include the following.

- ***Bending:*** The ability to bend or kneel to pick up something from the floor and straighten up again.
- ***Climbing:*** The ability to walk up or down a flight of 12 stairs without holding on or resting.
- ***Communicating:*** The ability to answer the telephone and take a message for someone.
- ***General health:*** The ability to independently arrange to see a doctor and take routinely prescribed medication.
- ***Lifting:*** The ability to lift, carry or otherwise move everyday objects using either hand. Everyday objects would include a kettle of water, bags of shopping, an overnight bag or briefcase.
- ***Manual dexterity:*** The ability to use hands and fingers with

precision, including the ability to pick up and manipulate small objects, such as pens or cutlery.

- ***Reading:*** The ability to read, with spectacles or contact lenses if necessary, ordinary newspaper print, or to pass the standard eye test for driving. This activity would be failed if the relevant life assured is certified as blind or partially sighted by an ophthalmologist.
- ***Walking:*** The ability to walk a distance of more than 200 metres on flat ground without stopping or without severe discomfort.

Source: Skandia Protect, Skandia Life, 2001

Functional assessment tests **21.32**

Where functional assessment tests (FATs) are used, the insured is unable to carry out ⅔, or more of typically ⅝ FATs. FATs are similar to ADWs (see 21.31 above) and measure an individual's ability to perform everyday tasks.

Personal capability assessment **21.33**

Personal capability assessments are now used as the test for state incapacity benefit (IB), and may be adopted by some insurers for consistency. However, it should be noted that insurer disability definitions are often more generous than those now adopted by the state for IB purposes.

Exclusions **21.34**

The ABI has developed a standard set of exclusions that its members may adopt. However, these are not compulsory, and more or fewer conditions may be included. Exclusions will normally start with a preamble such as: 'We will not pay an income protection claim if it is caused directly or indirectly from any of the following'. Example conditions include the following.

- ***Aviation:*** Taking part in any flying activity, other than as a passenger in a commercially licensed aircraft.
- ***Criminal acts:*** Taking part in a criminal act.
- ***Drug abuse:*** Alcohol or solvent abuse, or the taking of drugs except under the direction of a registered medical practitioner.
- ***Failure to follow medical advice:*** Unreasonable failure to seek or follow medical advice.
- ***Hazardous sports and pastimes:*** Taking part in, or practising for, boxing, caving, climbing, horse-racing, jet skiing, martial arts, mountaineering, off-piste skiing, pot-holing, power-boat racing, under water diving, yacht racing or any race, trial or timed motor sport.
- ***HIV/AIDS:*** Infection with Human Immunodeficiency Virus (HIV) or conditions due to any Acquired Immune Deficiency Syndrome (AIDS).

- ***Self-inflicted injury:*** Intentional self-inflicted injury.
- ***War and civil commotion:*** War, invasion, hostilities (whether war is declared or not), civil war, rebellion, revolution or taking part in a riot or civil commotion.

Source: ABI Critical Illness Exclusions, Association of British Insurers, 2000

Chapter 22

Long-Term Care Insurance

- **Overview of long-term care insurance**
- **Types of policy**
- **Benefits**
- **Activities of daily living definitions**
- **Exclusions**
- **State funding of long-term care**

Overview of long-term care insurance 22.1

Long-term care (LTC) insurance is a relatively new product to the UK, having first been marketed in 1991 by Commercial Union (now Norwich Union). Policies are usually designed to pay a regular monthly sum towards care fees, whether these are incurred at home or in a care home.

Types of policy 22.2

Pre-funded protection 22.3

Pre-funded protection policies operate in a similar way to income protection policies (see 21 INCOME PROTECTION INSURANCE) and are taken out while the insured is still in relatively good health. If care is subsequently needed, then once a particular threshold has been reached benefit becomes payable, usually after a deferred period of three months. Payment usually continues until death or until care is no longer needed, which is unlikely in most cases. However, in some cases there may be a limited payment term, for example up to five years.

Activities of daily living **22.4**

The care threshold is usually determined by reference to activities of daily living (ADLs). Typically, the insured must fail two or three out of six ADLs in order for the benefit to be payable. In some cases, a policy will pay out a lower level of benefit upon failure of two ADLs and then a higher level of benefit upon failing three or more. ADL failure will usually be tested by an independent medical practitioner or nurse appointed by the insurer. Typical ADLs are set out at 22.17 below.

In addition to being payable on failing physical ADLs, benefit is usually payable on cognitive or mental impairment. The Association of British Insurers' (ABI) standard wording for this is set out in 22.18 below.

Additional benefits **22.5**

In addition to the main benefit which, depending on the policy, is paid either to the policyholder or to the care provider, pre-funded protection policies often also provide the following.

(*a*) **Assistive devices benefit**

Usually linked to the main benefit (for example being up to three times the monthly benefit payable), assistive devices benefit can be used to pay for devices to help the insured cope with their disability. These can range from a walking stick or Zimmer frame to a stairlift to be installed in the home.

(*b*) **Access to a care counselling service**

For some people, this benefit can be as important as the financial benefit. Services vary but will typically include a helpline, personal counselling for the insured and their family, help and advice, including on what state and other benefits may be available (and even help with filling in the forms), and information to help the insured choose the best care package to meet their needs. Where this is an independent service, the contract will usually be between the insured and the care provider.

Premiums **22.6**

Policies may be funded by a regular (usually monthly) premium, or from a lump sum single premium. Plans do not usually have a cash value on death or surrender, although some insurers offer such options as a paid-for additional benefit, when the value is usually on a decreasing basis.

Pre-funded investment **22.7**

Although the benefits package follows the same lines as that of pre-funded protection policies (see 22.3–22.6 above), pre-funded investment policies include an investment element. These policies are often set up using an overseas insurance company, and in such cases the provisions of the *Policyholders Protection Act 1997* will not apply. Such policies aim to offer tax and investment benefits as well as long-term care benefits.

Critical illness policies **22.8**

Some critical illness policies have long-term care insurance attached as a rider benefit. These policies will pay benefit on the loss of independent existence or upon the insured needing long-term care, usually based on ADL failure.

Unlike 'true' LTC insurance, such policies will pay a cash lump sum once the need for care is established.

Typically, whereas most LTC insurance policies are taken out by people in their 60s or older, critical illness policies are mostly taken out by younger people. As such, LTC insurance is usually seen as an add-on rather than as a core element of the policy.

Whole life conversion option **22.9**

During 2001, life assurers have begun to develop a new form of LTC insurance benefit whereby life assurance which is no longer needed may be swapped for LTC insurance cover. For example, one company would allow an insured to surrender £100,000 worth of life cover and to replace it with a benefit of £2,000 a month payable for 50 months. In this example, the policy has a two year waiting period before a claim can be made. After the first two years from conversion, the policy has a more usual three month deferred period before benefit is payable. In the event of early death, the balance of the sum assured becomes payable.

Immediate need policies **22.10**

As the name suggests, immediate need policies – also known as point of need policies – are taken out by people who already need care. The insured will pay a single premium to the insurer who will assess the individual's health and, most importantly, their likely life expectancy, and offer a monthly benefit, usually until death. In most cases this will be a higher sum than could be obtained from a traditional annuity; otherwise there would be little point in having this type of policy.

In effect, the policyholder is getting an enhanced annuity, although, for technical reasons the policy may be written as an endowment rather than as an annuity.

Policies may also include:

- a care counselling service;
- higher benefits becoming payable if the care needs increase; and
- a capital guarantee so that, in the event of death before a certain date, part of the original capital is returned, therefore minimising the risk that if the individual dies early they would have gained no benefit from the policy (this is usually on a sliding scale, decreasing as benefits are paid).

Equity release schemes **22.11**

Often not insurance-based, equity release schemes are a funding mechanism whereby the unmortgaged value or equity of a domestic property is used to fund either an LTC insurance policy or to pay a regular income to the client.

In April 1999, Mortgage Interest Relief At Source (MIRAS) was discontinued, making equity release schemes less attractive, as tax relief could no longer be obtained on the mortgage interest paid. MIRAS was the system by which tax relief was given at source on qualifying mortgage interest payments. Such relief was restricted to interest on the first £30,000 of capital for home purchase or improvement, or for home income plans. As a general rule, equity release is most effective for older people – typically singles in their 70s and couples in their late 70s and older. However, each case needs to be assessed on its merits to determine whether it makes best sense financially.

Two main types of equity release scheme exist and are set out at 22.12 and 22.13 below.

Home reversion schemes **22.12**

With a home reversion scheme the property is sold to a third party, who then pays the client an income until their death. Upon their death the property reverts to the third party lender but until then the client has a right to continue living in the property.

Home income schemes **22.13**

Home income schemes involve the property being mortgaged rather than being sold outright. Typically the mortgage sum is invested into an annuity, which pays for the fixed interest on the deal plus a regular monthly income to the insured. On death, the property is sold and the mortgage redeemed. Any remaining equity forms part of the client's estate. Although this method usually generates a lower benefit than a home reversion scheme, ownership is retained as are rights to any increase in value of the property in the future. One variation of this is a shared appreciation mortgage, whereby the lender gives up the right to part or all of the interest payable in exchange for a share of the property's growing value in future years.

Surviving relatives and vulnerable consumers **22.14**

Experience on equity release schemes shows that disputes can arise where an elderly person dies soon after paying a lump sum into an arrangement designed to provide them with future income, which may have a lower or no value on death.

To protect themselves, some equity release organisations now insist that elderly people take independent legal advice before entering into such arrangements, and that they notify any family members who might be affected of what they have done and why. The same logic applies where an elderly person is investing any large capital sum that will have little or no value on their subsequent death.

The Government has recognised that elderly people may be vulnerable consumers so far as long-term care insurance is concerned, and in 2001 consulted on making all LTC insurance arrangements subject to some form of regulation, probably by the Financial Services Authority. The consultation period for this has now closed and observers are currently awaiting the Treasury's proposals on regulation.

Benefits **22.15**

The main benefit from any LTC insurance policy is a regular sum to pay towards care fees. If benefit is only paid to a care provider then in effect the policy is an indemnity, with benefit not capable of exceeding the actual care costs. Otherwise, benefits may be paid direct to the insured who will themselves be responsible for paying the care provider.

In most cases, the benefit to be insured will be significantly less than the expected cost of fees (nursing home fees or care at home could well cost around £20,000 a year at 2001 levels). This is because other monies will be available to go towards the fees including the following.

(*a*) ***Age Allowance:*** This state benefit is payable once an individual aged 65 or over has been hospitalised or in care for more than six weeks.

(*b*) ***Nursing fees:*** Under the *Health and Social Care Act 2001*, from October 2001 local authorities in England, Wales and Northern Ireland will pay towards nursing fees in nursing homes (see 22.23 below). Although full details have not been finalised at the time of writing, it is expected that the maximum payment will be around £110 a week (£5,500 a year) and that a sliding scale will apply based on the severity of the disability. (See 22.25 below with regard to the situation in Scotland.)

(*c*) ***Local authority contributions:*** Local authorities will pay part or all of the care fees if the individual's capital (including the value of their home unless a dependent relative lives there) is below £18,500 and they have insufficient income to pay the fees themselves. Since April 2001, the value of the home is now ignored for the first twelve weeks of needing care.

(*d*) ***The insured's state and any occupational pensions.***

(*e*) ***The insured's investment and any other income:*** In addition, they may also use any capital they have to help pay towards fees.

As a very rough guide, an individual may not need to insure for more than about a quarter to half the expected cost of care fees, although this figure will vary considerably depending on personal circumstances.

Other benefits have been listed in 22.3–22.10 above, under specific product types.

Activities of daily living definitions 22.16

Physical activities 22.17

The following are the standard ADLs as recommended by the ABI.

(*a*) **Washing**

The ability to wash in the bath or shower (including getting into and out of the bath or shower) or wash by other conventional means.

(*b*) **Dressing**

The ability to put on, take off, secure and unfasten all garments and, as appropriate, any braces, artificial limbs or other surgical appliances.

(*c*) **Feeding**

The ability to feed oneself once food has been prepared and made available.

(*d*) **Toileting**

The ability to use the lavatory or manage bowel and bladder function through the use of protective undergarments or surgical appliances if appropriate.

(*e*) **Mobility**

The ability to move indoors from room to room on level surfaces.

(*f*) **Transferring**

The ability to move from a bed to an upright chair or wheelchair and vice versa.

Mental impairment 22.18

In addition, mental impairment will also trigger benefit to be paid. This is defined by the ABI as the deterioration in or loss of mental capacity which results in a need for continual care or supervision and:

(i) results from an organic cause; and

(ii) is shown by a deterioration in the insured's short and long-term memory, knowing who and where they are, the identity of others, an awareness of time and the ability to solve simple problems and make rational decisions.

Exclusions 22.19

Standard exclusions under LTC insurance policies may include some or all of:

- intentionally self-inflicted injury or illness;
- the effects of the use of alcohol or drugs (unless these are taken in

accordance with a prescription given by a registered medical practitioner and they are not themselves prescribed in connection with the effects of the use of alcohol or drugs);

- any mental or nervous disorder where no organic cause can be shown, for example depression;
- unreasonable failure to seek or follow medical advice;
- infection by any Human Immunodeficiency Virus (HIV), Acquired Immune Deficiency Syndrome (AIDS) or AIDS-related complex (ARC);
- assistive devices where the insured can obtain an equivalent device free from their local health authority, the social services department of their local authority or from the residential care home or nursing home in which they are living; and
- living outside the United Kingdom, Channel Islands or Isle of Man.

Source: PPP Lifetime Care Bond (IZ7I/C2758/KNP), PPP Lifetime Care, 1997

Many exclusions will now follow the model exclusions adopted by the ABI on critical illness and income protection insurance (see 20 CRITICAL ILLNESS INSURANCE and 21 INCOME PROTECTION INSURANCE). However there will usually be additional exclusions for non-organic mental disorders and for assistive devices which can be obtained free elsewhere.

State funding of long-term care 22.20

NHS responsibilities 22.21

The NHS has a responsibility to provide medical care to UK residents, but it has never had a responsibility to provide long-term care. In practice, prior to 1993, long-term care was often provided through the NHS. However the *NHS and Community Care Act 1990*, which came into effect in April 1993, passed over responsibility for paying for long-term care to local authorities or their equivalents, who apply means testing to determine whether help is due.

In spite of the 1990 Act, the law remains unclear on exactly where NHS responsibilities end and local authority responsibilities begin.

Local authority responsibilities 22.22

Although local authorities have a statutory responsibility under the *NHS and Community Care Act 1990* to assess individuals needing care and to provide free means-tested care, there have been many examples of local authorities not providing such services. However, it is not acceptable for a local authority to refuse to help where it is legally obliged to do so and the authority may be sued if it is in breach of its obligations.

It can also be difficult to determine where NHS responsibility ends and local authorities' responsibility begins. The leading case on this is *R v North and East Devon Health Authority, ex parte Coughlan [1998] 47 BMLR 27*. The NHS position is now set out in Health Service Circular 2001/015 (also published as Local Authority Circular 2001/18), which was published in June 2001. Each health authority is responsible for establishing its own eligibility criteria, but essentially where an individual has a need for 'continuing NHS health care' the NHS remains responsible for providing it.

In the *Coughlan* case it was held that the NHS did have a continuing responsibility to provide such care (as it had since she was seriously injured in a road traffic accident in 1971) and that her health authority did not therefore have the right to close the Newcourt Hospital where she was being cared for and to transfer her care to the local authority services.

Nursing care 22.23

Under the terms of the *Health and Social Care Act 2001*, from October 2001 local authorities in England, Wales and Northern Ireland will be responsible for paying for nursing care, but only where this is received in a registered nursing home and provided by a registered nurse. Although details of how this scheme will work have not yet been published at the time of writing, it is expected that the maximum payment will be around £110 a week (£5,500 a year) and that a sliding scale, based on the nursing care needed, will apply.

Third party services 22.24

Both care counselling and care services themselves are likely to be provided by a third party rather than by the insurer. As with private medical insurance, any contract is likely to be between the claimant and the provider rather than with the insurer.

In the event of a dispute, any claim would be against the third party and not the insurer.

Personal care (Scotland only) 22.25

Scotland has determined to adopt the main recommendation made by the *1999 Royal Commission on Long-Term Care Funding* and to pay for all personal care costs, not just for nursing care. Again, full details of how this will work have not been announced at the time of writing.

One possibility is that English residents who are able to qualify under the Scottish rules could choose to move to Scotland in order to enjoy the higher benefits which apply there. It is not yet known what, if any, rules will apply to stop them from doing so.

Chapter 23

Private Medical Insurance

- **Overview of private medical insurance**
- **Types of policy**
- **Benefits**
- **Definitions**
- **Conditions and treatment**
- **Exclusions**

Overview of private medical insurance 23.1

Private medical insurance is designed to pay for private medical costs incurred when the insured needs treatment for an acute medical condition. It is an indemnity product and is usually written as an annually renewable contract by a general insurance company.

Private medical insurance can trace its roots back to the late 19th century, although the peak of its growth was in the 1970s and 1980s.

Types of policy 23.2

There are no hard and fast rules to determine what constitutes a particular type of private medical insurance policy. However, the main types of cover available are set out at 23.3–23.11 below.

Comprehensive cover 23.3

Comprehensive plans have the highest benefits and will typically include all in-patient and out-patient costs, together with specialist fees and other benefits.

Standard cover 23.4

Standard plans will normally cover both in-patient and out-patient costs, but will not include all the additional benefits which are contained in comprehensive plans.

Budget cover **23.5**

Budget plans usually just provide basic cover; they will often not cover out-patient costs or other benefits that are likely to have a high cost to the insurer.

Six week plans **23.6**

Another form of budget cover (see 23.5 above), six week plans only pay benefit if the NHS waiting list for the treatment required is six weeks or more. If not, the insured is expected to elect to have NHS treatment or to pay for it themselves.

International plans **23.7**

International plans are fundamentally the same as UK plans except that they are designed to cover treatment received abroad. They include emergency evacuation and repatriation (usually back to the UK) and may pay for primary care such as visiting a General Practitioner (GP), maternity and dental services.

Plans are targeted at expatriates – people living or working abroad – and are sold to both UK and non-UK nationals. International private medical insurance premiums are not usually subject to insurance premium tax.

Plans often have different price bands for different parts of the world, for example:

- Europe;
- rest of world (excluding North America); and
- rest of world (including North America).

Voluntary schemes **23.8**

A voluntary scheme is one where the prices are based on individual rates, often with a discount as such schemes are offered by companies and affinity groups to large groups of people. The underwriting requirements are the same as for individuals, with any pre-existing conditions excluded. The individual will be responsible for paying premiums, even if they do so through a salary payroll scheme.

Company and corporate schemes **23.9**

Company schemes are set up by and premiums paid by a company, usually the individual's employer. For larger schemes, typically those with 20–50 members or more, pre-existing conditions may be covered, while rates will typically be based on the scheme's previous experience. For these larger schemes the total annual premium is likely to be the anticipated cost of claims, plus an administrative fee payable to the insurer, plus insurance premium tax – this is known as a cost plus arrangement. There is therefore a direct incentive for employers to help minimise claims costs.

Employees may be able to choose higher benefits or to cover other family members such as spouses, partners or children at extra cost and to pay that extra premium themselves.

Flex schemes **23.10**

Flexible benefits, or flex, schemes allow employees to choose from a menu of benefits to create a package of employee benefits that best suits their personal needs. The constituent insurance covers will however follow the norm for that product type.

Employees may be given a choice of how much cover as well as what type to have; they may be able to add spouse, partner or children's cover and to change cover periodically. In many cases, changes will be subject to fresh underwriting.

Health and medical trusts **23.11**

Health trusts are an alternative to corporate private medical insurance and have the major advantage that they avoid paying insurance premium tax.

A trust is set up and funded by the employer. The terms of the trust are such that employees are entitled to have treatment and other costs paid on application to the fund, with the net effect for the employee being similar to that of a conventional private medical insurance scheme.

The trust is funded to pay for treatment costs plus the fees of the administrator – who may be an insurer or a third party administrator. In order to minimise the risk of unexpected claims increasing costs to an unacceptable level, stop loss insurance may be arranged which pays out if or when the benefits payable in any year exceed a pre-set threshold. Except to the extent of any stop loss insurance purchased, payments into the trust will not attract insurance premium tax as the arrangement is not an insurance scheme.

Self-pay **23.12**

Although this is not insurance at all, many people choose to self-pay for medical costs. Around a third of all private treatment is self-pay.

Many hospitals offer fixed price surgery or treatment, or can arrange loan facilities. Such arrangements may be combined with a savings plan in order to create a health fund to pay for future treatment. As such, this type of arrangement could be seen as an alternative to an insurance policy for some people.

ABI and GISC codes of selling practice **23.13**

The Association of British Insurers (ABI) represents around 96 per cent of all UK insurers, the major exception being Lloyd's, and its Codes of Practice are adopted by all its members.

At the time of writing in mid-2001, private medical insurance sales are regulated by an ABI Code of Selling Practice. However, it is anticipated that this will be replaced by a new Code of Selling Practice drawn up by the General Insurance Standards Council (GISC). GISC is a self-regulatory organisation which is expected to dominate the UK general insurance market. In particular, its Rule F42 requires its members to deal only with intermediaries who are themselves members of GISC. In effect therefore, and subject to any last minute legal challenges, from 2002 almost all general insurance policies will be written by GISC-regulated insurers, who will be subject to its codes and standards of practice.

Benefits 23.14

A typical benefit schedule for a comprehensive private medical policy may be set out along the following lines.

Typical private medical insurance benefit schedule 23.15

Benefit	**Maximum payment**
A Hospital costs	
Accommodation, nursing care, operating theatre intensive care and other ancillary charges	Full cover
In-patient diagnostic tests and services, radiotherapy, chemotherapy, physiotherapy and appliances employed in the course of an operation	Full cover
Day care treatment	Full cover
Accommodation for one parent to stay in hospital with an insured dependant under 14 years old	Full cover
In-patient treatment for psychiatric and mental conditions	Full cover up to 28 days per policy year
B Specialist fees	
Surgeons' and anaesthetists' fees for in-patient and day care operations	Full cover
Physicians' fees for in-patient treatment	Full cover
Consultations for acupuncture, osteopathy chiropractic and homeopathy	Up to £1,000 per policy year
Out-patient treatment i) Specialist consultations, chemotherapy, radiotherapy and diagnostic procedures such as pathology, radiology, CT and MRI scans ii) Physiotherapy iii) Specialist consultations and diagnostic procedures for psychiatric and mental conditions	 Full cover Up to £1,000 per policy year Up to £1,200 per policy year

C Other features	
Nursing at home – skilled nursing care under the direction of a specialist, which would otherwise be provided in hospital and which immediately follows in-patient treatment covered by the plan	Full cover up to 13 weeks per policy year
Complications of pregnancy – available after ten months' membership	Full cover
Private ambulance	Full cover
NHS hospital cash benefit for each night spent in an NHS hospital as a non-paying patient for a condition covered by the plan	£100 per night up to £2,000 per policy year
Maximum overall limit	None
D Optional add-on benefits (available for an additional premium	
i) Critical Illness ii) Dental Expenses iii) Hospital Cash iv) Personal Accident	

Source: Primecare, Standard Life Healthcare, 2001

Other benefits under private medical insurance policies may include any or all of the following.

(*a*) ***Home nursing:*** Usually after in-patient or day case treatment.

(*b*) ***Maternity grants:*** Policies usually exclude normal deliveries (although complications of pregnancy are usually covered including caesarean section, forceps and induced births), but some plans now pay a maternity grant of a cash sum for each child born.

(*c*) ***NHS cash benefit:*** The policy will pay a cash sum (typically £25–100 a night) for each full night or day where the insured has NHS paid-for treatment when they could have had private treatment paid for under their policy.

(*d*) ***Ambulance cover:*** This covers necessary road ambulance movements between hospitals. It does not cover ambulance journeys to or from hospital.

(*e*) ***Overseas cover:*** Covers emergency treatment overseas, which may include necessary evacuation and repatriation to the UK.

(*f*) ***Complementary medicine:*** Usually on a GP referral to a qualified practitioner (which will be defined, usually as being a member of their recognised professional body) for acupuncture; chiropractic; homeopathy, osteopathy or one of a number of other complementary therapies.

(*g*) ***Health screening:*** Some policies will pay for or towards a health screen (an approved medical test which is essentially a health check and aims to help spot serious illness at an early stage), often every two years.

(*h*) ***Travel insurance:*** Full travel insurance may be offered, although winter sports may be excluded and there may be some geographic and hazardous pursuit exclusions.

(*j*) ***Dental and optical cash benefits:*** In effect these are health cash plan type benefits.

(*k*) ***Critical illness cover:*** Usually for a relatively small sum assured and covering core conditions only.

(*l*) ***Psychiatric cover:*** Many policies now exclude in-patient or out-patient psychiatric cover. However, some policies will provide full or limited cover on either an out-patient or in-patient basis, although this may be subject to an initial period before such cover applies.

On some policies, the benefit schedule will refer to 'full refund'. In practice, most insurers now pay benefits direct to the provider, but in some cases the patient still pays the bill to the hospital, consultant and anaesthetist and then reclaims the sums paid from the insurer. This may apply where the insured does not contact the insurer before undergoing treatment (most insurers now have a claims helpline and some insist that this be used for a claim to be paid, except in an emergency) or where the hospital is in a different price band to the one which the insured has elected under their policy.

Many insurers now offer concessionary terms where the insured uses a network hospital, and in some cases a network consultant too. Network hospitals are those that have agreed terms or procedural pricing with the insurer.

Insurers will generally pay all consultant and anaesthetist fees where they meet one or more of the following criteria. The fees must be:

- agreed in advance with the insurer;
- within the insurer's published maximum fee scale; and
- normal and reasonable.

Definitions 23.16

There is no common set of definitions used in private medical insurance, but those set out at 23.17–23.19 below represent the practice of some of the major insurers in this market. In particular it is important to look at the treatments covered by a policy. Another key element of cover is that private medical insurance is designed to pay for acute treatment but not chronic treatment. There is as yet no common definition of what these terms mean, although it is possible that the ABI may develop standard conditions for its member companies in the near future.

'Treatment' 23.17

'A surgical procedure or medical procedure carried out by a specialist. This includes:

- Diagnostic procedures – consultations and investigation needed to establish diagnosis.
- In-patient treatment – treatment at a private hospital where the member has to stay in a hospital bed for one or more nights.
- Daycare treatment – treatment at a private hospital or daycare unit where the member is admitted but does not stay overnight and requires a period of supervised recovery.
- Out-patient treatment – treatment at an out-patient clinic, a specialist's consulting room, or in a private hospital, where the member is not admitted.'

Healthy Outlook, PPP Healthcare

'Surgical or medical procedures the sole purpose of which is the cure or relief of acute illness or injury. An acute illness or injury is characterised by an occurrence of brief duration, after which the Insured Person returns to his/her normal or previous state and degree of activity.'

Fair and Square (02/1999), Norwich Union Healthcare

'Surgical or medical procedures, including diagnostic procedures, the immediate purpose of which is the cure of acute illness and not the alleviation or management of long-term illness.'

BCWA Healthcare, May 1998

'Acute' 23.18

'A disease, illness or injury that is likely to respond quickly to treatment which aims to return you to the state of health you were in immediately before suffering from it, or which leads to your full recovery.'

Self-Pay Protect (2001), WPA

'Chronic' 23.19

'A disease, illness or injury which has at least one of the following characteristics:

- continues indefinitely and has no known cure;
- comes back or is likely to come back;
- is permanent;
- means you need to be rehabilitated or specially trained to cope with it;
- needs long-term monitoring, consultations, check ups, examinations or tests.'

Self-Pay Protect (2001), WPA

Conditions and treatment 23.20

Acute versus chronic conditions 23.21

Private medical insurance will pay for acute treatment and for treatment for acute episodes of chronic conditions, but not for treatment of chronic conditions.

In some cases however, it can be difficult to determine what is meant by the terms 'acute' and 'chronic'. For example, cancer is usually regarded as an acute condition. However, in its end stages, cancer may become a chronic condition, even though the oncologist is giving treatment with a view to extending the life expectancy of the patient.

Pre-existing conditions 23.22

Individual private medical insurance does not cover pre-existing conditions, although large corporate schemes generally will. The policy conditions or rules will usually define 'pre-existing' along the lines of a condition of which the insured was aware or should have been aware.

For example, an individual may suffer a sore throat for which they obtain medical treatment. After a few days, the sore throat goes away. Subsequently, the individual takes out an individual private medical insurance policy but does not notify the insurer about their sore throat. A few months later, the insured suffers another sore throat and, on a third occasion, their GP advises that their tonsils should be removed. It may be held that the sore throat was in fact a symptom of diseased tonsils and, even though the patient was never told that their tonsils might have to be removed, the condition would nevertheless not be covered under their private medical insurance policy. Such situations often occur with children, although adults may be affected too.

Moratorium underwriting 23.23

In its 1996 and 1998 reports on health insurance, the Office of Fair Trading (OFT) was critical of the practice of moratorium underwriting used by some private medical insurance insurers.

Moratorium underwriting will typically not cover conditions arising in the five years before a policy starts, until the patient has been free of any treatment for two complete years from the start of the policy. Treatment will usually include any medically necessary check-ups. Moratorium underwriting can alleviate the need for an insured to answer any medical questions when applying for private medical insurance.

The OFT was particularly concerned that consumers would not understand the implications of the moratorium and was concerned that this could result in consumers believing themselves entitled to treatment that, in practice, they would not get.

An ABI working party looked into the OFT's concerns and it was eventually agreed that moratorium underwriting could continue to be used provided that:

- the insured was given an underwriting leaflet explaining how the moratorium would work on that particular policy; and
- the insured had the option to elect for full medical underwriting instead.

An uneasy truce has now broken out with the industry still divided to some extent about the value of moratorium, or point of claim, underwriting.

Hospital treatment – disputes over treatment 23.24

Any dispute over treatment given to an insured is between the insured and the provider, and does not involve the insurer. So, where say a hernia operation was carried out negligently or complications arose because of some deficiency in the operating theatre, the patient would have a right of redress against the hospital, consultant or anaesthetist as appropriate. All medical doctors are required to have appropriate medical negligence cover and this will usually be provided through a specific insurance policy or through the doctor's medical defence union. In the latter case, cover is provided on a discretionary rather than contractual basis although, in practice, cover can be considered as though being provided by an insurance policy.

An exception to the general rule would be where a consultant was following a medical protocol dictated by an insurer and where the protocol itself is the subject of any negligence claim. Such protocols are often part of a managed care agreement on some group private medical insurance schemes. They are usually drawn up by the insurer's chief medical officer (CMO) and agreed with consultants who are accepted by the insurer under such arrangements. No examples of legal cases in this area are known to exist in the UK to date.

Treatment overseas and repatriation 23.25

Some policies will cover treatment abroad, usually where this is previously agreed with the insurer. This might be taken up where perhaps treatment is unavailable in the UK or where treatment is cheaper abroad. Generally though, overseas treatment is only covered where the policy also includes travel insurance.

Third party rights 23.26

The *Contracts (Rights of Third Parties) Act 1999* gives third parties such as individual employees rights under contracts made by others, such as their employer, and which affect them. However, it may be made a condition of the contract that the terms of the Act do not apply to it.

In practice, most group private medical insurers will grant rights to employees so far as claims under a policy are concerned. This means that, in the event of a dispute, the claimant can deal direct with the insurer rather than having to go through their employer – who, on cost grounds alone, may have an incentive not to wish to see a claim succeed as that might affect the premium they pay in future.

Confidentiality **23.27**

Where a group scheme is being re-brokered, the new insurer will usually require evidence of claims paid recently under the current scheme. Traditionally, this was obtained by the old insurer (or the scheme secretary at the insured employer) passing on claims details, including of individual claims and claimants.

Under the *Data Protection Act 1998*, this is now outlawed. Consequently both insurers and scheme secretaries need to ensure that data is not passed on which would enable an individual employee to be recognised, unless that employee has given written permission for that to happen.

Exclusions **23.28**

Private medical insurance exclusions may include some or all of the following.

- Any medical condition which the insured knew about, or that existed, or for which they received treatment before the policy start date unless they had given full details and the insurer had accepted the medical condition.
- Treatment of any psychiatric, psychological or mental illness, or any other condition normally treated by a psychiatrist or psychologist.
- Treatment which arises from, or is in any way related to, alcohol, drug or substance abuse.
- Chronic and long-term illness which, in the opinion of the insurer's medical adviser, cannot be cured.
- Rehabilitation for more than 14 days.
- Cosmetic surgery or a procedure carried out solely to change or improve the insured's appearance, whether or not for psychological purposes. However, reconstructive surgery will be covered as long as it is carried out to restore the insured's appearance or function after surgery for a medical condition or after an accident for which the insurer has paid benefits. Treatment must take place as soon as possible and be listed in the insurer's schedule of procedures
- Human Immunodeficiency Virus (HIV) infection and any associated medical condition (for example the AIDS virus).
- Kidney dialysis, other than acute, reversible kidney failure.
- Medical conditions arising through an intentional self-inflicted injury or suicide attempt.

- Pregnancy or childbirth except where childbirth complications arise. (There is usually a ten month waiting period before any pregnancy-related treatment would be payable).
- Termination of pregnancy.
- Investigating and treating infertility.
- Hormone replacement therapy (HRT).
- Organ transplant operations.
- A dental surgical operation unless a general anaesthetic is needed, the procedure is listed in the insurer's schedule of procedures and the operation is performed by a consultant oral surgeon.
- Orthodontic procedures and/or appliances whether or not for psychological purposes.
- Treatment arising from, or in any way attributable to, a sex change or gender reassignment.
- The services of a general practitioner except where stated in the benefit schedule.
- Treatment received following an emergency admission into hospital unless the insured and his/her specialist agree to their being transferred to private patient status. The insurer must authorise the transfer before it takes place.
- Treatment received outside the United Kingdom or the costs of being transported back to the United Kingdom to receive treatment.
- Treatment or listed hospital charges incurred in nature cure clinics, spas, health hydros or similar places even if they are registered as, or part of, a listed hospital.
- Routine or occupational medical check-ups carried out at screening centres, or similar facilities, whether or not they have been approved by a general practitioner or specialist.
- Treatment for injuries or illnesses arising out of nuclear or chemical contamination, war, invasion, act of foreign enemy hostilities (whether war be declared or not), civil war, riot, civil commotion, rebellion, revolution, insurrection or military or usurped power.
- A stay in hospital or registered nursing home which is arranged wholly or partly for domestic reasons.
- Treatment of any injuries arising from, or relating to, taking part in any form of professional sport or hazardous pursuits such as private flying, parachuting, mountaineering, rock climbing, potholing and any form of motor sport.
- Experimental or non-proven treatment. Procedures, tests, drugs and treatment will not be covered that is not proven and does not conform to normal and customary practice in the UK unless the insurer's medical advisor gives authorisation beforehand.

- Treatment which arises from, or is related to, a general exclusion listed or treatment which arises from, or is related to, a surgical procedure which is not covered.

Based on Lifetime Comprehensive (October 1998), Legal & General Healthcare policy terms, 2000

Where a private medical insurance policy contains other benefits, such as travel insurance or critical illness benefits, additional or different exclusions may apply.

Chapter 24

Accident, Sickness and Unemployment Insurance

- **Overview of accident, sickness and unemployment insurnace**
- **Types of policy**
- **Benefits**
- **Exclusions**

Overview of accident, sickness and unemployment insurance 24.1

Accident, sickness and unemployment insurance (either as individual products or as one or more of the constituent parts of a product) is a major market for UK insurers, and is commonly used in creditor insurance. Creditor insurance pays regular credit costs, such as the monthly interest and capital repayment under a typical repayment mortgage, in the event of the insured suffering one of the specified events.

Types of policy 24.2

Personal accident insurance 24.3

Personal accident insurance pays either a cash lump sum or a weekly or monthly benefit if the insured suffers an accident which results in:

- death;
- permanent and total loss of the use of one or more limbs;
- total and permanent loss of sight in one or both eyes;
- permanent total disablement preventing the insured from following any occupation; or
- other injuries such as a broken arm or leg.

Capital benefits **24.4**

Capital benefits are usually on a sliding scale – £100,000 may be payable on death, going down to £500 for a simple fracture of an arm or the loss of a small toe. This may be expressed either as a cash amount or as a percentage of the main benefit. More serious conditions such as death must usually arise within 12 or 24 months of the accident occurring. Permanent and total disability is usually only payable 12 or 24 months after the accident, so as to ensure that the condition is, in fact, likely to be permanent.

Weekly benefits 24.5

Weekly benefits are usually payable for up to 52 or 104 weeks and have a deferred (waiting) period of between 7 and 30 days. Some policies will pay a lower benefit if the insured is only partially disabled. Policies are written for a fixed term or until a specified retirement age.

Sickness policies 24.6

Sickness policies pay either a weekly or a monthly benefit where the insured is unable to carry on any or their own occupation as a result of illness or disability. The benefit is usually payable after a deferred (waiting) period of between 7 and 30 days, and typically pays out for up to 52 or 104 weeks. Policies are written for a fixed term or until a specified retirement age.

Unemployment insurance 24.7

This is usually written as an annually renewable policy as part of another policy such as mortgage payment protection insurance (see 24.8 below). The policy will pay a monthly benefit for up to twelve months if the insured becomes involuntarily unemployed.

Mortgage payment protection insurance 24.8

Mortgage payment protection insurance (MPPI) is an annually renewable policy that pays a monthly sum in the event of the insured becoming:

- ill;
- disabled; or
- unemployed,

and being unable to work.

MPPI is now taken out by one in four new mortgagors and the monthly sum is usually sufficient to pay the insured's:

- mortgage interest;
- monthly capital repayment (if a repayment or capital and interest mortgage); and
- monthly insurance premiums, for example for a mortgage endowment policy.

Benefits **24.9**

Benefits may be either based on the actual payments made by the mortgagor (which may go up or down as interest rates change), or based on current costs today and then uplifted by a certain percentage, for example 25 per cent.

Single premium policies **24.10**

Although most policies are annually renewable, it is possible to obtain single premium MPPI. In effect, the mortgage is increased by the single premium, and although this can result in a lower monthly payment, the cover will last as long as the mortgage does, which may be disadvantageous if the insured moves home or takes out a new mortgage.

Payment of benefit **24.11**

Benefits are usually payable after a deferred period of between 14 and 30 days, and will pay out until whichever occurs earliest out of:

- death;
- the end of the mortgage term;
- the insured's normal retirement date; or
- the insured being able to return to work.

Minimum standards **24.12**

The Council of Mortgage Lenders (CML) and the Association of British Insurers (ABI) have drawn up minimum standards which should apply to MPPI. Most insurers, and all ABI member companies, now follow these standards.

Conditional lending **24.13**

Conditional lending is where a loan is offered subject to the borrower agreeing to do certain things, such as take out the insurance offered by the lender. Although it is not illegal, conditional lending is generally regarded as being bad practice, and most reputable mainstream lenders no longer insist on borrowers having their insurance. However, they may insist that any policy meets objective minimum cover requirements, and may charge a one-off or annual fee to the borrower.

Accident, sickness and unemployment insurance **24.14**

Accident, sickness and unemployment (ASU) insurance is simply MPPI which is not directly related to a mortgage. The maximum benefit is normally restricted to 75 per cent of the pre-event income up to a specified total monthly maximum, for example £2,500.

Rider policies 24.15

Policies are often included as a rider benefit to a main insurance, for example to travel or motor insurance. In most cases, the add-on policy will be part of the main contract, although in some cases it may be written as a separate contract and sometimes even by a separate insurer.

Cancellability 24.16

Annually renewable policies may be cancelled, usually by the insurer giving 7–30 days notice to the insured. In addition, the insurer may refuse to offer new terms or may offer only revised terms on renewal.

In practice, it is rare for insurers not to renew or to cancel a policy part-way through its term, unless there is some evidence of non-disclosure or fraud. However, unemployment cycles can be volatile and, where a sudden economic downturn becomes evident, terms can and have changed rapidly or cover has been withdrawn at short notice.

Benefits 24.17

Benefits are usually expressed as either a monthly cash amount or as a capital sum, and are payable direct to the insured.

Usually either a maximum overall benefit, for example £2,500 a month, is specified, or a percentage of pre-event income (see 24.18 below) is set, for example 75 per cent.

Pre-event income 24.18

Pre-event income is defined as:

- income as evidenced by information such as P11D forms or three months' pay slips for employed people (bonuses and overtime will usually be excluded unless guaranteed); or
- taxable profits (not turnover) of self-employed people.

Exclusions 24.19

Sickness and accident exclusions 24.20

Exclusions for the sickness and accident elements of the policy may include some or all of the following:

(*a*) any claim made more than six months after the event;

(*b*) where the insured knew at the start date of the policy that they would become disabled or had any reason to believe that they might become disabled;

(*c*) any disability caused by self-inflicted injury, alcohol abuse or drug abuse, or if the insured fails to follow any medical advice;

(*d*) disability caused by stress, anxiety, depression or any nervous disorder unless a consultant certifies that the condition prevents the insured from working;

(*e*) pre-existing conditions;

(*f*) any disability caused by pregnancy or a normal pregnancy-related condition, other than a medical complication which happens as a result of the insured's pregnancy;

(*g*) any disability caused by a back-related condition unless there is radiological evidence of a medical abnormality or visible wound, or a consultant certifies that the condition prevents the insured from working;

(*h*) any disability arising from any operation which is not medically necessary including any cosmetic or beauty treatment; and

(*j*) any disability caused by any of the unemployment exclusions.

Source: Based on Berkeley Alexander Insurance Services policy conditions, and reproduced with their permission.

Unemployment exclusions **24.21**

Unemployment insurance exclusions typically apply where the insured:

(i) has prior knowledge of forthcoming unemployment or has reason to believe that they will be made unemployed;

(ii) is on a short-term contract (although this may not apply if they have been on short term contracts which have previously been renewed and which they expect to be renewed again – the precise terms will be defined in the policy conditions);

(iii) resigns;

(iv) is dismissed, for example for gross misconduct;

(v) is already in a period of notice;

(vi) accepts payment in lieu of notice;

(vii) is made unemployed during any initial waiting period specified under the policy;

(viii) is receiving benefit under any other part of the insurance;

(ix) is a member of an excluded occupation group; or

(x) is self-employed or a share-holding company director unless the business goes into involuntary liquidation.

Chapter 25

Other Health-Related Insurances

- **Introduction**
- **Health cash plans**
- **GP schemes**
- **Dental insurance**
- **Major medical expenses insurance**
- **Health insurance as a rider benefit on other policies**
- **Waiver of premium**
- **Viatical settlements**
- **Terminal illness**
- **Permanent and total disability**

Introduction 25.1

As well as the major types of health and related insurances already covered in CHAPTERS 20–24, other health insurance policies and benefits also exist. Some of these are marketed as standalone policies, others are riders to policies or affect other types of policy.

Health cash plans 25.2

Health cash plans, although not as well known as private medical insurance, actually cover about the same number of people in the UK, that is around seven million. Plans are also known as healthcare cash, hospital cash or simply cash plans.

These plans pay a cash benefit if the insured incurs costs in one or more of a number of specified events. Most benefits are written on an indemnity basis, typically paying 50–100 per cent of a cost, up to a pre-defined annual limit.

Originally plans paid just for hospital in-patient treatment, but the main benefits today, in terms of benefits paid, are for dental and optical care. Policies are usually low cost, starting from around £1 a week, and have simplified premium structures, usually with no additions for age or sex. Typical maximum annual benefits are set out in the table at 25.3 below.

Typical health cash plan benefits per £1 weekly premium **25.3**

Benefit	Benefit range
Each day spent in hospital	£18–30 per night
Sight tests, glasses, contact lenses	£50–60 per year
Dental treatment	£50–60 per year
Specialist consultations	£35–250 per year
Maternity cash payment	£50–150 per birth
Illness at home	£50–70 per week
Disablement/accidental death	£8,000–£10,000
Physio/osteopathy/acupuncture	£50–250 per year
Convalescence	Paid in full for 2 weeks

Source: British Health Care Association (BHCA), 2001

However, up to 30 or more separate benefits may be offered including:

- accommodation costs for a parent to stay with a young child (under age 8–14) in hospital;
- allergy testing;
- alternative therapies (for example homeopathy);
- ambulance (private);
- day surgery;
- discount card offering lower prices on a range of goods and services;
- double hospital benefit for certain conditions or for a couple both being in hospital at the same time;
- double maternity benefit for birth of twins;
- emergency medical cover in other European Union countries;
- GP minor surgery;
- health screening;
- hearing aids;
- helplines offering medical, legal and domestic help and information;
- home help costs;
- invalid care equipment;
- home nursing;

- out-patient treatment costs;
- permanent and total disability cash lump sum;
- personal accident lump sum payment (on a sliding scale based on severity);
- prescriptions (usually up to 2–4 a year); and
- surgical appliances.

Although many individuals have a health cash plan many providers report that the majority of their business comes from voluntary schemes set up by employers with contributions or premiums paid by employees.

GP schemes 25.4

Only an estimated 2 per cent of the UK population consults a GP privately rather than going through the NHS. However, insurance and capitation schemes do exist which pay for or towards GP services.

Typical benefits may include some or all of:

- consultations at short notice on demand, usually the same day and with no waiting;
- a specified maximum number of free consultations each year;
- separate, more luxurious waiting rooms from NHS patients, or the use of a private GP facility (these mainly exist in large cities);
- a 24 hour medical helpline;
- cover up to a specified amount, say £250 a year, for diagnostic tests; and
- home call outs at a fixed extra cost.

Dental insurance 25.5

Dental insurance may take two forms: dental capitation plans (see 25.6 below) and dental insurance plans (see 25.7 below).

Dental capitation plans 25.6

Dental capitation plans are a form of insurance but are not written as an insurance policy. Often sold by dentists themselves, the patient undergoes a dental examination and is categorised in one of a number of dental health categories. These take account of likely dental work required in the future.

The patient pays a monthly premium to the plan which, after deducting an administration fee, then pays the dentist a regular sum, regardless of what work they actually carry out. Plans may include an element of insurance in the form of accidental dental damage or a cash sum payment on diagnosis of some conditions such as oral cancer.

The main benefit of a dental capitation plan is that it enables patients to budget for their dental treatment. For dentists, it helps smooth their income, avoid bad debts or arguments about treatment costs and is marketed as a patient service. Some insurers accredit their participating dentists, who are subject to dental audit and must meet certain criteria with regard to their practice and practices.

Dental insurance plans 25.7

Dental insurance is typically only offered on a group basis. Usually underwritten for free, they pay all or a proportion of dental costs up to pre-set annual or treatment limits. Policies may cover regular check-ups and routine dental work as well as accidental dental damage, overseas treatment and conditions such as oral cancer.

Major medical expenses insurance 25.8

Major medical expenses insurance ('major medex' for short) pays a cash lump sum if the insured has to undergo specified surgery under a general anaesthetic. Benefit is usually on a sliding scale, typically from £1,500 for a minor operation up to £15,000 for complex major surgery. Examples are set out in the table below.

Procedure	Payment
Complex major	£15,000
Major plus	£12,000
Major	£8,000
Intermediate	£4,000
Minor	£1,500

Major medex has not proved to be a major success in the UK but is sometimes written as a rider on another policy. Where written on a long term policy, major medex will avoid insurance premium tax on the premiums.

Benefit is paid direct to the insured and is not an indemnity policy. Payment is usually made regardless of whether the insured chooses to have NHS or private care, although in some cases, a lower payment is made for treatment paid for by the NHS.

Health insurance as a rider benefit on other policies 25.9

Health insurance benefits may be included as a rider on another policy. For example, most travel policies will include overseas medical benefits; motor insurance and health cash plans may include personal accident cover; and critical illness benefit may be included on a private medical insurance policy.

Insurers and intermediaries are constantly striving to create new consumer propositions and this is often achieved by combining different types of cover. This can become confusing, especially where the rider does not use the generic name for that type of cover.

Examples of new consumer propositions include long-term care conversion options on whole life policies (Zurich Life, Whole Life and Skandia Life Protect 2001), paying only a percentage of private medical insurance treatment costs (WPA Self-Pay Protect 2001) and offering a twelve year money-back guarantee on mortgage payment protection insurance (Insurety Sovereign 2001).

Waiver of premium **25.10**

Waiver of premium means that the insurer will waive premiums in the event of the insured being unable to work due to illness or disability or, in some cases, involuntary unemployment. The definition of being unable to work is usually very strict – the insured must be unable to carry on their own or any other occupation. Exclusions are generally the same as for the rest of the policy.

The benefit usually has a deferred period of three or six months and premiums are waived until the earliest of the following occurs to the insured:

- returning to work;
- dying;
- reaching normal retirement age; or
- reaching the age at which the benefit stops – usually 55 or 60.

The benefit is paid for by an addition to the premium, usually a percentage increase based on age and sex.

Viatical settlements **25.11**

A viatical settlement is where a policy is sold for greater than its then cash value where the insured expects to die during the policy term. The value will depend on their life expectancy at the time of sale. Viatical settlements are common in some countries, for example the USA, but are relatively rare in the UK. A viatical settlement could be used with any in-force UK assurance policy which has a sum assured payable on death (see SECTION A: LIFE ASSURANCE).

For example, a £100,000 whole life policy may have a cash value of say £5,000 if surrendered to the insurer. If the insured has a life expectancy of just a few months, they may be able to sell the policy for a much higher amount – perhaps £60,000. In determining the price, the buyer will need medical and actuarial evidence about the insured's condition and will take into account the in-built uncertainty about predicting medical outcomes, even on patients with terminal illnesses.

Terminal illness 25.12

Terminal illness benefit is often included on life assurance and critical illness policies (see SECTION A: LIFE ASSURANCE and 20 CRITICAL ILLNESS INSURANCE). The benefit becomes payable if, in the opinion of a qualified consultant, the insured has a life expectancy of less than 12 months.

If the insured does not die within 12 months, the benefit is not repayable.

Permanent and total disability 25.13

Permanent and total disability (PTD) insurance (although the benefit is also known as total and permanent disability (TPD)) is added to many life, critical illness and income protection policies (see SECTION A: LIFE ASSURANCE, 20 CRITICAL ILLNESS INSURANCE and 21 INCOME PROTECTION INSURANCE).

PTD insurance pays a cash lump sum where the insured is totally and permanently disabled and unable to continue their occupation. A range of occupation definitions is used by insurers including:

- own occupation;
- any occupation;
- any occupation which the insured is capable, by reason of experience or training, of undertaking; and
- failing a prescribed number of activities of daily working (ADWs) or a functional assessment test (FAT).

Generally, an 'own occupation' definition provides the highest benefit. For example, under an 'any occupation' definition a barrister or engineer would not be able to claim if they could be employed as say a car park attendant. (For more details on these definitions see 21 INCOME PROTECTION INSURANCE.)

Flex schemes 25.14

Flex schemes, or flexible benefits schemes, allow employees to choose from a menu of insurance and non-insurance benefits to create a package of employee benefits which best suits their personal needs. The constituent insurance covers will however follow the norm for that product type.

Flex is usually only offered by large employers due to the costs associated with the necessary administrative systems.

Employees may be given a choice of how much as well as what type of cover to have; they may be able to add spouse, partner or children's cover and to change cover periodically. In many cases, changes will be subject to fresh underwriting.

Chapter 26

Taxation and Health-Related Insurances

- **Introduction**
- **Permanent health insurance**

Introduction 26.1

There is on-going political debate over possible degrees of tax relief for private health insurance. Lump sum benefits under critical illness policies are tax-free. However, the area where there are current tax implications in the field of health-related insurances is permanent health insurance, and this area is concentrated on below at 26.2 *et seq*.

Permanent health insurance 26.2

Permanent health insurance (PHI) policies sit rather uneasily in life office business as they are not dependent upon human life. The same can be said about annuities certain (see 19 TYPES OF ANNUITY).

All benefits under a PHI policy, and certainly those which continue for over twelve months, are taxable as annual payments under general tax legislation. However, tax exemptions are available under the *Income and Corporation Taxes Act 1988* (*ICTA 1988*).

Tax exemption requirements 26.3

Exemption from tax is given under *sections 580A* and *580B* of *ICTA 1988* where the policy meets certain requirements. Under *section 580A(2)* of *ICTA 1988*:

(*a*) the insurance must cover a qualifying risk, defined by *section 580A(3)* of *ICTA 1988* as:

  (i) a risk that the insured may become subject to, or suffer a deterioration in, a condition resulting from any physical or mental illness or disability, or

  (ii) a risk that as a result of any of the above the insured will cease to be employed or to carry on a trade;

(*b*) the risk must be self-contained (*ICTA 1988, s 580A(2)(b)*); this is an anti-avoidance measure designed to ensure that where there are multiple benefits under the policy, or multiple policies, the PHI element charges an adequate premium (*ICTA 1988, s 580B*);

(*c*) under *section 580A(2)(c)* of *ICTA 1988*, benefits are payable only in respect of a period in which relevant conditions of payment are satisfied; these conditions are satisfied as long as any of the following apply (set out by *ICTA 1988, s 380A(4)*):

  (i) the illness, disability or unemployment continues, including convalescence or rehabilitation,

  (ii) the insured is unemployed or not carrying on a trade,

  (iii) the income of the insured is reduced as a result of the illness or disability, or

  (iv) benefits are payable for a period after death of the insured following any of the above; and

(*d*) provision has at all times been of a qualifying type (*ICTA 1988, s 580A(2)(d)*), meaning that the insurer must have been at risk of loss under the policy; benefits must not for example be limited to a return of premium plus profits or interest (*ICTA 1988, s 380A(5)*).

If the conditions are met, benefits under the PHI policy, or the PHI element, should be free from tax.

As always, the policy conditions are paramount.

Other provisions **26.4**

A policy may pay benefits if the spouse of the insured is sick or unemployed (*ICTA 1988, s 580A(9)*).

A lump sum may be payable free of tax under the policy upon the occurrence of an accident, or in commutation of a right to future payments (*IR 153, para 10*).

Where the premiums are deductible as a business expense by the individual the benefits are not exempt from tax (*ICTA 1988, s 580A(6)*).

If the individual's employer pays the premiums and the employee does not pay tax on these amounts, then benefits are taxable; if he does pay tax then the benefits are exempt. If the employee pays the premiums, or makes a contribution to these, then benefits are wholly or proportionately free from tax, even if as a matter of mechanics the employer actually makes the premium payments (*IR 153, paras 17, 19, 20*).

The policy may include provision to continue benefits under an employer's group policy after an employee has left the employment as a result of the illness or disability, but benefits will be taxable to the extent that the employer has paid premiums (*IR 153, para 18*).

Bibliography

A Practitioner's Guide to Trusts (3rd Edition)
John Thurston
Butterworths Tolley

Dread Disease – The Critical Facts
Mercantile & General Reinsurance (now Swiss Re Life & Health)

General Principles of Insurance Law (6th edition)
E.R. Hardy Ivamy
Butterworths Tolley

Healthcare Insurance Report
Andy Couchman
Bank House Communications

Kluwer Handbook of Insurance
Croner: CCH

Kluwer's Income Protection Insurance: The Unique Annual Review
Croner: CCH

Insurance and UK Healthcare
Andy Couchman
Informa

Laing's Health Care Market Review 2000/01
Laing and Buisson

Law of Life Assurance (11th edition)
Houseman and Davies
Butterworths Tolley

Law and Practice of Life Assurance Contracts
Andrew McGee
Sweet and Maxwell

Life Assurance
Chris Marshall
CII Publications (published as Coursebook 735)

Life Assurance Law and Practice
Peter Hamilton
Sweet and Maxwell

Life Assurance and Pensions Handbook
Chris Marshall
Tax Briefs (in London)

MacGillivray on Insurance Law (9th edition)
Sweet and Maxwell

Pensions Law and Practice
Robin Ellison
Sweet and Maxwell

Pensions Law, Taxation and Administration
Sylvia and Leslie Tutt (Chapters 1–5)
CII Publications (published as Coursebook 740)

Permanent Health Insurance Claims
Mercantile & General Reinsurance (now Swiss Life & Health)

Personal Insurance
Len Barnett
CII Publications (published as Coursebook 760)

Taxation of Insurance Business (4th edition)
Macleod and Levitt
Butterworths Tolley

The Complete Guide to Long-Term Care
Capital ERC Francona

The Facts of Life and Health Insurance
Andy Couchman
Tax Briefs (in London)

Tolley's Income Tax 2001-02
Glyn Saunders, David Smalles and Gina Antczak
Butterworths Tolley

Tolley's Insurance Handbook (2nd Edition)
Barlow Lyde & Gilbert
Butterworths Tolley

Tolley's Tax Planning 2001–02
Butterworths Tolley

UK Health and Welfare Insurance
Andy Couchman
Informa

Yellow Tax Handbook 2001–02
Butterworths Tolley

Useful Addresses

Associated Scottish Life Office
15 Dalkeith Road
Edinburgh
EH16 5BO
Tel: 0131 655 6000
Fax: 0131 662 4053

Association of British Insurers (ABI)
51 Gresham Street
London
EC2V 7HQ
Tel: 020 7600 3333
Fax: 020 7696 8999
Website: www.abi.org.uk
Email: info@abi.org.uk

Association of Consulting Actuaries
1 Wardrobe Place
London
EC4V 5AG
Tel: 020 7248 3163
Fax: 020 7248 1889
Website: www.aca.org.uk

Association of Taxation Technicians
12 Upper Belgrave Street
London
SW1X 8BB
Tel: 020 7235 2544
Fax: 020 7235 4571

Association of Unit Trusts and Investment Funds
65 Kingsway
London
WC2B 6TD
Tel: 020 7831 0898
Fax: 020 7831 9975
Website: www.investmentfunds.org.uk

Assurance Medical Society
11 Chandos Street
London
W1M 9EB
Tel: 020 7636 6306
Fax: 020 7580 5793

Chartered Institute of Taxation
12 Upper Belgrave Street
London
SW1X 8BB
Tel: 020 7235 9381
Fax: 020 7235 2562
Website: www.tax.org.uk

Chartered Insurance Institute (CII)
20 Aldermanbury
London
EC2V 7HY
Tel: 020 8989 8464
Fax: 020 7972 0157
Website: www.cii.co.uk
Email: info@cii.org.uk

Council of Mortgage Lenders
3 Savile Row
London
W1S 3PB
Tel: 020 7437 0075
Fax: 020 7434 3791
Email: info@cml.org.uk

Faculty of Actuaries
Maclaurin House
18 Dublin Street
Edinburgh
EH1 3PP
Tel: 0131 240 1300
Fax: 0131 240 1313

Financial Services Authority
25 The North Colonnade
Canary Wharf
London
E14 5HS
Tel: 020 7676 1000
Fax: 020 7676 1099

Friendly Societies Commission
15th Floor
25 The North Colonnade
Canary Wharf
London
E14 5HS
Tel: 020 7676 9610

HM Treasury (Insurance Directorate)
Parliament Street
London
SW1P 3AG
Tel: 020 7270 4558

Institute of Actuaries
Staple Inn Hall
High Holborn
London
WC1V 7QJ
Tel: 020 7632 2100
Fax: 020 7632 2111

Insurance Ombudsman Bureau
South Quay
183 Marsh Wall
London
E14 9SR
Tel: 020 7964 1000
Fax: 020 7964 1001
Website: www.theiob.org.uk

Personal Investments Authority
25 The North Colonnade
Canary Wharf
London
E14 5HS
Tel: 020 7270 1000
Fax: 020 7676 1015

Pension Management Institute (PMI)
PMI House
4/10 Artillery Lane
London
E1 7LS
Tel: 020 7247 1452
Fax: 020 7375 0603
Website: www.pensions-pmi.org.uk
Email: enquiries@pensions-pmi.org.uk

Society of Financial Advisers
20 Aldermanbury
London
EC2V 7HY
Tel: 020 7417 4419
Website: www.sofa.org.uk
Email: info@sofa.org.uk

Worshipful Company of Insurers
20 Aldermanbury
London
EC2V 7HY
Tel: 020 7600 4006
Fax: 020 7972 0153

Table of Cases

Table of Statutes

Table of Statutory Instruments

1981	**Insurance Companies Regulations**	
	SI 1981/1654	6.5
1991	**Retirement Benefit Schemes (Restrictions on Discretionary Approval) (Small Self-Administered Schemes) Regulations**	
	SI 1991/1614	15.25
1994	**Insurance Companies Regulations**	
	SI 1994/1516	9.9
1994	**Unfair Terms in Consumer Contracts Regulations**	
	SI 1994/3159	5.3, 11.25
1999	**Unfair Terms in Consumer Contracts Regulations**	
	SI 1999/2083	5.3
2000	**Stakeholder Pension Schemes Regulations**	
	SI 2000/1403	17.9
	Reg 22(4)	17.12
2001	**Stakeholder Pension Schemes (Amendment) Regulations**	
	SI 2001/104	17.9
2001	**Stakeholder Pension Schemes (Amendment) (No 2) Regulations**	
	SI 2001/934	17.9

Table of European Material

Equal Treatment Directive (76/207/EEC)		15.11
Life Establishment Directive (79/167/EEC)		6.5
1992	**Treaty on European Union**	
	Art 119	15.11

Index